DIABOLICAL DISORIENTATION

THE ROOTS OF THE CRISIS IN THE CHURCH, FAMILY, NATION, AND CULTURE

By Ted Flynn

Maxkol Communications

Cover of St. Peter's lightning storm: Shutterstock
Book design: Paul McNamara Graphic Design
Published and printed in the USA
© Copyright, MAXKOL, 2020
ISBN Number: 978-0-9634307-4-8

Publisher:
MAXKOL, All Rights Reserved.

For bulk or case orders contact: tflynn3@cox.net

Distributor:
Signs and Wonders for Our Time
P.O. Box 345
Herndon, Virginia 20170
E Mail: signsorders@gmail.com
Phone: 703. 707. 0799
Web site: Sign.Org

"No one captures the truth of our times and puts it all together better than Ted Flynn. Penetrating in his vision and forceful in his assessments, Flynn is the spiritual Alex de Tocqueville of our age, a prophet walking among us who has the courage to abandon all fear in saying what needs to be said. Read DIABOLICAL DISORIENTATION *from the beginning to the end, ponder its epiphanies, and be prepared to strike the moral high ground in the battle that approaches."*

Dr. Tom Petrisko, author of 25 books,
his most recent is *Triumph, Medjugorje and the
Fulfillment of the Prophecies of Fatima.*

"I first discovered the importance of our Blessed Mother's apparitions and messages given to our Church when I had read Ted Flynn's book The Thunder of Justice *twenty five years ago. This was before I converted to the Catholic Church. Today, now as a Catholic priest, I find his new book* Diabolical Disorientation *to be very timely and prophetic for any Catholic seeking to better understand the roots of the current trials facing our Church and world today, and God's plan of remedy in this escalating crisis."*

Pastor, Father John Paul Shea

"Bravo! In the last two years I have read many books on the confusion and troubles in the Church. But, not one of these gave a full view of the reality of what is afflicting the Church and the world. Ted has done something in this book which literally takes the lid off of this pressure cooker we call the modern Church. I am sure there are some who will disagree what is revealed in this book, but truth is truth. Thank you for your courage. There are many who are asleep today when it comes to God and the topics addressed in this book. I believe it can bring even the walking dead back to life. I am convinced of the value in this book, and I will be the first to buy a case when they come off the press."

Pastor, Father Ron Stone

iv

Table of Contents

Acknowledgments

Hours of conversations went into the content of these articles on many diverse subjects by many people. They have been forged through study and experiences. We are who we are because of environment, education, travel, stimuli, relationships, our neighborhood, events, culture, family, and many things we absorb consciously and subconsciously. I have also had many wonderful friends over a lifetime.

Most of all, it is family that shapes us. Spoken, unspoken, and in silence. I have been blessed with an outstanding family. As I get older, I realize all the more that what matters most is family. We often lose sight of that and can take it for granted.

Having a hand in this process in different capacities was Maureen, Colleen, Meredith, and Danny Flynn. They all live life to the fullest and there is seldom a dull moment, which is exactly the way it should be. It reminds me of the verse when Jesus said, *"I come to give you life and give it more abundantly"* (John 10:10). I have lived that life beyond expectations, and I appreciate the opportunities the Lord has given me.

A very special, warm, and grateful thank you to Kimberley Welter. If she were in a trade, she would be a finish carpenter. The finish carpenter has to be the best and the most accurate at the end of the job, lest imperfections be seen in any light. She spent dozens of hours polishing, cutting, adding, researching, clarifying, and refining the articles that were first on the internet with no intention of putting them into a book when I started nearly eight years ago. It is a much better product because of you.

I am grateful for all of you.

Foreword

During their basic training, U.S. naval aviators are taught what to do if they find themselves suddenly under water after ejecting from an airplane. It's very easy to become confused or disoriented in such a crisis, thereby causing someone beneath the waves to swim even deeper in his desperate but misguided attempt to find breathable air. Aviators in this situation are therefore trained to avoid panicking, to exhale slowly, and then to follow the direction of their bubbles to the surface and safety.

This analogy speaks to our own age: in the midst of societal crisis and confusion, marked by the decline or outright abandonment of traditional morals and values, it can be very hard to make sense of things and know where to turn. In unsettled times such as ours, it's therefore all the more essential we learn to lift up our hearts and voices to God, letting our prayers and expressions of faith rise up or point us in the right direction. Panic and despair accomplish nothing; trusting in the Lord leads to inner peace and salvation.

God never abandons those who call upon Him; moreover, He reveals His plans to His prophets (Amos 3:7), so that His children may be forewarned and not be caught unaware or unprepared. Scripture and Church teachings serve as reliable guides; furthermore, numerous saints, mystics, and contemporary visionaries have received messages from Heaven, warning of coming events and helping believers learn to read the "signs of the times" (cf. Luke 12:54-56) — while also offering much-

By compiling much of this Heaven-sent information, Ted Flynn's new book *Diabolical Disorientation* serves as a valuable resource for anyone trying to make sense of an increasingly frightening and confusing era—a time marked by divisions in society and in the Church, political corruption, economic uncertainty, ever-increasing immorality, and numerous indications we may indeed be in the age of the "mass apostasy" foretold in the Bible (Matthew 24:12; Luke 18:8; 2 Thessalonians 2:3).

As the Fatima visionary Sister Lucia (d. 2005) warned some years ago, Satan is in the mood for a "decisive battle"— one, however, he is destined to lose, for the power of Almighty God will bring about the Triumph of the Immaculate Heart of Mary and a prophesied Era of Peace. Jesus has reserved to His Mother the central role in the coming victory of righteousness, and Our Lady has promised — at La Salette, Fatima, Medjugorje, and elsewhere — to shield under her mantle all who call upon the Name of her Son in faith.

May the information provided in these pages deepen the faith of many readers, while helping them obey the Lord's command: *"When these signs begin to happen, stand erect and raise your heads because your redemption is at hand"* (Luke 21:28).

REV. JOSEPH M. ESPER

A priest of the Archdiocese of Detroit, and author of over a dozen books.
He has spoken at numerous conferences, and written several dozen articles.

Introduction

This book is comprised of a series of articles that were first written in early 2011 and continue to this day. They have been posted on SIGN.ORG on a variety of subjects, but for the most part, they all have in one way or another, a Biblical or Magisterial Catholic historical perspective. Heaven has clearly taken the speculation out of where we are headed. It may be a surprise to many what is happening in the world, but Heaven warns its people in advance of events. Those following the messages of the Blessed Mother are not finding anything they haven't seen coming. She provides a glimpse into the future and she has told us, *"I have given you the full and entire truth."* Heaven has given us clear instructions for our conduct in turbulent times, as well as an intricate roadmap of what awaits us. But, this is only if we take the time and the effort to listen to the still small voice of God.

The articles vary in length. The culture, faith, the Church crisis, the assault on traditional values, the apostasy of faith and its ramifications as root problems, a liberal group within the Catholic hierarchy with an insidious agenda to bring the country and the Church into socialism and worse, are just a few topics addressed. Socialism is the prerequisite first step towards Marxism/communism, and we are marching at a greatly accelerated pace to a godless pagan culture. We are witnessing a global socialism using migration and immigration under a false banner of social justice, compassion, and tolerance. Leading the charge is an educational system with government indoctrination from Hell, designed to dumb down students so they can control them in this dystopian nightmare. Based on the results, this may be their crowning achievement. The utopian goals of the left will never be achievable because they ignore Original Sin as a reality, and as importantly, lower human nature.

We have a public nearly impervious to the fact that many in the Roman Catholic hierarchy are working with governmental agencies on this plan to usher in global government. The planning has been generational, but in the last fifty years it has been well organized and heavily funded. It is now in the open for all who choose to see it for what it really is. This battle is for all the marbles as the political and ecclesiastical agendas have merged with the same goals for the first time in history. That alone makes our times unique. The enemy is inside the gates of the Roman Church and they are firmly entrenched in positions of leadership promoting and protecting one another.

A central focus of many articles is to show the evil of Freemasonry being the primary enemy from within and outside the Church. This diabolical group maneuvers behind the scenes with goals to virtually reshape and transform our world with a humanistic manifesto void of God in the public square. They are very close to achieving all they have worked for over the last one hundred years, and this is why the fight is so ferocious. They have penetrated the very highest positions in Rome and government. Few believers understand how evil operates and how its roots are so vast and deep. Most believers have been naïve, subservient to government propaganda, brainwashed, and worse lazy, while this diabolical agenda has been going on under their noses. It reminds one of the verse when Jesus said to His disciples, *"I send you out as lambs among wolves."*

However, the Blessed Mother said, *"right when it appears Satan is the victor, I will snatch his victory away in a trice"* (quickly). The fight in all ages is the people of God versus the forces of darkness — two cohorts in constant battle. It is not a conspiracy theory as it is now in the open with those who have ears to hear, and eyes to see. The darkness is an organized cabal of men from the political, ecclesiastical, and industry ranks. They have had a well thought through stealth agenda to end the Primacy of Peter, promoting women's ordination, married clergy, install a supranational governmental body of rulers, end the sovereignty of nations, with the ultimate goal to abolish the Holy and Perpetual Sacrifice of the Mass. Rest assured, Heaven has given us the remedy to what ails us, and instructs us how to fight this evil. We are told the gates of Hell will never prevail against it.

This is a battle of epic proportions in this bareknuckle fight where in the end there will be only one party left standing. It is a war, and diabolical forces will not stop until they achieve depopulation, and a global socialist/Marxist government. In addition, climate change was ultimately designed to limit energy use to control the population, which will in turn levy a tax for another global slush fund. It will be similar to the United Nations pressuring countries to acquiesce to their godless social policies as a condition for funding. The United Nations has openly said for the last thirty years the Catholic Church needs to change it policies towards abortion rights, climate legislation, LGBTQ acceptance, and more control by government. Many in the Roman Curia want global government with the Church under it. The question is, *"who runs it?"* Their agenda has no ambiguity. It is clear they not only want to remove all reference to Christianity, but to eradicate it as a way of life.

Many articles were published before Cardinal Bergolio of Argentina became Pope Francis on March 13, 2013, and Donald J. Trump became the 45th President of the United States on January 20, 2017. Both are herculean players on the global stage in this battle regardless of your opinion of them. Change is taking place and the after shocks under both are seismic, rippling across the landscapes of the world. Confusion reigns and the drama and chaos will increase, not decrease. The wildly bizarre will increasingly become the daily news, and believers will gasp in disbelief and shock at what they are hearing.

The material is not dated, on the contrary, it shows how those closely following the messages of Heaven can have peace of heart, mind, and soul, as there is a plan for the salvation of mankind. This is precisely why someone can maintain their wits about them as institutions topple around us. The Church and Western Civilization as we have known them, has eroded so significantly, that in the coming years it will be unrecognizable from what we have known in the past. Just look at the last several years alone. Before the New Times arrive, by definition the old must pass away. It is happening everywhere, in every profession, in every milieu. The word *Apocalypse* means *Unveiling,* and the curtain is presently being pulled back to rid those money-changers ransacking the Temple. They were present in the time of Jesus, and they are among us today.

The word crisis that is used in the sub title of this book has an emotional connotation. A crisis for one is not a crisis for another. If a tsunami in Thailand kills five thousand people and destroys fifteen thousand homes, it is a crisis for them. But to one not affected, they may go out that night for dinner and a movie, and not give much thought to it the next day. It is the same with the crisis in the government and the Church. Many are aware historically where this present crisis will bring us. However, most people are indifferent because they are either unchurched, don't believe, ceased to believe, or written off the Church as irrelevant and outdated, and want nothing to do with it due to the corruption and scandals. To them it is not a crisis, and they go about their day not giving a thought to it. But, to the thinking person, the crisis we face today is of monumental proportions with incalculable repercussions on the street, schools, and at the family hearth. Political and religious division and animosity will continue to be a cause of fractured relationships.

The battle over ideologies and what we expect from government versus personal responsibility are at the center of the conflict. If one listens, the verbal battle is, *"what do we expect from government in our lives?"* Overall, the anxiety and stress is felt because there is great uncertainty in this societal shift of values. It is uncertainty that makes an individual feel unsafe. The battle is about people in power trying to push the world in a new godless direction versus those with biblical and traditionally accepted values. Legislative victories will make one or the other governmental policy. It is a principal reason for the division we see around us.

Never in the history of the United States have the clergy given so much cause to state authorities to investigate their behavior. Some clergy have been abusive beyond any sense of decency, and it has caught up to them. The bad actors are no longer able to hide in plain sight. The pus is being exposed, and it is painful to watch. However, only when the disease is identified and treated, can the body heal — and this is a necessary step to healing the Mystical Body of Christ. The Church will schism before it heals, as the differences are so great with neither side budging an inch. There is little middle ground anymore. The faithful remnant will be increasingly marginalized and will in time move to home or small venue worship with Mass being said in those settings.

God knows there are many good men in the rank and file of clergy. But at the top, the rot, the stench of corruption has taken the edifice down with it, in what is generally called clericalism. Arrogance is a better word because some clergy have abused their rights as ordained priests. They have a higher calling to proclaim the Word of God commissioned by a vocation to protect the defenseless. Jesus called men like them, *"a brood of vipers"* and *"white watered sepulchers."* The Church is well on its way to becoming poor as its assets are incrementally being stripped and steadily litigated away. An estimate of $4.3 billion and counting has taken place in Church settlements on and off the books, and it shows no sign of slowing down. Priests and laity alike were complicit in their silence rather than deal with the mess in front of them. People have reached the breaking point by no longer donating to the Church and its mission, having decided enough is enough. The Church will become poor in its humility and poverty as in ages past, but it will blossom again in holiness. It will become pure again in the Divine Light of Truth. The liberals will take the property, believers will keep the faith. Maybe that isn't all bad since vibrant faith is hard to find in many parishes anyway.

Growing up in America in past generations provided normalcy and safety. Institutions worked, the home was generally a safe place, neighborhoods were not violent (there were exceptions), there was civility in schools, and teachers and clergy were respected. The living room was where the family could watch television without making Grandma blush. In several generations we arrived at a place not just pagan, but outright barbaric, often with public funding. Thousands of aborted babies kept in freezers and jars in the homes of abortionists is even new for America. If that is not barbaric, then I don't know what pagan and barbaric mean. These actions rival the worst in all previous civilizations. These are abominations that will make us desolate.

People transitioning to another sex is now only possible through modern science. It is an act against nature itself, and rebellion against God. It is the deep wounds and hurts from youth manifesting itself in this behavior. It is an utter sense of being lost without a vision and purpose in life. Infanticide is virtually sanctioned, endorsed, and accepted by millions of people, and promoted in many state legislatures. Live births are taking place, and then killed, so live organs can be harvested and sold at a premium price. For a large segment of the U.S. population they refuse to talk about it. It is the classic story of the frog dropped in a pot of water. All the while many faithful laity cower in fear of speaking out when these atrocities are taking place. The life of Jesus was a contradiction, and we are called to the same. If the drift of the culture doesn't bother you, you must ask yourself, *"What will it take to be bothered?"*

The difference from yesterday and today is that if there were a glitch in the system with something not working properly, it could be fixed with bipartisan political support. That concept is now history. Today, little is working anywhere as designed. People are resorting to lawlessness, because they know that many leaders and politicians are stealing as much as they can, as fast as they can. They know better than most the ship is about to go down. So the thinking is, let's take while the taking is good.

People know there is a two-tiered system of justice, those with connections and money, and everyone else. And everyone else is tired of watching media expose the indiscretions of authority figures stealing from programs their tax dollars are funding. It is why when you walk in a room today with people you don't know, everyone is guarded in their speech. The conversation can easily get out of control with a single phrase said to the wrong person. People are consumed with media to minimize social contact, and it is one reason NetFlix has had explosive growth. There is emotional safety curled up on a sofa watching a movie at night all alone.

There is a global push towards Marxism/communism. Unsuspecting people simply don't know the horrors it has brought to previous countries. The intentions may be noble in a freshman college philosophy course with the professor not having any knowledge of what socialism, Marxism, and communism will bring. But, as history has shown us, the outcome will bring pain and suffering to all. Worst of all, is how any adult could not understand its evil. Anarchy is the end result that will usher in a fascist state to control the unbridled abuse of a democratic republic.

Pope Benedict resigned on February 28, 2013 at 8:00pm. Just several hours later, lightning struck St. Peter's Dome not once, but twice. It makes one ponder. What Mother would not warn her children to prevent peril? At Fatima, Our Lady of Good Success, Our Lady of America, Our Lady of Nations, La Salette, Akita, Pontmain, Medjugorje, and many other apparition sites, she speaks as a loving mother warning her children. She instructs us how to maintain peace with a practical remedy. That is what the articles over the last eight years are about — for those with the humility of heart to listen. The Blessed Mother provides solutions for her children. While the vast majority of people are addressing the problems, few are providing real solutions. In the Old Testament there were three stages before the downfall of the people. They are Idolatry, rampant immorality, infanticide, and then destruction. You decide where America is at this point in time.

"The fear of the Lord is the beginning of wisdom, and knowledge of the Holy One is understanding" (Proverbs 9:10). The phrase "Fear of the Lord" is often misunderstood when people discuss it. It doesn't mean fear as we most often use the word, but it translates to *"awesome respect or awesome majesty."* Because we have lost the sense of the Divine, we find ourselves in this moral malaise. But we are told, at Fatima, *"In the end, My Immaculate Heart will Triumph."*

TED FLYNN
January 1, 2020
Feast of the Mother of God

"In the beginning was the Word, the Word was with God, the Word was God."

John 1:1

———

"Now you are able to appear before him holy, pure and blameless, as long as you persevere and stand firm on the solid base of the faith, never letting yourselves drift away from the hope promised by the Good News, which you have heard...."

Saint Paul to the Colossians 1:22-23

———

"The final battle between the Lord and the reign of Satan will be about marriage and the family. Don't be afraid, because anyone who works for the sanctity of marriage and the family will always be fought and opposed in every way, because this is the decisive issue."

Sister Lucy of Fatima (1907-2005) in a letter to Cardinal Carlo Caffarra after he had been appointed by Saint John Paul II with founding the Pontifical Institute for the Studies on Marriage and the Family.

———

*"People must recite the rosary every day. Our Lady requested this in her apparitions, **as if to arm us in advance against these times of diabolical disorientation,** so that we would not let ourselves be fooled by false doctrines, and that through prayer, the elevation of our soul to God would not be diminished.... **This is a diabolical disorientation invading the world and misleading souls."***

Sister Lucy of Fatima on April 12, 1970.

Cardinals Opposing Cardinals,
Bishops Against Bishops, Priests Against Priests...

"The work of the devil will infiltrate even into the Church in such a way
that one will see cardinals opposing cardinals, bishops against bishops.
The priests who venerate me will be scorned and opposed by their confreres
(other priests); Churches and altars will be sacked; the Church will be
full of those who accept compromises and the demon will press many priests
and consecrated souls to leave the service of the Lord."

Message of the Blessed Mother, Akita, Japan, October 13, 1973

The message of Akita is approved by the Catholic Church. It was given to an ill Japanese nun who bore the stigmata. Her name is Sister Agnes Sasagawa. Cardinal Joseph Ratzinger as head of the Congregation for the Doctrine of the Faith (CDF) under Pope John Paul II, who had read the Third Secret of Fatima, said that *"the messages of Fatima and Akita are essentially the same."*

The collective messages of Akita are arguably the most severe to humanity in the history of the Catholic Church, and the direct consequence of sin. The accuracy of this portion of the Akita message is borne out in the daily press around the world. Many people believe the Church has had a silent schism going on now for approximately two generations. There are some priests who with a wink and a nod (father friendly) have allowed their parishioners to cherry pick what they choose to follow. If one priest is not amenable to a certain doctrine, the individual can simply travel to another neighboring parish and find another priest who will allow them to feel comfortable with their views on just about any subject.

However, with Pope Francis we now see that the battle is more in the open. All can see the whites of the eyes no matter where one stands on any issue. Thus, the vitriol and division not seen for ages are present in the pews of the world. There is little charity and tolerance one for the other — and it is building faster and more ferocious than ever before. Some people who have had a hidden agenda contrary to Church teaching are now brazenly flaunting their views. This confusion and lack of discipline has not been seen for as long as one can remember. Woe and behold if one disagrees with another who promotes a homosexual agenda as you will be banished to the marshlands and considered intolerant. Don't expect a Christmas card or dinner invitation if you express a view not their own.

The Reformation five hundred years ago was fought principally over doctrine. The division we see today is being fought over morals. Even the Reformers didn't try to change the words of Scripture, yet that is precisely what is going on now. Sister Lucia of Fatima said before she died that the last battle in the Church would be fought over marriage and family. We are now in that battle and it is separating the men from the boys. Those who truly uphold Magisterial teaching, and those who want a watered down faith to conform to the culture of the day are engaging in a great spiritual war.

We presently have Cardinals and Bishops in the U.S. and other world cities not only allowing in-stealth an LGBT agenda, but actually promoting it. Often speakers and advocates at Church convocations are the leading crusaders for homosexual rights throughout the land. No longer shrinking violets, but the bold and bolder homosexuals now openly promote a godless and anti Scripture agenda. Cardinal Muller, former head of the Congregation for the Doctrine of the Faith (CDF) under Pope Francis said, *"Dubia Cardinals raise legitimate questions."*

Many immoral agendas are implemented a step at a time. I am reminded of the holocaust of the Jews in Nazi Germany and Europe prior to, and during World War II. Jews all over the world after the war, wondered how the holocaust could have happened. Historians wrote in amazement there was no early uprising with the signs around European Jews pointing to what inevitably happened. History tells us people of good will found it unfathomable that any nation or race could ever do something as heinous and in the open for all to see. Jews being driven to the gas chambers said, *"Can this be happening? It is not possible."* There was a complete denial of the facts in spite of what had been going on for a generation in Germany; with a progressive loss of faith starting with brain washing the youth on the humanistic philosophies of George Hegel and Friedrich Nietzsche. Win the youth — win the country. In the last fifty years the USA and the West have similarly been indoctrinated by godless philosophies and have been brought down morally by the breakdown of solid teaching on marriage and family. This has been a huge agenda of practical atheism. If a nation removes God from the classroom, the state can then easily manipulate the profession of teaching.

Each day after we see the news, many of us ask ourselves the same question: Can you top this? Did you see the news today? Is this really happening with the moral decay in our culture? Where does it stop? When does this end?

The answer is, it does not stop until courageous people express the truth rather than accept the moral slide as inevitable. The problem is that most people lack the conviction to speak up for fear of what others think. Witnessing to the truth requires that we pay a price and many are unwilling to do so. They opt to go along so they can get along.

As Timothy wrote to the faithful, *"Do your best to present yourself to God as one approved, a workman who has no need to be ashamed, rightly handling the word of truth. Avoid such godless chatter, for it will lead people into more and more ungodliness"* (II Tim. 15-16).

JESUS I TRUST IN YOU

The Secret Meaning of the Number 18 and Our Lady

How It May Pertain to the Prophesied Warning and the Great Miracle

When all is lost, a child goes to the mother. It is with the mother that the child finds the solace, gentleness, forgiveness, and understanding only a mother can give. Mankind has cried out many times in history to the Blessed Mother, and it has been through her direct intervention that history has been altered on many occasions.

At the moment, we are a morally rudderless world, and it will be again through the Blessed Mother that life-changing events will set us back on course. Sister Lucia of Fatima once used the emotive phrase that the world was in a state of "**diabolical disorientation**." Heaven is going toe to toe with the enemy, and the gates of Hell will not prevail against the Church. That is the promise of Scripture. The chosen instrument for that task by the Most Holy Trinity is the Blessed Virgin Mary — the Daughter of the Father, the Mother of the Son, and the Spouse of the Holy Spirit.

Catherine Laboure' was a twenty four year old novice in a Daughters of Charity convent at Rue du Bac in Paris when the Blessed Mother first appeared to her on July 18, 1830. The Miraculous Medal, revealed to Catherine, has been distributed around the world in the billions since 1830. The apparitions of the Virgin of the Globe, as Rue du Bac is officially called, ushered in the Marian Era as we now know it.

Our Blessed Mother appeared **18** times to Bernadette Soubirous at Lourdes, France. These apparitions began February 11, 1858 when the Blessed Mother prayed the rosary with Bernadette. On February **18**, the Blessed Mother spoke for the first time and said, *"I do not promise to make you happy in this life, but in the next."* It was at Lourdes where the Blessed Mother said for the first time: *"I am the Immaculate Conception."* The **18**th and final apparition occurred on July 16, 1858 on the Feast of Our Lady of Mount Carmel, a sacred site to the Jewish people as well as Christians.

Mirjana Soldo is one of six visionaries who have been receiving apparitions and locutions from the Blessed Mother since 1981. Three visionaries have all ten secrets, and the other three have only received nine of the ten secrets. A total of fifty-seven secrets have been given thus far by the Blessed Mother to the visionaries. The visionaries themselves don't know if there is overlap in the messages, as Mirjana said they do not discuss the secrets when they are together.

The Numbers 18 and 2 — Our Lady is Planning on Saving the World

Medjugorje has been an on going Marian apparition for the last thirty-five years. There hasn't been any Marian apparition like this in world history. The number and frequency of the messages is a story in itself and deserves honest inquiry. Why so long — and why so many? Those frequently asked questions are addressed in Mirjana's book. Mirjana is known for her depth of character, joy, wit, and laughter, but there has been intense suffering in her life. She makes it clear that Heaven has given her all the tools necessary for dealing with the rigors and mysteries of life. She has thrived in the midst of adversity touching millions in the process. With so many yearning souls making a pilgrimage to Medjugorje, there has been incalculable consolations to life's ills for those that have made the time, the effort, and the expense to make the journey.

In a new book written by Mirjana named *My Heart Will Triumph,* and released August 15, 2016, Mirjana states that March 18 will be a date of great significance that we will only understand when the events prophesied start to happen. She also mentions specifically August 2 as another important date. Mirjana regularly receives messages she conveys to the world on the second of every month. Again, only when these events happen will we understand the importance of the 2nd of the month, but more importantly the 18th, as some sort of major announcement and one of great significance.

The fact that this book by a Medjugorje visionary has been released now after thirty-five years of apparitions and messages is very significant. The Blessed Mother said very early at Medjugorje, *"I have a great plan for the salvation of mankind, and I come to tell you God exists."* Heaven has a plan and the Blessed Mother has said time and again fear does nothing to enhance our spiritual state. Joy, peace, contentment and laughter are characteristic of Mirjana that emanate from her and her family life. Mirjana said when the visionaries are around each other, the common denominator is joy and laughter.

The Blessed Mother appeared daily to Mirjana for only 18 months. Now three visionaries have all ten secrets, and three have received nine secrets thirty-five years later. Mirjana received all of the ten secrets by the 18th month from the start of the Blessed Mother's appearances. Mirjana emphaizied that her secrets deal in some capacity with the priesthood. She said, *"priests will be the bridge to the Triumph."*

The Blessed Mother visits Mirjana on her birthday March 18, *"but the Blessed Mother has never said to me Happy Birthday."* Mirjana said the Blessed Mother promised to appear on her birthday for the rest of her life. The date of March 18 will be very significant for a future event.

Mirjana said, *"only when the things contained in the secrets start to happen will the world understand why she chose the 18th of the month... When everything starts happening, then you will be able to understand why the 18th of March, why every second of the month, and why Wednesdays and Fridays are days of fasting. The significance of the date will be clear."* Mirjana's secrets are written on a scroll or parchment. Mirjana said, *"I can not divulge much about the secrets but I can say this, Our Lady is planning on changing the world."* Here is a young girl who has experienced considerable hardship in her life, and on March 18, her birthday, the Blessed Mother has never come with a greeting of Happy Birthday. Heaven's ways are not our ways.

Mirjana said August 2nd is another important day for the world. The Church celebrates August 2nd as the feast day of Our Lady of the Angels, which is connected with Saint Francis of Assisi. Mirana said, *"it was on August 2 in 1981 that Our Lady allowed the villagers to touch her dress."* Mirjana adds little else why August 2nd or the second day of the month is important.

Mirjana said, *"Our Lady is preparing us for everything that is going to take place in the world. She is training us for victory. When the events in the secrets begin, everything will be clear. You will see, for example, why she chose to appear to me on the 18th of March every year, and why I experience the other apparitions on the second day of the month. You will understand the importance of these dates, and you will realize why she has been appearing for so long."* Mirjana said, *"At this moment, according to Our Lady, we are living in a time of grace. After this will come the time of the secrets, and the time of her triumph. God-willing, you will hear from me then."*

None can doubt that the confluence of events in the world has pushed us beyond the tipping point. The world is out of control, and people are anxious and discouraged. Uncertainty and anxiety grip households. However, as Mirjana says in her book, Heaven has a plan and needs our cooperation to fulfill that plan.

Medjugorje is the Continuation and Fulfillment of Fatima

Saint John Paul II said on March 25, 1984, *"Medjugorje is the continuation of Fatima, it's the completion of Fatima."* On several occasions the seers of Medjugorje have said, *"Medjugorje is the continuation and fulfillment of Fatima."*

The main visionary of Fatima, Sister Lucia dos Santos not only confirmed, but also reported experiencing apparitions of Our Lady of Medjugorje in the convent. In Sister Emmanuel's book, *Triumph of the Heart,* she said Sister Lucia's nephew, Father Salinho, a Salesian priest who lives in Portugal, said that Sister Lucia received visions of the Blessed Mother long after 1917. According to Father Salinho, the Blessed Mother confirmed her mission in Medjugorje.

On August 25, 1991 the Blessed Mother in a message to the world from Medjugorje said, *"I invite you to renunciation for nine days so that with your help everything I wanted to realize through the secrets I began at Fatima may be fulfilled."*

In Message 357 (m) of the Marian Movement of Priests with a message titled, *My Times Have Arrived,* the message is about God's mercy and love. The Blessed Mother revealed, *"Already during this Marian Year, certain great events will take place concerning what I predicted at Fatima and have told, under secrecy, to the children to whom I am appearing at Medjugorje."* She said to Mirjana, *"What I started in Fatima, I will complete in Medjugorje. My heart will triumph."* Mirjana emphasizes in her book, that Heaven has a plan for all mankind, and the visionaries who are knowledgeable of the secrets are at total peace. At Fatima, through Mary, Jesus pointed to the significance of the Immaculate Heart in our times and emphasized that Russia is a central part of the Fatima message.

In 1981 at Medjugorje the Blessed Mother said, *"Russia will come to glorify God the most, the West has made civilization progress but without God, and acts as if they are their own creator."* Russia has always been the key to the Fatima message. It would seem logical that if Medjugorje is the completion of Fatima, then it may in some way have a strong connection to the Triumph of the Immaculate Heart.

Some Sort of Climax Awaits Mankind

On the very last page of Mirjana's book, she provides a metaphor what we may expect in the future. It is handled tactfully and with elegance to not frighten people, but she also makes a significant point what may lie ahead. She writes,

> *"Our Lady told me many things that I cannot yet reveal. For now, I can only hint at what our future holds, but I do see indications that the events are already in motion. Things are slowly starting to develop. Our Lady says, look at the signs of the times, and pray.*
>
> *I can compare it to spring-cleaning. If I want my home to be spotless, I know that I first need to turn everything upside down. I move the sofa; I stack the chairs on the table; I open all the cupboards — nothing remains in its place. My home is thrown into chaos and disorder. It's unrecognizable to my children and the peace is gone. But then I clean under everything. I wipe away all the grime. I put every piece of furniture back to its rightful place. In the end, my home is more immaculate than ever.*
>
> *This is how I see all the confusion in the world today. This is how I see Our Lady's apparitions and God's plan. A truly clean house starts with a big mess. Will you be like most children who stand back while Mom cleans, or will you not be afraid to get your hands dirty and help her? Like Our Lady said in one of her messages, 'I desire that, through love, our hearts may triumph together.'*
>
> *May the triumph of her heart begin with you."*

Several things are significant in this message. First, she is the first visionary in nearly forty years to ever publish a book on Medjugorje, and this is exactly how Heaven must want it. Second, the sub theme of the book is how through the grace of Heaven Mirjana has dealt with much suffering, and still maintains a vibrant life of joy and peace in the midst of what she does. Few people would have had the grace to wake up in the morning to have thousands of pilgrims standing outside your front door since 1981. Third, Mirjana uses a metaphor of very emotive words like: *"upside down, chaos, disorder, wipe away all the grime, and a big mess"* concerning where the world is headed. Let those who have ears hear.

Women will be able to identify more than men with this, but what we are witnessing on a global basis is like the birth of a baby. As the baby nears delivery, many women experience fear like they have never experienced before. Many don't know what to expect, and the anxiety of what may or may not happen very soon is something the couple has never experienced. There is blood, guts, tearing, shots, screaming, anxiety, fear, cursing (ask any OB-GYN) and just about every emotion imaginable for the soon to be mother and father. After the birth, there is great fatigue and relief, yet joy. The ordeal is over, and it is often as if nothing happened due to the new child and the miracle of life. Tranquility is there with the triumph of the newborn. The day that we are now in is the like the birth of a child. World events may get painful and messy before they get better.

JESUS I TRUST IN YOU

Heaven's Messages Foretold the Current Crisis and Scandal in the Church

S he is the most venerated, misunderstood, and often the most vilified woman in the world. For those who venerate her, she is called The Blessed Mother. She also has the unique distinction with one of many titles called, The Immaculate Heart of Mary. In other sects and religions, it is often called Mary idolatry, for those who do not choose to soak in all she has to offer. To those who know her, she is the most revered creature ever born on earth. She is the short cut to the heart of the Father. She is the surest, safest, and quickest way to the Trinity. Yes, she is a mystery.

Our Lady is the Daughter of the Father, the Mother of the Son, and the Spouse of the Holy Spirit. In the book of Revelation she is the Woman Clothed with the Sun (12:1), who in the end days battles the serpent and crushes its head. She is the woman mentioned in Genesis 3:15, and she is the prophetess of these times with a role ordained by the Most Holy Trinity for the salvation of mankind. Her role is unique by all measurements. Her humility towards the Will of God is unmatched in all of human history as we read in Luke chapter 2 chronicles her submissive and obedient will. Saint Augustine called her, *"the mold of God."*

Below is a general synopsis of just a few of the major mystics and approved apparition sites that Heaven has used to send messages to mankind. In pulling together the material for this article, several things became crystal clear. First, Heaven uses imagery, metaphor, simile, analogy, and parables much in the same way Jesus did in Scripture to make a point. Secondly, the material Heaven is presenting leaves little doubt on the outcome of the turmoil of the Church in particular, and the world in general find themselves. Third, many profound societal changes have occurred in the last one hundred years, and they will now happen more rapidly. Events that largely affect an interconnected world will see a quickening. Fourth, *the Deep State spoken of in the press is Freemasonry. It is insidious, hidden, and the work of Satan, which is why in the teaching of the Magisterium for hundreds of years, it has been consistently forbidden.* Dozens of edicts, instructions, papal bulls, and encyclicals mention it as an enemy of the Church. It is the malevolent force behind the curtain wrapped in stealth and deception.

Although just a sample of prophecies are presented due to space and time, the messages are that the Church will be thrown into a state of confusion that will utterly and absolutely change its character forever. Combined with many scandals presently rocking the Church that has germinated for several generations, the Church will be maintained, small in number, yet simultaneously restored to one of beauty and majesty. Therein lies our hope.

Saint Louis de Montfort presents in his masterpiece **True Devotion to Mary** one of the most potent images of the end time Church when he said, *"with one hand they shall fight, overthrow and crush the heretics with their heresies, the schismatics with* *their schisms, the idolaters with their idolatries, and the sinners with their impieties. With the other hand they shall build the temple of the true Solomon and the mystical City of God, that is to say the most holy Virgin, called by the Fathers The Temple of Solomon and the City of God.*" Due to the modern heresies we are witnessing at the present moment, we may be seeing this come to fruition.

A small sample of Heaven's messages to all of mankind is listed below.

Our Lady of Good Success, Quito, Ecuador, beginning in the late 16th to the 17th Century

Christopher Columbus, financed by Queen Isabella of Spain, had just sailed to the new world in 1492 proving to the world that the earth was not flat. Just over one hundred plus years later, a nun from Spain sailed on faith to set up a mission in Ecuador. Soon after, Heaven appeared to Mother Mariana de Jesus Torres while praying in front of the Blessed Sacrament where a lamp that had been previously lit went dark with no explanation. The Blessed Mother then appeared with a foreign source of light, and gave a prophecy that is especially relevant for our times, as it specifically mentioned the 20th century when important events would take place. She said that faith would be incrementally extinguished in the 20th century, and that impurities of the flesh would envelope the world, and this is how the demon would control mankind. Remember this prophecy was made over four hundred years ago. The Blessed Mother on one occasion cast away the infernal serpent from tormenting Mother Mariana *"with such a great roar that it caused the earth to tremble throughout the city and the convent."*

At 3:00 AM on January 11, 1611 the sisters in the convent witnessed a miracle as the archangels Michael, Gabriel, and Raphael with Saint Francis built a statue that was asked to be processed into the convent. The Blessed Mother also said:

Thus I make it known to you that from the end of the 19th century and shortly after the middle of the 20th century, passions will erupt and there will be a total corruption of morals...Unbridled passions will give way to the total corruption of customs and Satan will reign through the Masonic sects, targeting children in particular to insure total corruption... unhappy times will come wherein those who should fearlessly defend the rights of the Church will instead, blinded despite the light, give their hand to the Church's enemies and do their bidding. **But when evil seems triumphant, and when their authority abuses its power, committing all manner of injustice and oppressing the weak, their ruin shall be near. They will fall and crash to the ground.**

...The effects of secular education will increase, which will be one reason for the lack of priestly and religious vocations.... "The Sacred Sacrament of Holy Orders will be ridiculed, oppressed and despised... The demon will try to persecute the Ministers of the Lord in every possible way and he will labor with cruel and subtle astuteness to deviate them from the spirit of their vocation, corrupting many of them. These corrupted priests, who will scandalize the Christian people will incite the hatred of bad Christians and the enemies of the Roman, Catholic, and Apostolic Church to fall upon all priests....

The sacrament of matrimony, which symbolizes the union of Christ with the

Church, will be thoroughly attacked and profaned. Masonry, then reigning, will implement iniquitous laws aimed at extinguishing this sacrament. They will make it easy for all to live in sin, thus multiplying the birth of illegitimate children without the Church's blessing."

Comment: Vatican II took place over four plenary sessions opened by Pope John XXIII in 1962, and ended in 1965. The Council was contemporaneous with the apparitions at Garabandal, Spain. This was the latter half of the 20th century stated above when events saw a rapid deterioration in the Church. The Blessed Mother only had two major messages as it pertained to the Church. First was the sacredness of the priesthood, and the other stating that the Eucharist as the Body, Blood, Soul and Divinity of Jesus Christ.

It can be argued with the attack on the culture since the 1960's, there is widespread evidence that the onslaught of continued apostasy has been relentless with discernible loss of faith and moral corruption. The introduction of the birth control pill in the late 1960's seems to give more importance to the above prophecy. No other event in all of human history has had such an impact on human relations than the pill. As of October 2018, the Unites States had approximately equal births (50%) with married couples, and those out of wedlock. By comparison, in 1970 out of wedlock births were 10%.

Blessed Anna Katharina Emmerick, 1774–1824

She was an Augustinian nun who lived only fifty years. She spent most of her life in solitude; and had visions of the future of the Church. She bore the wounds of Christ with the stigmata, and lived a life of multiple sufferings in her native country of Germany.

These are just a few of her prophecies:

April 23, 1820. *I had another vision of the great tribulation. It seems to me that a concession was demanded from the clergy that could not be granted. I saw many older priests especially one, who wept bitterly. A few younger ones were also weeping. But others, and the lukewarm among them readily did what was demanded. It was as if people were splitting into two camps.*

May 13, 1820. *I saw also the relationship between the two popes... in size; heretics of every kind came into the city of Rome. The local clergy grew lukewarm, and I saw a great darkness... Then, the vision seemed to extend on every side. Whole Catholic communities were being oppressed, harassed, confined, and deprived of their freedom. I saw many churches close down, great miseries everywhere, wars and bloodshed. A wild and ignorant mob took to violent action. But, it did not last long.*

Once more I saw that the Church of Peter was undermined by a plan evolved by the secret sect, while storms were damaging it. But I also saw that help was coming when distress had reached its peak. I saw again the Blessed Virgin ascend on the Church and spread her mantle over it. I saw a Pope who at once was gentle, and very firm... I saw a great renewal, and the Church rose high in the sky.

September 12, 1820. *I saw a strange church being built against every rule...No angels were supervising the building operations. In that church, nothing came from high above. There was only division and chaos. It is probably a church of human creation. Following the latest fashion, as well as the new heterodox church of Rome, which seems of the same kind. There was nothing holy in it. Everything was done according to human reason.*

September 27, 1820. *I saw deplorable things: they were gambling, drinking, and talking in church; they were also courting women. All sorts of abominations were perpetrated there. Priests allowed everything and said Mass with much irreverence. I saw that few of them were still Godly, and only a few had sound views on things.*

October 4, 1820. *When I saw the Church of Saint Peter in ruins, and the manners in which so many of the clergy were themselves busy at this work of destruction — none of them openly willing to do it in front of the others... it was also shown to me that there were almost no Christians left in the old acceptation of the word.*

August to October, 1820. **When the Church had been for the most part destroyed (by the secret sect), and when only the sanctuary and the altar were still standing, I saw the wreckers (the secret sect) enter the Church with the Beast. There, they met a woman of noble carriage who seemed to be with child because she walked slowly. At this sight, the enemies were terrorized, and the beast could not take another step forward. It projected it neck towards the Woman as if to devour her, but the woman turned about and bowed down (towards the Altar), her head touching the ground. Thereupon, I saw the Beast taking to flight towards the sea again, and the enemies were fleeing in great confusion... Then I saw the Church was being promptly rebuilt, and she was more magnificent than ever before.**

Comment: It is fascinating that Emmerick saw two popes. At the moment, two popes are living at the same time, a very rare phenomena in the Church. The secret sect is Freemasonry, which was a constant theme of Emmerick. The plan to destroy the Church was constructed by the highest order of Freemasonry with a plan called, *The Permanent Instruction of the Alta Vendita.* The plan is breathtaking in its detail for execution, and now in hindsight, we can see the validity of the document. St. Maximilian Kolbe saw this plan in Vatican Square in 1917, and immediately launched the Militia Immaculata on October 16, 1917 to combat this heresy not even knowing about the apparitions at Fatima on October 13, 1917. The plan of the *Alta Vendita* was to place Masons in high-ranking Church positions and ultimately elect a Masonic pope. The name of the Masonic lodge in Rome where many leading clergy are members is called the Propaganda Due (P2) Lodge.

La Salette, France, 1846

Wherever the Blessed Mother speaks about freemasonry or corrupt clergy, there is an immediate movement from the Church to suppress the messages and the place it came from. Consecrated clergy are held to a higher standard than others because of who and what they represent. Laity do not take vows. It is for this reason that clerical sexual abuse is so heinous because there is a commitment of consecrated souls to protect the innocent, rather than be perpetrators involved with such a crime. La Salette is a prime example of that fidelity to the priesthood. We have also seen that in many valid apparitions in the modern era. As we look at the scandals of today at the senior level of the hierarchy, it is not difficult to go back in time to see how clergy abused their privileges of position. With a class of people highly illiterate at that time in history in France, abuses from the clergy were much easier to hide.

The destruction of the Roman Catholic Church was well under way since the French Revolution (1789) that has wreaked havoc on the Church with ramifications to this very day. It was one of the most important dates in all of Western Civilization. The *Alta Vendita* was being implemented for the demolition of the Church from within. *Masons asserted that the Church was too powerful, too large with so many land holdings, and wealth yielding so much authority, so the best strategy was to dismantle it from within. It was simply not feasible to take it head on as it would crush those that came against it due to its influence and social structure for 1,800 years.* The venomous writings of Voltaire against the Church inciting the masses had a profound impact on people as the abuses of the French and European monarchies were exposed and were no longer tolerable. The abuses of the French monarchy were real and substantial upon its citizenry.

The Alta Vendita states that, *"Our final end is that of Voltaire and of the French Revolution, the destruction forever of Catholicism and even of the Christian idea which, if left standing on the ruins of Rome, would be the resuscitator of Christianity later on."* The Masons published these instructions in 1822.

For those that may think this is the material of conspiracy theorists and the hob-goblin of minds in altered states, it has been Church teaching for centuries. Catholics are not permitted to be Masons. Many, however, are unaware of the Church's long-standing position. The secret papers fell into the hands of Pope Gregory XVI (1765-1846) and were published at the request of Saint Pope Pius IX (1792-1872) by Jacques Cretineau-Joly in his work published in 1859 called *The Roman Church and the Revolution.* Pope Pius IX guaranteed the authenticity of the documents in his approbation of February 25, 1861 when he said to the author that the letters are proof of the existence of this conspiracy against the Catholic Church. **Monsignor George E. Dillon, D.D., reproduced the *Permanent Instruction* in his work, *Grand Orient Freemasonry, Unmasked as the Secret Power Behind Communism* (1885). Pope Leo XIII Was so Impressed by the Book he Had it Published in Italian.**

At the time of the La Salette apparitions, the Church and French government were in chaos because of the French Revolution (1789). France had been previously called the Elder Daughter of the Church because it had such a rich Catholic heritage. Thousands of clergy left France in fear of their lives prior to La Salette, thousands were murdered during the reign of terror and beyond the French Revolution, and many that did stay in France capitulated to state dictates for survival. The French Catholic Church was rudderless and corrupt. It was not an easy time to be a believing Catholic, and this was understandable as war ravages nations for a long time after the event. It takes a long time for a nation to find its equilibrium after a revolution — if ever. This was the atmosphere of France when the apparitions began. The revolution whose ideas spread had destroyed the civility, normalcy, and governance of a large portion of Europe.

There is confusion to this day around the messages and the apparitions of La Salette. On September 19, 1846 the Blessed Mother appeared to two young mountain children by the name of Melanie and Maximin. Pope Pius IX was made aware of the messages, and they were neither approved nor disapproved at the time, which is customary and prudent in the Church. The local bishop said that the events did occur. Due to the controversy surrounding the apparitions, the approval came, but years later. The confusion around the events were significant at the time, because freemasonry set out to destroy the messages with cooperation from some bishops. The messages were highly critical of the corrupt clergy and the Blessed Mother said, *"the clergy was a cesspool of impurity."* This is no small thing to be said by the Queen of Heaven and Earth about her beloved priest sons.

The messages of La Salette were ultimately approved by the Catholic Church and given the imprimatur by Bishop Zola of Leece, France on November 15, 1979. The message read in part: *"The priests, ministers of my Son, the priests, by their wicked lives, by their irreverence and their impiety in the celebration of the holy mysteries, by their love of money, their love of honors and pleasures, and the priests have become cesspools of impurity. Yes, the priests are asking vengeance, and vengeance is hanging over their heads. Woe to the priests and those dedicated to God who by their unfaithfulness and their wicked lives are crucifying my Son again! The sins of those dedicated to God cry out towards Heaven and call for vengeance, and now vengeance is at their door... God will strike in an unprecedented way...in the year 1864, Lucifer with a large number of demons will be unloosed from Hell...Evil books will be abundant on earth...Woe to the princes of the Church who think of piling riches upon riches to protect their authority and dominate with pride...France, Italy, Spain, and England will be at war...the mountains and all nature will tremble in terror, for the disorders and crimes of men have pierced the vaults of Heavens... Rome will lose the faith and become the seat of the Antichrist...The demons of the air together with the antichrist will perform great wonders on earth and in the atmosphere, and men will become more and more perverted..."* And in the end, *"God will be served and glorified."*

The message of LaSalette are severe ones for mankind. They were precipitated by grave sin, yet end with a promise of great hope. The Blessed Mother said to the Marian Movement of Priests, *"the times in which we are living is 1000 times worse than at the time of the flood."* The message of La Salette in its totality is a lengthy one that deserves attention because Heaven makes it clear there are repercussions for sin as it was then, and is now.

Fatima, Portugal, 1917

For anyone who has ever studied apparitions, locutions, or messages from Heaven, it would be hard to find one more significant than Fatima. After the failed assassination attempt on his life in 1981, Pope John Paul II told his friend Slovakian Bishop

Paul Hnilica, SJ the following, *"Paul, in these three months I have come to understand that the only solution to all the problems of the world, the deliverance from war, the deliverance from atheism, and the defection from God is the conversion of Russia. The conversion of Russia is the content and meaning of the message of Fatima. Not until then, will the Triumph of Mary come."*

Fatima is the key Marian apparition of the 20th Century. It is the cornerstone the others build upon and compliment. Pope Pius XII noted that the message is one of the greatest interventions of God through Mary in world history since the death of the apostles. Only in the name of God does the Blessed Mother intervene. She does not say a word, does not take a step without the explicit will of God. The message of Fatima cannot be understood if you do not know atheistic communism, if one does not know what happened in Russia.

Pope Pius XI said, *"Today we see something in world history that has never been seen before: the waving of the flag of Satan in the battle against God and religion, against all peoples, and in all parts of the world, a phenomena that outdoes all that happened before."*

In the history or mankind, nothing in our past rivals the brutality of man against man like communism. It surpassed in scope all former persecutions of the Church. Hitler was responsible for the deaths of approximately twelve million people, including the holocaust and all war victims. Lenin, Mao, Stalin, and others after them are responsible for hundreds of millions of deaths under the banner of communist rule. Nearly 300 million inhabitants in what was the former USSR, and the 1.4 billion living in China were under communist governments with a firm doctrine of life without God. To openly express faith in God would cost you your life. It is mind numbing to think that at one point thirty-six nations embraced the ideology of communism. The sad reality is that the world was heavily colored pink or red under atheistic rule.

Since the Bolshevik Revolution of 1917, Satan has worked ferociously to control a country spanning eleven time zones from Saint Petersburg bordering Europe in the west, to Vladivostok in the east, a brief ship ride away from Alaska. The Soviet reach was dominant and brutal to its friends, foes and neighbors alike without discrimination, if they were to cross the plans of the hammer and sickle. To have even a remedial understanding of Russia will enable the individual to understand Fatima. Since the world did not pay attention to what was asked at Fatima, the repercussions to the loss of faith and destructions to families was incalculable. Even with a spectacular miracle of the sun on October 13, 1917 the world still paid little attention to Heaven's request.

Marian people know the issue of communism spreading its errors throughout the world, **but few know that the Soviet system spread abortion as a tenet of their ideology long before it was done in the west in a more common way — legal or illegal.** It was another facet of Russia *"spreading her errors throughout the world."* In every respect communism was the epitome of a godless and ruthless existence for people. At any one time up to three million people were in labor camps or in transport to camps by rail. Communism was the definition of human horror.

There are two major aspects to Fatima that still bring confusion and often division to well intentioned people to this day. **One is the issue of the Consecration of Russia, and the other is information around the release of the Third Secret and its exact content.** Multiple hundreds of thousands of pages (yea verily) have been written on each of these subjects for a very long time and authors are only as good on either subject as the footnote they use, and what source they believe. The disinformation from leading hierarchy in the Church seeking to discredit the messages has been intense, deliberate, and calculated with precision.

On the 13th of the month from May to October of 1917, the Blessed Mother came to three young illiterate children in a remote and sparsely inhabited small city in Portugal called Fatima. Messages were given for all mankind that would radically change world history. Directives were given to the Church at large that were generally ignored, thus we see the severe consequences for not obeying. Pontiffs since 1917 were acutely aware of the contents of the Third Secret, and for reasons only open to speculation, the Church has chosen not to release it to the satisfaction of all. When the faithful gather and speak on this issue, it is often like a conversation on who killed JFK.

Was the Consecration of Russia Accomplished?

The first major controversy is the issue of the Consecration of Russia. Father N. Gruner of the *Fatima Crusader* campaigned and wrote his entire adult life about Fatima. He was resolute until his death that the Consecration of Russia as asked by the Blessed Mother was not done properly. He felt the forces of evil entrenched in the Vatican had an agenda to destroy what the Blessed Mother was asking and false information was continually being disseminated. Others believe that on March 25, 1984 the Consecration by Pope John Paul II was done as asked. Because it was NOT done in union with all the bishops of the world, many feel the event was inconsequential because it did not follow the specific rubrics as the Blessed Mother specifically asked. Those denying it was done properly failed to see the CONVERSION of Russia, thus it was incomplete of the requirements to fulfill the Blessed Mother's request. Since it was not done as asked, then Russia had several generations to spread her errors throughout the world.

Was the Third Secret Fully Revealed?

The second major controversy revolved around The Third Secret and the release of its full content. With the dawn of the Third Millennium, Pope John Paul II visited Fatima, a place of apparitions of Our Lady to which he had a deep devotion. On stage with Pope John Paul II at Fatima were Cardinal Ratzinger, the head of the Congregation of the Doctrine of the Faith (CDF), Sister Lucia, and many other high ranking officials including Cardinals Sodano and Bertone. After hearing what was read concerning the secret immediately after the Mass at Fatima, Mother Angelica said on live television, *"I don't think we got the whole thing."*

On May 13, 2010, while celebrating Mass at Fatima, Pope Benedict said, *"We would be mistaken to think that Fatima's prophetic mission is complete."* In addition, he said, ***"to those who think the full measure of the text of the secret has been revealed, you*** *are deceived."* The issue at hand is what exactly is the drama in the Vatican for disinformation. What is known for sure is that a portion of the secret is indicated that there would be widespread apostasy in the Church.

Garabandal Spain, 1961-1965

Once again, the Queen of the Cosmos chose a remote mountain hamlet and gave messages to pure souls that are unable to interpret messages on their own. To four young girls from the Cantabrian Mountains in northern Spain, not far from the Bay of Biscay, the Blessed Mother warns humanity in 1961 that, *"the cup is filling up,"* and by 1965 added that, *"the cup is flowing over." The apparitions of Garabandal and what was said there were contemporaneous with the four major sessions of Vatican II that altered the Church in major ways from all historical precedent. Thousands of clergy incrementally left all forms of religious life after the sixteen documents of Vatican II were released for public consumption.* These men and women felt the Church was going in the wrong direction so they left. However, there were profound seismic events that were taking place in the world, not just in the Church. The outcome of Vatican II has generated enormous controversy in their own right. What may have been the intent of the Church in writing, was heavily distorted by liberals to reform the Church wanting to steer the Church in a more modern direction. At this point in time with writings released by senior Church officials, this is no longer a debatable fact.

The messages of Garabandal are about two major things. The importance of the priesthood, and the sacredness of the Eucharist were Heaven's major themes. Both aspects of these fundamental aspects of Catholicism changed dramatically at Vatican II and came under attack from all directions around this time as modernism slammed into long held doctrine. The conflict intensified in the Church. Parallel to the time of Vatican II was the sexual revolution in the western world and undue emphasis on materialism and pleasure. Long held sacred doctrine of theology were distorted by left leaning clergy.

In addition to the messages, there were major events prophesied at Garabandal that are so spectacular, it is difficult to grasp. John Haffert, founder of the Blue Army wrote a book in 1958 titled, *Fatima: There is Nothing More.* Although the Fatima messages had not had their full impact on the world, the messages of 1917 had not changed and there was not much more to come. Six major messages over six months in 1917 are at the core of the messages of Fatima. At Garabandal, the Blessed Mother appeared over 2,000 times to the four young girls. Heaven will move with or without us, but one thing is certain. Heaven is dynamic and not static. The future of prophetic events shifted to Garabandal after Fatima, and those who journey there with a knowledge of apparitions realize that major events are on the horizon.

Prophesied are miracles to occur that have never happened before. Those who travel there at a certain time will be healed of all illness, a World Wide Warning where every man, woman, and child on earth will see the state of their soul as God sees it at judgment. A Great Miracle that defies all reason much like the Miracle of the Sun at Fatima, where the sun hurtled towards earth and the 70,000 in attendance felt the earth was coming to an end. ***However, this Miracle of Garabandal will be greater than the one at Fatima, and it will be Eucharistic and Marian.*** One can only guess. One of Saint Padre Pio's favorite verses in the bible was *"we all see through the glass darkly"* (I Cor. 13:12). Saint Pio and Saint Mother Teresa were firm believers in Garabandal. Our finite minds cannot fathom the enormity of Heaven's mysteries. Once we realize that, we will live the mystery of life in greater peace that Heaven is in complete control.

With the confluence of confusion and chaos in the world, events are mounting in severity and frequency. In short, man is running out of answers to solve problems through human reason and actions. We are now waiting on Heaven's intervention to remedy this disordered existence, and we may be getting closer to the fulfillment of the events prophesied for the last several hundred years.

The Blessed Mother said at Garabandal to the visionaries, ***"Many cardinals, many bishops, and many priests are on the road to perdition and bringing many souls with them."*** Perdition means Hell, a concept many feel is no longer real even though Jesus spoke of it by name several times. With the crisis in the Church of all faiths, challenging Sacred Scripture by many leading clergy promoting alternative lifestyles, with new additions to nomenclature about what constitutes the definition of a family, a crisis is here. Fatima has passed, and the new is being ushered in. We are in times of change.

When then Bishop Ratzinger was a young professor at Regensburg University in Germany, in 1969, he spoke about the future of the Church. It was four years after Vatican II closed its final session and he articulated where he thought the Church was headed. He felt the changes coming to the Church would be greater than those of the French Revolution. He wrote that the Church would be reduced to a tiny remnant of what it once was, and become a very poor Church that would lose all of its possessions that it took centuries to build. As Pope Benedict XVI, he modified his opinion and said he felt the changes to the Church would be far greater than what he said in 1969, with changes as great as the Church functioning under Roman times. That is why Heaven will intervene because God never abandons His people.

There is Akita (1973), Medjugorje, (1981) and other sites where Heaven speaks to those willing to listen. The messages of the Blessed Mother always point to her Son Jesus as she said at the miracle at Cana where her request ushered in His public ministry, *"Do whatever He tells you."* We have Saint John Bosco speaking of the barque of Peter going though turbulent waters where the **Twin Pillars of the Eucharist and the Blessed Mother** are at either side of the boat giving it safe passage.

Saint Louis de Montfort in his timeless masterpiece, **True Devotion to Mary** speaks of the end day Marian apostle fighting with one hand, and building with the other. It is she now in her appointed time at the direction of the Most Holy Trinity, to fight the Deep State of Freemasonry, and free the Church from the shackles of deceit at the interior of the Church.

The answer and solution for the United States to fulfill the Blessed Mother's request to process the statue of Our Lady of America into the Basilica of the Shrine of the Immaculate Conception in Washington, D.C. The request arose in an approved apparition that began on September 24, 1956, with messages to a nun by the name of Sister Mary Mildred Neuzil, from Fostoria, Ohio. It has been ignored by the bishops of the U.S to do as she requested, much in the same way the bishops of the world did not consecrate Russia as asked for the remedy of what ailed the world in the last century. What is the force behind the bishops of the U.S. not fulfilling a simple request where the United States would be restored to purity, with promised miracles at the Shrine greater than those granted at Lourdes, and Fatima if we did as Our Lady asked? **A request so simple — with a promise so great.**

Indeed, a battle behind the scenes of fierce ideological differences and worldly allegiances, with the cohort of Satan battling that of God.

Believers have the tools at their disposal daily to correct the tide of filth and violence consuming our culture. These include Mass, confession, the rosary, prayer from the heart, fasting Scripture reading, adoration, community, and the things we know we should be doing. We have at our disposal the remedy. Now we need to act and apply the remedy!

JESUS I TRUST IN YOU

What Does the FBI, The DOJ, the Secret Society, and Our Lady Have in Common? More Than You Think. More Than You Know.

After the United States saw the carnage of World War II, where an estimated 60 million people died in all theaters of the war, the United States Congress established the National Security Act of 1947. The goal of the Act was to monitor world events and not be caught off guard with any foreign power having ill intent against the U.S. A secret government had just been established, and undoubtedly, the politicians assumed they had America's best interests in mind. The head of the Office of Strategic Services (OSS) during the war was a man by the name Wild Bill Donovan, and he was commissioned to set up a new agency to monitor these world events. It was called the Central Intelligence Agency (CIA). No one ever dreamed in 1947 the hydra would grow so many heads.

Over time, the now seventeen U.S. intelligence agencies and other bodies of institutional governance in the United States has become a group of subversive secretive government unto themselves, accountable to no one. It is called by many the Deep State, or the Shadow Government, and it is a virulent cancer on the United States and the world. The darkness behind this cabal of secret agencies is now being exposed to the light precisely at this point in time.

Is this a Conspiracy Theory as many could claim? No, it is an informed opinion based upon historical facts that are now being brought to the forefront for exactly what it is: a corrupt cabal collapsing in front of our eyes — in real time. It has run its course, and Heaven is intervening. The fight is ferocious. Powerful people and organizations don't give up their positions lightly without a battle. The battle is between the sons of darkness and the sons of light, because it is the fiercest battle of all time.

These intelligence agencies appeared to have the best interests of America in mind, when instituted at their genesis, but over time they have morphed into the shadow government we see today. In these last 70 years, the intelligence community combined with big government, big business, interlocking directorships of corporations, and The Secret Society has become a destructive force in the United States undermining the democratic rule of law. How did this happen?

The answer to that spiritually is quite simple. It is rooted in what lies in the human heart. It happens when power and authority remain unchecked by another person, or entity. The original framers of the U.S. Constitution were aware of unchecked authority that would ultimately result in the abuse of power, so a system was set up with checks and balances to counter the abuse they knew would come without a system of oversight. As the common adage says, *"Power corrupts, and absolute power corrupts absolutely."* Founding Father James Madison said, *"men are not angels, and that is why we need oversight of government."*

A republic can only endure when there is voluntary compliance with the law. The pursuit of virtue and combined with sincere religious instruction and belief is necessary. Today, we have little of either in the public square, and especially in government schools (public schools) that have been on the fast track to expunge God from the life of mankind in every possible way. Hitler was clear that if you brainwash the youth, you'll own the next generation. Hitler's feared SS was heavily Catholic Swabians from the affluent south of Germany, who had been fed a constant stream of evil teaching for several generations by the time Hitler came along. Thus his godless tyranny was accepted by the general population.

President John F. Kennedy: Understanding the Threat

On April 27, 1961 President John F. Kennedy addressed the Newspaper Publishers of America at the Waldorf Astoria Hotel in New York City. He spoke about how Secret Societies undermine a democracy. Listening to that speech today on You Tube will send shivers up your spine on the validity of his informed statements concerning a subversive body of people having a profound influence over the U.S. Congress. He said this group exerts control through financial largesse and their loyal secretive interconnected networks. All the while operating with impunity in plain site enjoying the sumptuous feast of *"easy careers."* Even in 1961, just sixteen years after the establishment of the CIA and the birth of the modern leviathan intelligence community, this community had become entrenched as bloated arrogant entities with off the book black op budgets. A body of people had emerged in a short amount of time to stage a coup d'etat to rule government.

Patrimony and privilege from The Secret Society were placing people in power to ultimately control the government through stealth networks — namely Freemasonry, which answers to an organization outside government and operates with their own set of rules. At the Waldorf with speechwriters from **The Best and the Brightest** the world had to offer, President Kennedy said, *"the very word secrecy is repugnant in a free and open society and we are as a people inherently and historically opposed to secret societies, to secret oaths and to secret proceedings. We decided long ago that the dangers of excessive and unwarranted concealment of pertinent facts far outweigh the dangers which are cited to justify it. Even today, there is little value in opposing the threat of a closed society by initiating its arbitrary restrictions. Even today, there is little value in insuring the survival of our nation if our traditions do not survive with it.* **And there is very grave danger that an announced need for increased security will be seized upon by those anxious to expand its meaning to the very limits of official censorship and concealment...**"Kennedy was directly addressing the issue of a body of people who had an agenda of their own outside the constitutional process. One doesn't have to be an historian to see that a constitutional crisis is in our midst.

What Exactly is THE Secret Society? The Black Beast?

Before Donald Trump was the GOP nominee for president, former Speaker of the House of Representatives Newt Gingrich said to Bill O'Reilly on *The O'Reilly Factor,* *"Bill, you have to remember, Trump has not been initiated, he is not a member of The Secret Society."* He used the definite article **THE**. So what exactly is **THE** Secret Society where if you address it, you may be labeled the village idiot spewing conspiracy theories? It is Freemasonry. Freemasonry is the most virulent, diabolical, and destructive source of power working against the Catholic Church from within and without, having an active agenda to dismantle the existing form of ecclesial and civic government. The name of the lodge in Rome where an estimated one-third of the leading Curia is Masonic is called the P2 Lodge, Italian for *Propaganda Due.*

In message 405 to the Marian Movement of Priests, Our Lady instructs, *"Above all, my Immaculate Heart becomes today the sign of my sure victory, in the great struggle which is being fought between the followers of the huge Red Dragon and the followers of the Woman Clothed with the Sun. In this terrible struggle, there comes up from the sea, to aid of the Dragon, a beast like a leopard.*

If the Red Dragon is Marxist atheism, the Black Beast is Freemasonry. The Dragon manifests himself in the force of his power; the Black Beast, on the other hand acts in the shadow, keeps out of sight and hides himself in such a way as to enter in everywhere. He has the claws of a bear and the mouth of a lion, because he works everywhere with cunning and with the means of social communication, that is to say, through propaganda. The seven heads indicate the various Masonic lodges, which act everywhere in a subtle and dangerous way."

The FBI and the Intelligence Community Today

It had been found out primarily through the emails of FBI staffers Peter Strzok & Lisa Paige that there was an attempt to impede Trump from being elected at the highest levels in the intelligence community. Once Trump was elected there was an agenda to remove him through impeachment under the ruse of Russian collusion. Since they were unable to block Trump's victory, the cabal of the Shadow Government went the next step with plans to impeach him. Peter Strzok in that widely known email wrote that a meeting was to take place the day after the election **off site** to begin a campaign to strategize how to remove Trump. Strzok specifically said, *"THE Secret Society was to meet off site."* Coincidence? I think not. We didn't end up where we are today by accident. The attempted coup was orchestrated by a network of evil men who have been planning this for a long time. Indeed, a long time.

There has been an internal war of opposing ideologies in the intelligence community and how America should be governed for several generations. As we now know, there are many good people in the rank and file in the intelligence community who believe in its originally designed mission. However, we are also learning there are many powerful well placed people who adhere to the mission of **The** Secret Society and their ideology. The Foreign Intelligence Surveillance Act (FISA) memo's are the tip of the iceberg concerning how deep this issue really runs throughout business and government. It has been reduced in life to no longer being a democrat or republican, but believers versus unbelievers — light vs. darkness.

During Watergate, Deep Throat approached Bob Woodward in a parking garage and told him, *"It is deeper than you can imagine. The FBI, Justice, and the entire intelligence community are involved, your life is in danger."* And this was in 1973/1974 this cabal were running a secretive collaborative government with significant authority in agencies throughout government and industry. Remember, President Richard Nixon was a Republican.

Nixon had fallen out of favor with the global elite and he had to be removed because he wasn't going along with their plans. Nixon had a delusional moment and thought he was in charge. As long as leaders go along, they will get along. Think Bill Clinton with two terms, George W. Bush with two terms, and Obama with two terms to carry the water for **The** Secret Society and the global elite. Cross them, and it is tough sledding going forward, or criminal indictment. Trump is fighting over more than one hundred years of institutional rot, and it won't be turned around except for the prayers of the faithful and divine intervention at this point. Our Lady is involved in exposing the evil plans of the Masons in a significant way on behalf of her people.

Heaven is Intervening at This Point in Time—Her Target

Much of the entire intelligence community and senior levels of government and business are thoroughly embedded with each other. The revolving door of government and big business promote each other from within to ensure loyalty to their secret oaths to achieve their goals in anonymity. Heaven at this point in time is dismantling it. We have some strong indications that the Divine Plan for humanity is coming into play in incremental steps, pointing to a possible turn around in the direction of the country.

The Lord is hearing the cries of His people who have been in prayer and fasting. His remnant, God's people faithful to the gospel have been mobilized and are in spiritual battle. The veil of lies and deceit is presently being lifted, and a joyful and glorious day is upon us. The Lord and His Blessed Mother are now shining a spotlight exposing the enemies of truth.

We have a track record from a very reliable source — The Blessed Mother — as the prophetess of our age who has been appointed by the Trinity for this role at this moment in time to take on Freemasonry, the same way she won other battles for her children in the past.

So what exactly does the Blessed Mother say about her next target of evil? To the Marian Movement of Priests, she identifies her next target of conquest. In message number 456, *In The Name of Mary,* delivered just before the fall of the former USSR in 1991 from Slovakia, Our Lady says:

"In the name of your Heavenly Mother, yes, in the name of Mary, the Turks were defeated, when they laid siege to the city of Vienna, and threatened to invade and destroy the whole Christian world. They were far superior in strength, in numbers and in weapons, and they felt that their victory was assured. But I was publicly invoked and called upon: my name was inscribed upon their banners and shouted out by the soldiers, and thus through my intercession, there took place the miracle of this victory which saved the Christian world from its destruction. It is for this reason that the Pope, instituted on this day, the feast of the name of Mary.

In the name of Mary, Marxist communism, which for decades had been exercising its rule and holding so many of my poor children in oppressive and bloody slavery, has been defeated in these countries. Not because of political movements or persons, but through my personal intervention, has your liberation finally come about.

It will again be in the name of Mary that I will bring to completion my work with the defeat of Masonry, of every diabolical force, of materialism, and of practical atheism, so that all humanity will be able to attain its encounter with the Lord and be thus purified and completely renewed, with the triumph of my Immaculate Heart in the world.

It is for this reason that I desire that the feast in honor of the name of Mary be restored, now that you are entering into the fiercest moments of the struggle and the most painful stage of the great tribulation."

Several very important things are being said.

1. This message is about her agenda, not about Russia as Fatima was, it is not about the region of the Persian Gulf, North Korea, the Korean Peninsula, China, Iran, Iraq, Saudi Arabia, or counties in the forefront of geopolitics that dominate the news. She did not say, LGBTQ, Islam, migration, immigration, sex trafficking, or apostasy of faith. It is specifically about Freemasonry. How interesting a subject under the radar to the average person knowing its hidden agenda. Its tentacles run far, wide, and deeper than most can imagine — always operating in secret. Man hacks at the branches of evil, Heaven goes to the root of evil.

2. The Christian world defeated the Islamic powers at the Battle of Lepanto (1571), and the Siege of Vienna (Turks, 1683), against great odds after invoking her name.

Similarly, under enormous odds, the Soviet Empire stretching from Vladivostok in the East, to St. Petersburg in the west were defeated without bloodshed. The USSR just collapsed, and no one saw it coming other than the Marian devotee following her messages. The CIA (an oxymoron) said they never saw its collapse coming.

3. When we march under her banner and shout out her name there is protection and victory. Victory is swift and decisive if we follow her directives under her mantle. It is her personal intervention that assures this victory, not the words of political rulers and pundits, but because of her love for all people.

4. It is Our Lady who will bring about to completion her work with the defeat of Masonry and all that comes with it; every diabolical force, practical atheism, and materialism. These events will take place.

5. We are in the fiercest moments of the struggle. Much like birth pangs that increase in intensity before the birth of a child, the battle at the moment will increase and will be painful (and is) for many.

We are witnessing evil v. good, virtue v. vice, God's cohort v. Satan's cohort, children of light v. children of darkness; and the fight is spiritual at the highest levels in Heaven. The reign of Satan as prince of this world is about to be broken by the heel of a woman who steps on the head of the serpent. Much like Queen Esther interceded to the King on behalf of her people with evil men around her seeking her destruction, the Blessed Mother is interceding on our behalf to the King of Kings, Our Lord Jesus Christ.

Also, in the same way the Third Secret of Fatima was not released with the support of the bishops of the world as Our Lady asked, so too the battle for Our Lady of America is being blocked by strong Masonic forces because Heaven's promise is so great. Her promise is one of purity being restored to America if Bishops do as Our Lady asks, when she is enthroned at the Basilica of the National Shrine of the Immaculate Conception in Washington, D.C. With a promise so magnificent for all America and the world, clergy in positions of great power are blocking her request.

In message 457 to the Marian Movement of Priests, Our Lady says, *"Thus, by means of you, I am able to continue my motherly work of mercy, which I have begun in these countries, but which I must still bring to completion in every part of the world, for the triumph of my Immaculate Heart."*

"Thus, by means of you." Our Lady as said she needs us to participate in her redemptive plan for mankind. Your prayers, your fasting, your sacrifices... Heaven needs you to speak up and stop the deceit. It is your time.

JESUS I TRUST IN YOU

When Did The 100 Year Reign of Satan Begin?

Speculation Continues in the 100th Anniversary of Fatima

On October 13, 1884, Pope Leo XIII heard Satan ask God for 75-100 years to have dominion over mankind. According to Pope Leo XIII, Satan was granted the time to test mankind in unknown ways. Pope Leo fainted after he heard the conversation between God and Satan. He immediately composed the Saint Michael Prayer, which was said after every Low Mass until Vatican II in the mid 1960's.

The problem many people have had with Pope Leo's vision is, *"What was the start date for the 100 years?"* Was it the first Fatima apparition on May 13th? Was it the last Fatima apparition on October 13, 1917 with the Miracle of the Sun? Was it the July 13th 1917 Fatima apparition where Russia was mentioned for the first time? Why not the beginning of World War I with the guns of August 1914? World War I began on July 28, 1914 and didn't end until November 1918. Over one million died or were injured at the Battle of the Somme (Somme Offensive) over a period of four and a half months in 1916, separating itself as one of the bloodiest periods in world history. An estimated fifteen million died, and for that time this was a significant percentage population for Western Europe. Is this a valid or generally accepted day for the start date of Satan's 100-year reign?

The world would recognize World War I as a more substantial event than three little simple illiterate children in a poor hamlet of Portugal receiving messages from the Mother of Jesus. Could Tsar Nicholas II of Russia abdicating the throne of Russia on March 15, 1917 (after having a royal family in Russia for over 300 years) be the start date? This was two months before the first apparition of May 13th at Fatima. Assuming the throne in 1894, on March 16, 1917, Tsar Nicholas and his family fled for their lives. The monarchy was overthrown with this act in March 1917. Could the October/November Revolution in 1917 be the start date of the 100-year reign? Maybe November 7, 1917 when Vladimir Lenin took control of Russia? To put in perspective how small numbers can effectuate change, there were only 10,500 card-carrying members of the communist party by mid-1917 that overtook a nation of approximately 150 million people. Lethargy has its consequences. Could the Spanish Flu of 1918-1920, that infected 500 million people worldwide and killed approximately 75 million people be the event?

Many Catholics point to 33 years after Pope Leo's October 13, 1884 vision to the start of the Bolshevik Revolution in October 1917. 1884 + 33 = 1917. Since Jesus walked the earth for 33 years, is it plausible that this is the commencement date that begins the 100-year cycle as some claim? We know Heaven sees things we do not see on a supranational level operating with preternatural gifts? Is there a deeper meaning behind the date of 1917? Fatima as the cornerstone of 20th Century apparitions plays a role with the Red Dragon of atheistic communism and the Black Beast of Masonry.

Consecration to the Sacred Heart Delayed

On June 17, 1689, Sister Margaret Mary Alacoque (Saint, 1647-1690) was asked by Our Lord to communicate to King Louis XIV of France to consecrate France to the Sacred Heart of Jesus for its protection. Several other things were asked which he did not do, including building a Basilica to the Sacred Heart in France. One hundred years later to the day on June 17, 1789, the monarchy of France fell in what was arguably one of the greatest events in world history ushering in a new age of intellectual enlightenment without God. On July 14, 1789, the symbol of French resistance took place with the storming of the Bastille. Liberty, equality & fraternity began a new time under godless secularism that spread throughout Europe and thus the rest of the world. France as the *"Elder daughter of the Church"* had not complied with a simple request for its own safety and welfare. The Sun King of France Louis XIV as the longest reigning monarch in European history did not respect a simple request. Much in the same way as France, the Blessed Mother asked for the Consecration of Russia by name at Fatima, and that was not done as asked in union with the bishops of the world.

While in Rianjo, Spain in August of 1931, Jesus communicated to Sister Lucia of Fatima that the failure of the Church would have dire consequences. The Lord said, *"Make it known to My ministers, given that they follow the example of the King of France in delaying the execution of My requests, they will follow him into misfortune."*

King Louis XVI was executed by guillotine in 1793 bringing to an end over one thousand years of continuous monarchy in France. Before death, he attempted to consecrate France as was asked during the reign of Louis XIV, but it was too late. The Lord said to Sister Lucia concerning Russia, *"They did not wish to heed my request! Like the King of France they will repent of it, and they will do it, but it will be late. Russia will already have spread its errors in the world. Provoking wars and persecutions against the Church. The Holy Father will have much to suffer."*

Could there be more to the one hundred year story on a deeper level than the obvious? Due to the ravages of World War I at its peak with carnage to the people of Europe, Pope Benedict XV asked for the Blessed Mother to intervene on May 5, 1917. The pope asked the people to pray a novena to Our Lady Queen of Peace to hear the cries of the people to end the war. Eight days later on May 13, 1917, the Blessed Mother made her first public apparition at Fatima, culminating with the Miracle of the Sun on October 13, 1917, the last public apparition. There were an estimated 70,000 people present with the world press in attendance. What is generally not known is the dominance of Masonry in Portugal in particular, and Europe in general at this time. Masonry has been a dominant political and economic force hidden behind the curtain. 2017 is the 300th anniversary of Freemasonry in its present form, and the 500th anniversary of the Reformation. Masonry is Satan's diabolical army or force on earth having rituals, laws, hierarchy, and customs for its members to battle against the forces of God.

Our Lady of Good Success: Quito, Ecuador

The Church approved apparitions of Quito, Ecuador, under the title of Our Lady of

Good Success, address the role of Masonry in the 20th Century. Mother Mariana de Jesus Torres (1563-1635) sailed from Spain to found a convent and promote a new order in Quito. Our Lord, the Blessed Mother, and the Archangels appeared to her and gave messages for her own edification and to the world. Three centuries after her death, her body was exhumed and found to be incorrupt. Mother Mariana said, *"... I make it known to you that from the end of the 19th century and shortly after the middle of the 20th Century... unbridled passions will erupt and there will be a total corruption of customs (morals), because Satan will reign through the Masonic sects, targeting the children in particular to insure general corruption... then through the faith of the just a 'complete restoration."* Reading her messages is like reading the news over the last sixty years. We especially see today how viciously the culture war has taken its toll on marriage and the family. Who would believe years ago that today we would be having a battle over gender identity? To even mention it shows how absurd we have become.

Maximillian Kolbe and the Militia Immaculata

On October 16, 1917, three days after the October 13th Miracle of the Sun, there was a young Polish seminarian in Rome by the name of Maximilian Maria Kolbe. He had called a meeting with three brother seminarians and three priests. That day through Rome and the Vatican, Masons in large numbers marched saying they would overturn the Church. Many know this story, but what is not generally known is that Masons had written on the banners and placards, ***"Lucifer will rule the Vatican in 2017,"*** as they looked to overthrow the Church. They had given themselves 100 years to accomplish their goal.

On October 16, 1917, Kolbe wrote, *"These men without God find themselves in a tragic situation. Such implacable hatred for the Church and the ambassadors of Christ on earth is not in the power of individual persons, but of a systematic activity stemming in the final analysis from Freemasonry. In particular, it aims to destroy the Catholic religion. Their decrees have been spread throughout the world, in different disguises. But with the same goal — religious indifference and weakening of moral forces, according to their basic principle — **We will conquer the Catholic Church not by argumentation, but rather with moral corruption."***

The Militia Immaculata was formed that night, and neither Kolbe nor the others knew of the apparitions at Fatima. Evolving in the next few years was his magazine by the name of *The Knights of the Immaculate,* which had over one million in circulation and the largest friary in the world in Niepokalanow, Poland. It had over 700 friars with their own printing presses and the most modern means of communication at that time, and enlisted the Blessed Mother as Mediatrix of Grace to overcome the evils in the world.

The Beast Like a Leopard, Secular Freemasonry

In message 405 to the Marian Movement of Priests on June 3, 1989, the Blessed Mother addresses the power of the Red Dragon calling it Marxist atheism, and calling the message, the Beast Like a Leopard. Our Lady says, *"The Dragon manifests himself in the force of his power; the Black Beast, on the other hand, acts in the shadow, keeps out of sight, and hides himself in such a way as to enter in everywhere. He has the claws of a bear and the mouth of a lion, because he works everywhere with cunning and with the means of social communication, that is to say, through propaganda. The seven heads indicate the various Masonic lodges, which act everywhere in a subtle and dangerous way.*

The Black Beast has ten horns and, on the horns, ten crowns, which are signs of dominion and royalty. Masonry rules and governs throughout the whole world by means of the ten horns. The horn, in the biblical world, has always been an instrument of amplification, a way of making one's voice better heard, a strong means of communication.

The task of the Black Beast, namely of Masonry, is that of fighting, in a subtle way, but tenaciously, to obstruct souls from traveling, along this way, pointed out by the Father and the Son and lighted by the gifts of the Spirit. ... The aim of Masonry is not to deny God, but to blaspheme Him. If the Lord has communicated his Law with the Ten Commandments, Freemasonry, spreads everywhere, through the power of its ten horns, a law completely opposed to that of God."

Sister Lucia of Fatima said that the final battle for mankind would be over issues relating to marriage and family, and how Satan was on a rampage to destroy both. In the recent past, we have witnessed the collapse of family life, rampant divorce, state control over children, LGBT acceptance, and morally corrupting doctrine.

The Beast Like a Lamb

In message 406 to the Marian Movement of Priests, the Blessed Mother addresses at great length (nearly five pages) the Beast Like a Lamb — ecclesiastical Freemasonry. She states, *"Above all, as Mother, I have wanted to warn you of the grave dangers which threaten the Church today, because of the many and diabolical attacks which are being carried out against it to destroy it. The black beast like a leopard indicates Freemasonry; the beast like the two horns indicates Freemasonry infiltrated into the interior of the Church, that is to say, ecclesiastical Masonry, which has spread especially among members of the hierarchy. This Masonic infiltration in the interior of the Church, was already foretold to you by me at Fatima, when I announced to you that Satan would enter in even to the summit of the Church. If the task of Masonry is to lead souls to perdition, bringing them to the worship of false divinities, the task of ecclesiastical Masonry on the other hand is that of destroying Christ and His Church, building a new idol, namely a false Christ and a false Church.... The aim of ecclesiastical Masonry is that of justifying sin, of presenting it no longer as an evil but as something good and of value.... The beast with the two horns like a lamb seeks to destroy the mystical Christ, which is the Church."*

The Blessed Mother has often referred to Masonry as *'the Synagogue of Satan'* to the Marian Movement of Priests. Our Lady addresses in message 456 in a message titled, In the Name of Mary, how it was in her name that the Turks (Ottoman Empire in 1529) *"were defeated when they laid siege to the city of Vienna as it threatened the Christian world even though they were far superior in strength and they felt their victory was assured."* She likewise says in the same message it was in her name that Marxist communism oppressed so many people in the world and was defeated. She says, *"Not because of political movements or persons, but through my personal intervention..."*

Then She says, *"It will again be in the name of Mary that I will bring to completion my work with the defeat of Masonry, of every diabolical force... and thus be purified and completely renewed, with the triumph of the Immaculate Heart in the world."*

We know the Battle of Lepanto had similar promises as the Battle of Vienna with Heavenly intervention to save the Christian world even though they were out-manned and outgunned by Islam. Considering every diabolical force in the world, the Blessed Mother does not say her next target is China, Trade, Russia, the Persian Gulf, the Islamic invasion of Europe and the America's, North Korea, immigration, unbridled capitalism, atheistic communism, the creep of godless socialism, state control from cradle to grave, or any other 'ism" or issue. Our Lady specifically says **Masonry**. The Blessed Mother says that before a renewal takes place, Masonry must be defeated, as it is a force of government on earth operating in the shadows.

As the Daughter of the Father, the Mother of the Son, and the Spouse of the Holy Spirit, the Blessed Mother is on another supernatural level than our logical and rational thinking. She is Coredemptrix, Mediatrix, and Advocate of all mankind. So, if Masonry is as powerful as the Queen of Heaven and Earth says, was October 16, 1917, the beginning of the 100-year reign of Satan? Time will tell. *The United States officially entered World War I on April 6, 1917. President Woodrow Wilson's campaign platform slogan was, He Kept Us Out of War.* On May 13, 1917, the Blessed Mother first appeared at Fatima to three young children.

Heaven has told us repeatedly the Church would go through a dark night. Heaven has a plan, and Jesus and Mary are asking for our participation in that plan for the salvation of mankind. The multiplicity of apparition sites around the world primar-ily ask people for a return to the faith through the sacraments.

The Blessed Mother has promised a triumph, and She said at Fatima, *"...in the end my Immaculate Heart will Triumph."*

JESUS I TRUST IN YOU

The Further Division Coming in the Catholic Church

"We do not really want a religion that is right where we are right.
What we want is a religion that is right when we are wrong."

G.K. Chesterton

At the moment we are seeing a full-scale war over the direction of the Holy Roman Catholic and Apostolic Church. The pull and tug of those involved in the battle is what surely went on during the Reformation as well as during Vatican

II. Make no bones about it, behind the scenes and often in stealth, there are those looking to aggressively change what has been taught by the Church for 2,000 years.

It has now been five years since March 13, 2013, the date when Pope Francis assumed his position as the Vicar of Christ on earth. Since then, the changes to the Church under his pontificate have been profound. The Reformation produced incalculable changes in the Church and the world, yet news traveled slowly because of the times in which they lived. When Martin Luther posted his ninety-five theses on a door for all to see in 1517, few could imagine the changes that came to the Church over time. With Vatican II from 1962-65, we saw a further delineation and separation of thought with the New Order of the Mass (Novus Ordo), and a different doctrine emerging from previous ages.

People at the moment are confused and finding it difficult to process all the language coming from leading clergy and what it actually means. With an estimated 1.3 billion Catholics in the word, naturally there are significant nuances and variations of thought. Neither the Reformation nor Vatican II had social media, but today what happens in Rome or Jerusalem can be seen in real time. With millions of bloggers, websites and reporters, people have an opinion on just about everything.

There is often more heat than light in most conversations on Church and politics. We have not seen as great a division among the faithful we see today since Vatican II. As a result of what is taking place now, people seem to be falling into one of three main camps since the white smoke went up the chimney of the Sistine five years ago.

Group 1

This group is threatening to leave the Church because it opposes what it considers to be heretical teaching by Pope Francis. These folks were put on guard over the number of homosexuals in key posts (where little seems to be done to rein it in), the direction of the Synods, and the ambiguous language of Amoris Laetitia (The Joy of Love) that many consider intentional. *Amoris Laetitia* was released on March 19, 2016 on the Feast of the Solemnity of Saint Joseph encapsulating the two Synods on love in the family. Many in this group were skeptical early in the pontificate of Francis with the first Synod being hijacked by a very liberal contingent of Bishops and Cardinals. This group is not sure where to go at the moment and are looking more and more to the Traditional Latin Mass for continuity or leaving the Roman Catholic Church outright for Orthodox or schismatic Catholic Churches. They have read *The Dictator Pope,* and *The Lost Shepherd, How the Pope is Misleading His Flock,* and other writings and they see their content as true. Also in this group are people leaving the Roman Catholic Rite or Traditional Mass, and joining other denominations.

Group 2

This body of believers is remaining in the Church and accepts the Synod writings of Pope Francis, appearing to have little problem with *Amoris Laetitia.* They do not speak against it, and accept it as true because it comes from the papacy. To question the papacy is not acceptable to this group.

Here is a fuzzy area. Many Catholics have a DNA strand that comes at birth prompting them to respect the authority of Rome as gospel. Many do not question it.

They are soccer moms, maybe a dad or mom working two jobs or putting in a lot of overtime to make ends meet, sacrificing for the love of family, as well as parents genuinely concerned about their kids' grades and keeping little Johnny and Mary out of trouble with the neighborhood kids. Commuting home from work, they wonder how they will pay the orthodontist bills. The parents coach little league and take the girls to ballet lessons. It is often beyond their emotional capacity and time to read magisterial documents on subjects they can't control or fully understand. They trust the Church because they have been taught to trust the Church. However, they are trying to get by in a culture deteriorating in front of their eyes.

Many in this group cannot tell you the language of encyclicals or the names of Church hierarchy promoting an agenda one way or the other. Often these people are the salt of the earth. They are being faithful to what they have been taught in the past and are sometimes unaware there is a hidden liberal agenda going on behind the scenes wanting to bring the Church into a new direction. Sometimes there is a virulent strain with these folks if someone disagrees with them. They may see the wholesale apostasy of faith in our midst, and the Church under attack, but they will stay the course with the papacy because they don't know where else to turn.

Group 3

Here is the smallest group. This group opposes some of the teachings of Pope Francis as heretical just like those in Group 1 does, but this group decides to stay in the Church because they believe they are standing on magisterial truth that has endured through thick and thin for millennia, where the gates of Hell will never alter the long-term direction of truth. This group considers the current confusion in the Church as just another bump in the long road of the Catholic Church. Often this group is persecuted and marginalized by group 2 for being critical of the Vicar of Christ. Pope Francis' five words of "Who Am I to Judge?" sent them over the edge early in his pontificate.

No one is now immune from this confusion. On April 7, 2018 there was a conference in Rome entitled, *The Catholic Church: Where Are You Heading?* Beyond the Cardinals who had issued the famous Dubia the conference was attended by bishops, priests, and lay faithful. They met to deal with the issues caused by statements and proclamations from Pope Francis. When all was said and done, the Conference was unsuccessful from their point of view and nothing changed.

The Answer

Heaven is always operating beyond our comprehension — and always well in advance. In 1830, the Blessed Mother appeared to a young novice named Catherine Labouré in a chapel at the Daughters of Charity Convent at Rue du Bac, in Paris. Between July 18 and December 1830 Saint Catherine received the extraordinary favor of conversing with the Blessed Mother on three separate occasions. One time Our Lady pointed to the altar where the tabernacle was and said, *"Come to the foot of this altar. Here, graces will be spread over all who ask for them with confidence and fervor."* Our Lady said that her message at the time was not listened to as she had asked. Our Lady as always was providing the answer for mankind and it was Her Son.

In 1846 she appeared in an isolated farming hamlet to two young children in the mountains of France by the name of La Salette. Here she gave one of the most severe messages in the history of Marian apparitions. She said, *"The priests, ministers of my Son, the priests by their wicked lives, by their irreverence and their impiety in the celebration of the holy mysteries, by their love of money, their love of honors and plea-sures...the priests have become a cesspool of impurity...the Church will be in eclipse... I gave you six days to work; I kept the seventh for myself, and no one wants to grant it to me. This is what weighs down the arm of my Son so much...Rome will become the seat of the anti-christ."* This was not exactly a casual message. On September 19, 1851 Pope St. Pius IX formally approved public devotion and prayers to Our Lady of La Salette referring to her messages as "secrets." In 1879, Pope Leo XIII granted Canonical Coronation to the Blessed Mother's image at the Basilica of Our Lady of LaSalette.

There are many similar authentic messages like this over the last hundred years. Our Lady announced to Father Gobbi of the Marian Movement of Priests: *"This ... infil-tration, in the interior of the Church, was already foretold to you by me at Fatima when I announced to you that Satan would enter in even to the summit of the Church."* (#406 g) She further warned in #407 *The Number of the Beast* that *"the apostasy will be ... gen-eralized."* (p) The question must be asked what exactly is The Summit of the Church? The summit of a mountain is the very top. You cannot say that you scaled Everest or any peak until you touch the very top.

The battle for souls is intense and the moral welfare of future generations are at stake, which is why we must focus on the cross and the fruits of Eucharistic Adora-tion. It is Heaven's medicine for the ills of mankind. It is time to double down and go deeper in prayer and Adoration. Our Lady exhorts us *"Take courage! Be strong, my little children. To you befalls the duty, in these difficult years, or remaining faithful to Christ and to his Church, putting up with hostility, struggle and persecution. But you are a precious part of the little flock, which has the task of fighting against, and in the end of conquering, the powerful force of the Antichrist"* (#407 r).

JESUS I TRUST IN YOU.

The Saint Who Visited Hell and Came Back to Talk About It

The Scriptures and tradition in the Church are clear that there is a place called Hell. People speak of Heaven all the time, but rarely mention Hell except in the vernacular, part of a curse, or as a matter of every day speech. It is often said that the devil's greatest accomplishment is getting people to think that Hell does not exist. That may be a correct assessment because if one really knew what mystics of old have said about it, they would be much more serious about their daily actions. Blaise Pascal the French Renaissance man had a similar thought about God. He said if there is no God then nothing matters, but if there is a God, then nothing else does matter. This became known as Pascal's Wager.

In the early part of the fourteenth century Dante Alighieri wrote the epic poem *The Divine Comedy.* For hundreds of years this was considered one of the greatest classics (not just Christian) ever written in western civilization. It is the story of the Roman poet Virgil guiding Dante through Hell first, then followed by Purgatory, and then Heaven (Paradiso). The description of Hell is vivid and graphic, and the source of many conversations and classes on what Hell may be like. Scripture mentions Hell on several occasions, but does not give much of a description of what it is like or takes place there. Dante describes Hell as being comprised of nine concentric circles of torment for those who do not acknowledge God in their pursuit of sinful appetites. Each circle gets significantly more severe with spiritual and physical torment than the last, as one journey's deeper into the abyss of Hades.

As a cradle life-long Catholic, I don't think I have ever heard a sermon from the pulpit on Hell, yet Jesus was clear that it exists. In a world of moral relativism, this is not surprising. The last time I remember hearing the word Hell frequently as a reality, was when the founder of *Playboy* magazine, Hugh Hefner died in September 2017. Many felt he would soon be a visitor there for the incalculable obscenity and moral corruption he brought to the culture on a worldwide basis. Hefner opened up the portal of sin for many young people at a vulnerable age, where a habit often became an addiction — which then leads to greater sin.

Saint Faustina's Visions of Hell From What Jesus Taught Her

In an age of widespread relativism, and lack of formation for the majority of Catholics, few are aware of the concept of sin as a physical reality. However, a young nun from Poland by the name of Sister Faustina (Saint Faustina) was given far more information by Jesus Himself than Dante could ever provide. Her description could move the most hardened soul. As a young novice in 1925 her guardian angel led her to Purgatory, and after that, in what became a life long practice she made it a routine to pray for the souls in Purgatory. Heaven also took her to Hell and she wrote, *"I, Sister Faustina, by the order of God, have visited the abysses of Hell so that I might tell souls about it and testify to its existence, it is a place of great torture.... The kinds of torture I saw:*

*The **first** torture that constitutes Hell is the loss of God;*
*The **second** is perpetual remorse of conscience;*
*The **third** is that one's condition will never change;*
*The **fourth** is the fire that will penetrate the soul without destroying it — a terrible suffering, since it is a purely spiritual fire, lit by God's anger;*
*The **fifth** torture is a continual darkness and a terrible suffocating smell, and, despite the darkness, the devils and the souls of the damned see each other and all the evil, both of others and their own;*

*The **sixth** torture is the common company of Satan;*
*The **seventh** torture is horrible despair, hatred of God, vile words, curses, and blasphemies.*

These are the tortures suffered by all the damned together, but that is not the end of the sufferings. There are special tortures destined for particular souls. These are the torments of the senses. Each soul undergoes terrible and indescribable sufferings, related to the manner in which it has sinned.

Faustina's description of Hell is as real as anyone can deliver in a written language. It puts everything in perspective concerning our earthly existence and our purpose for living, and the ramifications of our actions.

Faustina gives further elaboration that God instructed her to write these things *"so that no soul may find an excuse by saying there is no Hell, or that nobody has ever been there, and so no one can say what it is like....I noticed one thing, that most of the souls there are those who disbelieved that there is a Hell...."* Sister Faustina realized the need for more prayers for people to prevent this suffering so she would *"incessantly plead God's mercy upon them"* (Diary 741).

Further in her *Diary*, she wrote about the absolute essence of Divine Mercy and how grace is available to everyone even to the moment of death. Faustina writes, *"God's mercy sometimes touches the sinner at the last moment in a wondrous and mysterious way. Outwardly, it seems as if everything were lost, but it is not so. The soul illumined by a ray of God's powerful final grace, turns to God in the last moment, with such a power of love that, in an instant it receives from God forgiveness of sin and punishment, while outwardly it shows no sign either of repentance or of contrition, because souls (at that stage) no longer react to external things. Oh, how beyond comprehension is God's mercy!... The merciful God gives the soul that interior vivid moment, so that if the soul is willing, it has the possibility of returning to God. But sometimes, the obduracy in souls is so great that consciously they choose Hell"* (1698).

Hell is a deliberate choice of the proud. Notice how Faustina (words from Jesus) above says *"they choose Hell."* One can think of the two thieves on the cross next to Jesus as he was being crucified. Both were going to die within the hour, yet one asked for mercy, the other did not. Jesus never asked about the crime of the one asking for mercy. He immediately gave clemency because it was asked. The repentant thief is the only person in the entire New Testament who was specifically told he would go to Heaven. Jesus said, *"Truly, I say to you, I promise you today you will be with me in paradise"* (Luke 23:43). No apostle was ever specifically told this, not Peter, not John, not Andrew, not Matthew, not Paul. The thief stole Heaven through contrition at the moment of death, as he recognized Jesus alone could grant this request, and was humble enough to ask for mercy.

The Divine Mercy that Jesus instructed Sister Faustina to write about is the unfathomable mercy that Jesus has for people. It knows no bounds and is limitless. As Hell is an endless abyss, His mercy is also an endless abyss of mercy and love. There are virtually no limits to His forgiveness and mercy. No one is exempt from that mercy but the person has to ask for it. It is readily available all the way to the moment of death. Sin separates us from ourselves, from others, and from God. Sin is Hell. The Lord told Isaiah, *"it has been your sin that separates you from God"* (59:2). When souls are away from God, they often feel unworthy to approach Him. It is for this reason that so many stay away from God for 10, 20, 30, 40, or even 50 years before they realize that all that remains are the Four Last Things: **Death, Judgment, Heaven and Hell.** One may feel that he or she is not worthy to ask for Mercy due to previous sin. It may prevent such a person from receiving the abundant love the Lord wishes to bring into his or her life that the Lord Himself wants to restore and heal. This is a lie of Satan telling them that they cannot be forgiven.

Sin is like a bag of feathers being released in a windstorm. The sin happens and where it goes after that can affect lives for generations. It does harm even without the sinner knowing it. The feathers can never be organized the same way ever again. Jesus said that, *"Satan comes to kill, destroy, and steal, but I come to give you life, and give it more abundantly"* (John 10:10). It is the Lord's Divine Mercy that welcomes the sinner back into the arms of God. He never asks about the past, but always forgives when one asks in sincerity. No matter the severity of the transgression, no sin is too great for His Mercy.

JESUS I TRUST IN YOU

The 9/11 for Europe

Marie–Julie Jahenny (1850-1941), the French stigmatist, mystic, and victim soul, bore the stigmata from the age of twenty-three until her death. On December 8, 1874, she gave a prophecy that may now apply to our day. She said, *"In Rome the storm will be the blackest. The storm in Rome is worse than the storm in France. All the wrath of the ungodly is in Rome. All the anger of the wicked is focused on the Holy See. But, the chastisements will begin in Paris."*

Notre Dame (Our Lady) Cathedral located on the Ile de la Cité in the middle of the Seine in Paris went up in flames on April 15, 2019. The Cathedral is the embodiment of the word icon. It is old. The Construction started in 1163 under King Louis VII of France, and was completed nearly two hundred years later in 1345. It is central. All distances in Paris originate from Notre Dame. It is Catholic. France is the Elder Daughter of the Roman Catholic Church, and that Basilica is symbolic of its past faith. What went up in flames on April 15, 2019 was old Europe. The stone slabs of Notre Dame reflect the heart of a nation, and Western civilization itself. Notre Dame IS Paris, because so much of the city was built around it –and because of it. It survived warring nations in the Middle Ages, the French Revolution, Napoleon's exploits, two World Wars and the Nazi occupation.

Anyone who has been to Paris and seen Notre Dame remembers its Gothic architecture and flying buttresses. To see the Notre Dame Cathedral while on a boat on the Seine is breathtaking and inspiring. Notre Dame embodies past generations of Christendom, not just France. It is over 850 years old, and to put that in perspective, Saint Augustine, Florida the oldest city in the United States was founded in the year 1565, and Jamestown Virginia 1607. The cornerstone of the U.S. Capitol was laid in 1793. Yes, Notre Dame has been around for a long time.

What Notre Dame once was, it is no longer. Nor is the faith of its people any longer what is once was, not only in France but in all of Europe. It is a shell of its former self and a faithless one at that. The world is in a state of shock because in our souls we know that the Christian era has passed. Approximately three percent of Parisian Catholics today identify with orthodoxy and go to Church. For the rest of Parisians, Notre Dame is about culture, not heart or soul. It became a cultural icon in the past several generations and is now relegated to a tourist attraction, more of a museum and cultural heritage site, rather than what was in the heart of its French pilgrims and visitors who sojourned there to see its magnificence. FAITH made Notre Dame what it was.

Its aura was wrapped in the soul of man touching God. People have converted standing in front of it. Its architecture reflected what was in the heart of man seeking the transcendent. It elevated the spirit of man to gaze upon it. The commitment of heart, mind, soul, sweat, and faith built it to the glory of God. That was replaced long ago by a state that was not interested in the hereafter but in the tourist dollars that benefit the many surrounding cafes and restaurants and taxes derived from commerce. The fact is that for the vast majority of people who enter its sacred walls, faith has little to do with the religious structure. Go to any great religious shrine in the world today, and you will see the same phenomenon. Many people see the structures of beautiful buildings of a by-gone era, but not the soul of a people who built them, or the WHY they built it. They do not understand the meaning behind these beautiful edifices. There is a disconnect in a world that is increasingly distant from God.

The shock of seeing the spire fall to the ground against a darkened sky in real time and the subsequent mourning of people will be etched in minds of many for decades. Those of faith will remember where they were, just like it happened to those who saw images of the Twin Towers collapsing on 9/11. With the Pentagon hit and Twin Towers falling, mankind knew in their hearts that the world had changed. That created the emotion. It would have been different if lightening had struck the Twin Towers. It was so dramatic because there has been no remedy in sight for the warring factions of religion and strong ideological differences. Everyone knew that the world would be different from that day on.

The same applies to this. France has changed, Europe has changed, and so has everyone. It has to do with race and different religions. The Muslim invasion to take over Europe is at the heart of the conflict. Migration, invasion, legal, and illegal immigration, and caravans are the beating heart of the issue. Muslims and Arab nations are using mass migration to take over the world for Allah. Oil rich Arab nations are taking in virtually no migrants (zero) but choosing to promote Islam through invasion. It is a jihad, and the West is walking in a daze and hoping it goes away.

Let's see how far logic takes us.

• Col. Muammar Gaddafi, President of Libya, now deceased, said thirty years ago that Islam would take over Europe without a shot being fired due to mass migration and flooding Europe with migrants.

• Parts of Sweden, England, Germany, Belgium, and the Netherlands, now with large pockets of Muslims, and whole suburbs in Paris are *"no go zones"* for police due to possible violence against the *"intruder and infidels."* Streets in heavily trafficked suburbs have been closed at the call to Muslim prayer.

• In 2016 a car carrying seven gas cylinders was found near Notre Dame Cathedral in Paris. ISIS has continually said that Notre Dame was a target as is St. Peter's Basilica in Rome. As the Twin Towers and Pentagon were symbols of the power and might of New York and the U.S. military, Notre Dame is a symbol of Western Christianity.

• The intensity of violence in all of Europe is increasing each against Christian and Jewish establishments. At Notre Dame des Enfants in Nimes, the Consecrated Host was found in garbage outside the church, and human feces was used to draw a sign of the cross.

• In the year 2018, 875 French churches alone were vandalized.

• In March 2019, over a period of just one week, Saint Sulpice in Paris and eleven other churches were vandalized, with damage to one alone estimated at several million euros.

• *Le Parisien* reports in April of 2019 a 41 year old Pakistani immigrant was on trial for vandalizing the Saint Denis Basilica housing many of the tombs of past French Kings.

• Benjamin Mouton, former Chief Architect of Notre Dame said on French TV that in no way was this an accident. He said the fire broke out in an area where there was no renovation.

• In 2018, according to the French Minister of the Interior there were 1,063 acts against Christians and 541 anti-semitic acts. That is an average of 134 per month. Similar incidents are now being reported all over Germany. A German report in November 2017 said that in the Alps area alone, 200 churches were vandalized. If the Notre Dame fire was an accident, so be it. Many however, are skeptical that the French Government sponsored report will be forthcoming about the cause, just like the many Americans who don't believe the U.S. government sponsored 9/11 Report. If anyone believes the U.S government 9/11 Report, just ask gently, *"How did Building 7 fall six hours later?"*

• U.S. Congresswoman Ilhan Omar of Minnesota (D), a Muslim, has openly attacked the Christian views of Vice President Mike Pence. Thirty-seven years old and born in Mogadishu, Somalia, she states that his view of Christianity is unacceptable to her Muslim views.

• Cardinal Robert Sarah of Guinea in Africa has clearly stated what is at stake in a March 30, 2019 interview with the French weekly news magazine Culture a' Valeurs Actuelles, said, *"If the West continues down this disastrous road, there is a great risk that for the lack of replacement birth rate, Europe could disappear, invaded by foreigners as Rome was invaded by the barbarians. I speak as an African. My country has a Muslim majority. I think I know what I am talking about. If Europe disappears and with it the invaluable value of the old continent, Islam will invade the world and we will totally change culture, anthropology and moral vision."* However, globalist Western leaders are welcoming the migration for the new world they wish to mold in their image. If you have a different political opinion than many Muslims, you are labeled a racist or a bigot. Muslim leaders are schooled in classrooms and cafes around the world on how to speak to the press and the general public to control the narrative. Listen to just about any talk show and you will see them talking over the opposing view, hammering the message of intolerance if one disagrees with their talking points.

The Twin Towers and the Pentagon were symbols of U.S financial and military strength. When they were hit, it showed their vulnerability. The abandonment of faith in the West has allowed this to happen. Faith, when not properly taught and handed down can be lost in a couple of generations. Now in the year 2019, the West by biblical standards is pagan, with the massive killing of innocent children being the prime indicator of this reality. In the West, we are now two to three generations removed from proper education in the Faith. This has been the result. We reap what we sow.

Many people refuse to see the signs of the West's decline. It reminds us of the fact that in the 1930s and early 1940s, the Nazis in Germany made no bones that they wanted the Jews eliminated from Europe. They then proceeded to undertake a human carnage the likes of which had rarely been seen in history. Yet millions lamented the fact that they had ignored the obvious signs. Kristalnacht, the night of the broken glass in November of 1938, was a mere two-day duration in Germany, yet that was a warning. Today, there are thousands of instances of Muslim violence across all Europe, and people refuse to see the threat. Twice in past history Muslims have attempted to take over Europe and lost at the Battle of Lepanto (1571) and the Battle of Vienna (1683). In those times, there was a united Christian Europe. Today, despite the European Union's purported strength in numbers, it has sought to hide its Christian roots. For most in Europe, God has been banished from the public square, yet it ultimately may run to Him in time of crisis.

Yet many people believe that the U.S. is largely to blame for Muslim migrant unrest by sticking its nose in places it was not wanted. First and foremost, it was the Iraq War. Staged by the United States and the neocons from the People for the New American Century (PNAC) they fabricated a war in the Middle East, using the excuse that Saddam Hussein had Weapons of Mass Destruction (WMD). The charade of uranium from Niger with the Valerie Plame story proved to be a lie. The administration of George W. Bush (#43) used the former Secretary of State General Colin Powell to deliver before the U.N. General Assembly the lie regarding uranium from Niger in Iraq, thus justifying an invasion. The U.S. wanted a war to remake the world into its image of what ought to be. President George H. W. Bush (#41) in his message to the joint members of Congress said twice, **"The New World Order, [is] a big idea."** The goal of the global elite is to merge all nations into a utopian dream without borders or sovereignty.

There is a game being played far above the heads of most, with people who want war and unrealistic aspirations for mankind. At the heart of the matter is a Luciferian agenda dating back to Genesis with Satan saying, *"I will not serve."*

Some people know that the Notre Dame Cathedral fire is about the spiritual chaos and upheaval in the Church. That attack is particularly virulent against the traditional family. As the family goes, so goes the Church, and so goes the world. The family which is the domestic Church and the Church itself are under a great spiritual and diabolical attack.

A friend sent me a reflection on the Notre Dame fire he picked up off the net. It reads: *"First, what survived the fire? The cross, the altar, and the Crown of Thorns. Consider this for your own life, when our lives will be burned up and everything turned to ashes, what will survive? Will it be the crosses that made you holy, the altar where you offered yourself to God as a living sacrifice, or the Crown of Thorns in humility you wore that you may be worthy to wear a glorious crown of gold?*

"Second, the outside of the church looked completely destroyed, while the inside remained intact though damaged — a fitting metaphor for the universal Church. But, to those on the inside, we know that while damaged, it can never be destroyed.

Finally, the fire at Notre Dame is a powerful symbol of what is happening in Europe, and soon the United States. The flames of secularism seem intent on destroying it. Will a new generation rise up to save not their cultural heritage, but their very faith itself?"

"But, the chastisements will begin in Paris." Jesus was clear that the gates of Hell will never prevail against the Church. That is our hope — that is our destiny.

JESUS I TRUST IN YOU

A Glimpse into Tomorrow

For anyone who missed it, the first week of June 2017 witnessed a momentous event. The event will ripple not only throughout the vast Canadian provinces where it was implemented, but throughout the rest of the world as well. On June 1, Bill 89 called Supporting Children, Youth and Families Act in the Ontario legislature, was passed by an overwhelming majority of 63 to 23 giving the Ontario Government the right to seize children from their parents who oppose gender transition. Note that the vote was not even close with a near 3 to 1 margin.

The Minister of Children and Youth Services said that *"a parent's failure to recognize and support a child's gender identification is a form of child abuse, and a child in these circumstances should be removed from the situation and placed into protection."* This bill replaces Bill 28, and is a more aggressive law governing foster care, adoption, and child protection in general. Like an earthquake, the aftershocks will follow this morally abhorrent legislation.

Child protective services in Ontario are now required to include a host of new factors such as ethnic origin, citizenship, diversity of the family, sexual orientation, and other criteria giving the State a carte blanche to intervene in a family's affairs with little to no legal recourse of the family. Bill 28 gave the parents the right *"to direct a child's education and religious upbringing."* This Bill strips that right. If one looks over the last generation at the gradual erosion of religious liberties and rights under a totalitarian state, by all historical measures this is a gigantic assault on Christian values. It will produce a tsunami of heinous laws. At some point in America, the democrats will resume the administration and this will be voted into law immediately.

The ramifications of this legislation are breathtaking in scope, because of the legal precedent it is setting for the government to intrude in any area of family life, **WITH** the support of government. The ruthless tentacles of secular structures now legally reach into the classrooms choking the light and purity of faith, and are increasingly moving more virulently to the home. The vagueness of the Bill is as deceptive as the name of the Bill itself. This legislation is moral poison that will work its way throughout a lost and directionless western world.

This Bill does several harmful things, although we are just hitting the tip of the iceberg.

Bill 89:

1. *Sets children's rights over parental rights;*
2. *Gives the State the legal right to intervene at will in family decisions;*
3. *It is directed at parents who home school where the State has tried now for decades to rid them from the earth;*
4. *Teaches a pagan agenda;*
5. *Gives a legal precedent for much broader interpretation of laws;*
6. *Inhibits a parent or grandparent from teaching the authority of Scripture;*
7. *Will ripple throughout the world in a much broader fashion;*
8. *It is not a socialist, but a communist agenda;*
9. *Allows the courts to hold a political opinion to determine what is best for the child rather than the family, and;*
10. *Last, but not least, is intended to obliterate free speech.*

This list is just for starters with parental rights in complete jeopardy with an authoritarian and godless State.

A Primer on the Language of Political Philosophy

Over the last twenty plus years we have a seen a much more accelerated decline in morals than in previous generations. If the decline once galloped, it now a full-fledged horse race to the abyss. Words are often used incorrectly when discussing political views. Language manipulation is used as a tool to disguise the intended purpose of legislation. There are many terms used to discuss a political philosophy. Several are: Democratic, Progressive, Socialist, Fabian Socialism, National Socialism, Democratic Socialism, Marxism, Stalinism, Maoism, Leninism, Fascism,

Communism, and so forth. These all have specific meanings, but are often misused in discussions because young talking heads being told what to spew by bosses really don't know the difference. When a young broadcaster is making $500,000 or more a year, and has use of the corporate jet, don't expect independent thinking.

With the above, we'll just touch on socialism and communism. Socialism is the gradual destruction of society through a slower process than communism. Communism is in a hurry, socialism is more patient to carry out an agenda. Mikhail Gorbachev as the former General Secretary of the Communist Party in what was once the USSR, said at the one thousand year Anniversary of Kiev Rus in 1988 that *"if the communists had implemented more of a socialist agenda rather than the violence the communists imposed, the experiment of the USSR would have succeeded."* Speaking at the Presidio in California, he would repeat that many times in differing ways as he looked back on the failed state of the USSR. Principally, he said it failed because Russian roots were Christian, and the Soviet Union failed to rid Christianity from the Russian soul before it imposed political structures.

As T.S. Elliot said, *"The world will not perish with a bang, but it shall perish with a whimper."* Inch by inch socialists have used the politics of Antonio Gramsci. and the social and political structures of incrementally taking turf one yard at a time, year after year, decade after decade where national leaders are allowed to vote this type of law in motion — and then get elected again. Gramsci as head of the Italian Communist Party at the time of the Russian Revolution, went to Russia to see it for himself. After spending a year there observing the aftermath of the Bolshevik Revolution of 1917, Gramsci determined that Russian communism would fail because it was too violent. Therefore, in what was arguably one of the greatest political minds since Machiavelli, Gramsci determined the best way to advance communism was the slower path of socialism. A bite at a time can equal a sumptuous feast.

Communism by definition does not have to be violent as it was under Mao, Lenin, or Stalin. Communism by definition is simply a government without God. To achieve that goal, first it has to rid the soul of Christ to achieve State goals. Violence is used due to the fortitude of the believer fighting a godless state. Socialism with its indirect and slow approach to state control is like an anesthetic to a patient to numb the pain before a procedure.

The goal of socialism is to rid faith slowly like boiling the frog in water so it doesn't know it is boiling to death. The United States and Canada have died by a thousand cuts and been numb to the truth for several generations, so we end up with legislation like this. Not to be too tough on Canada, the USA leads the pack in many areas of moral legislation — or lack thereof. Scandinavia and other western countries are well along the path of no return. The United States is in hot pursuit with judges legislating from the bench.

Taking children from the home for teaching a biblical view is Communism at its finest. The LGBTQ community is moving forward with its promotion of a homosexual agenda now often sanctioned by churches of all denominations. One can now expect law on top of law legitimizing this behavior culminating in a more general acceptance through resignation and acquiescence. We fail to realize the treasure of our faith that brings peace and serenity in our homes, neighborhoods, and society—elements making up our culture. Many believers are culpable for not speaking up. Jewelers get used to fine stones.

Governments swing like financial markets. They go up down, cold hot, stable and unstable. One day a conservative agenda, and the next a liberal usually due to abuse of governing bodies in knee jerk reactions to previous administrations. History shows governments can be violent after one group feels it has no option but to start shooting. Too much of one thing breeds the opposite of its intended purposes. Too much sugar for the child, and we have a sick child. The parent appeasing the wish of the child for candy, will ultimately harm the child. No society can expect to last by giving everything away for free to its citizenry.

Likewise, democracy without boundaries and constraints breeds fascism. Democracy in excess breeds a lawless society to contain the abuses of the rule of law. It is for this reason that the framers of the U.S. Constitution said democracy can only exist within a Christian culture. Christianity has a belief system where one chooses obedience to God, and a belief system larger than the individual because the believer chooses obedience to God's laws because it is right, just and best for all. Democracy is based upon voluntary compliance of the law, and its biblical principles bring an ordered civil society.

Sister Lucia of Fatima said that the last assault of the devil would be on **marriage and the family.** Looking at the bold onslaught of the homosexual agenda in every area, it is now happening at a ferocious pace. **Years before Sister Lucia died, she said the world was experiencing "*diabolical disorientation*."**

In the June 2, 2017 the monthly message of the Blessed Mother at Medjugorje to Mirjana. She said something that may not have been articulated since the apparitions began in June of 1981. She said, *"Be ready, this time is a turning point. That is why I am calling you anew to faith and hope."* The Blessed Mother is speaking to us as the Daughter of the Father, the Mother of the Son, and the Spouse of the Holy Spirit. She speaks with the consent and the authority of Heaven.

It is time to speak up, because shortly you will have no voice if you don't speak up now.

JESUS I TRUST IN YOU

The Time of the Trial is Now

If one were to search the internet for "Purgatory", "what is Heaven like", "Hell", near "death experiences" (NDEs), "life after death" and similar subjects, you will find those categories get multiple millions of hits on the net. Subjects like NDEs have been a topic of fascination for over thirty years. Yet we rarely hear about Heaven,

Hell, Purgatory or the Four Last Things — Death, Judgment, Heaven, or Hell — from the pulpit. Is there a connection between not hearing the most fundamental of truths that were taught for nearly 2,000 years and the pablum we hear so much today as we watch in real time the destruction of our culture?

The data is clear that people are very interested in this genre of spirituality given that they research and read these subjects on their own. Many books on these subjects are best sellers. Jesus addressed Heaven and Hell in the Gospels and He was not ambiguous as to their reality. A person could go to Church for a life-time and not hear a sermon on Purgatory or Hell. A priest would be considered too extreme or negative as the talk may offend someone if he did address the subject.

In the same vein, people today know something is very wrong in our culture. Society is talking and operating on the extremes, with a festering civil disturbance on the horizon. Based upon nearly any conversation, we can often tell if someone we meet is on the same political and spiritual wavelength as us. Bring up Pope Francis, Hillary Clinton or President Trump, and the waters part as if Moses waved his walking stick over the Red Sea. It doesn't take long to find if one has a starkly contrary view from yours.

Which direction is the Church going? We now have authority figures writing books abdicating the Magisterium and its 2,000 years of teaching and openly discussing dissention going all the way up to Rome. Books like *The Dictator Pope*, authored by the Anglo-French historian H.J.A. Sire under the pseudonym of Marcantonio Colonna and released in 2017, present a compelling case for the auto demolition of the Church from within at a dizzying pace. Many other books are now written on the same subject. Long standing scriptural doctrine is being challenged, and sometimes tossed out the window wholesale by progressive groups within the Church. It is now cardinal against cardinal and bishop against bishop, prophesied in Akita, Japan in the early 1970s. The fulfillment of that prophecy is in our midst.

Some cardinals, bishops and clergy are in open dissent against some of Pope Francis' views, while others dissent in silence as to the direction the Church is taking. Many live in fear of their bishop's authority as it can be dangerous to have a different world-view than your boss'. Many clergy are frustrated and nearly despairing as they watch the direction of the Church and don't really don't know what to do.

We may get a glimpse of where we are now headed with a very powerful prophetic quote from Father Ratzinger when he was teaching theology and philosophy in 1969 at Regensburg, Germany. The quote that follows was a commentary he made four years after the final session of Vatican II. It may have been an insight based upon his knowledge of history, a prediction as a philosopher, or a prophetic utterance. Nonetheless, here is what the young theologian said nearly fifty years ago based upon what he saw for the future of the Church.

"The Church will be restructured with far fewer members that is forced to let go of many of the places of worship it worked so hard to build over the centuries. A minority Catholic Church with little influence over political decisions, that is socially irrelevant, left humiliated and forced to start over... a great power will emerge from a more spiritual and simple Church." Father Ratzinger said that he was convinced the Church

was going through an era similar to the Enlightenment and the French Revolution. He continued by saying that *"we are at a huge turning point in the evolution of mankind. This moment makes the move from the medieval to the modern times seem insignificant."* Professor Ratzinger compared the current era to that of Pope Pius VI who was abducted by troops of the French Revolution and died in prison in 1799. The Church was fighting against a force which intended to annihilate it definitively, confiscating its property, and dissolving religious orders.

> *"Today's Church could be faced with a similar situation, undermined by the temptation to reduce priests to social workers and it and all its work reduced to a mere political presence. From today's crisis will emerge a Church that has lost a great deal. It will become small and will pretty much have to start all over again. It will no longer have use of its structures it built in its years of prosperity. The reduction in the number of faithful will lead to its losing an important part of its social privileges. It will start off with small groups and movements and a minority that will make faith central to experience again... It will be a more spiritual Church, and will not claim a political mandate flirting with the right one-minute, and the left the next... It will be poor and it will be the Church of the destitute."*

One must not neglect these words from a philosopher, theologian, historian, priest, Bishop, Cardinal, the head of the Congregation for the Doctrine of the Faith (CDF), and then Pope Benedict XVI. The ramifications of today's proclamations from Rome will have a profound influence on future generations. We can be sure that changes will be staggering in all spheres of social milieu, similar to what happened after Vatican II when many within the Church took it upon themselves to implement their own stretched interpretations of the Vatican II documents and watered down Church teachings for a confused laity. Yes, the Rhine still flows into the Tiber. Rather than the most prominent Churchmen upholding Magisterial truth with a mandate to protect it, often they are the ones leading the charge against it from the very interior of the Church. It is difficult to fight a foe with powerful, organized, and influential enemies inside the gates.

One thing is certain. We have been told that the Church will never perish. The Blessed Mother said that we will know we are in the times spoken of by seeing the events themselves. She has been speaking at numerous apparition sites around the world warning us about this day and how to avoid catastrophic consequences. Some of those apparitions are genuine, while others are not. Discernment is obviously necessary. Is there a mother who would not warn her children of impending danger if given the chance? The events spoken of at the major apparition sites are all around us and are often ignored to the peril of the individual refusing to listen. The Blessed Mother has told us repeatedly where we are headed, and it is now obvious to those who have paid attention that the future is here. We are in the time of trials.

Saint John Bosco (1815-1888) saw in his vision the future of the Church, how the barque of Peter would be tossed from stem to stern, nearly capsizing. As the boat went through the **Twin Pillars** of the **Eucharist** on one high pillar, and the **Blessed Mother** on the other pillar of less stature — the Church was saved and calm was restored. As Mediatrix, Coredemptrix, and Advocate of mankind, we seek to follow the Virgin Mary's directives for safe passage, sustained by the Bread of Life, Our Eucharistic Lord.

JESUS I TRUST IN YOU

America on the Brink: Our Lady Will Triumph

Many years ago I learned a word that I had never previously known. It was a word that I thought best described America, and generally the world. It was the word acedia. I have thought of it often as I watch America's rapid descent sliding towards Sodom. *Acedia* has several meanings, but one is the *"Lack of respect for spiritual things."* As America descends into a moral abyss due to a lack of spiritual formation and an abdication of spiritual thinking, America is moving to a place it has never been before.

Growing up in a New England state not far from everything having to do with salt-water activities like boating, scuba, surfing, clamming and fishing was a simple and wholesome way of living with few complications. My mother kept her car keys in the ignition so she wouldn't lose them. I cannot remember having a key to our home, as we never locked the doors. One night I came home unannounced during my senior year of college and couldn't get in the house. I had to ring the doorbell because the house had been broken into the month before and I hadn't been told. In the span of twenty years a lot had changed.

When America decided by order of the Supreme Court to ban prayer in public schools on the fateful day of June 25, 1962, and one year later prohibited Bible reading in the classroom, the United States sealed its fate. The Lord being the gentleman He is gave mankind free choice — and man doesn't always make the best choices if they violate His statues and commands. The Trinity must have had a long discussion in Heaven before they ever gave man free choice. Free choice with an unbridled libido has caused a lot of problems over millennia.

The question is often asked whether *the United States is different from other civilizations and empires in world history?* One thing is certain among historians, and that is there are great similarities to the ascent and decline of empires. There have been twenty-two empires preceding the American empire, and the rise and fall have nearly identical similarities. Many know of the Greek, the Roman, the Persian, Mesopotamian, the Dutch traders, the mighty Spanish Armada, the French, the British sailing the world pillaging commodities like those that preceded them. These countries still exist, just not as empires. They all fell on the ash heap of history the same way.

America entered the Great War (World War 1) on European soil April 1917 after President Woodrow Wilson campaigned he would keep the U.S. out of war. Thus a largely rural, agrarian, and the vast United States tooled for war. The military industrial complex was in its nascent stage hatching for the next wave that began in December 1941, and at the end it claimed 418,000 American lives. With that war finished, America engineered having the dollar as the reserve currency of the world. The ability to print money from thin air with the world wanting it was a dream come true for central bankers of the United States as an industrial power. The U.S. was now unstoppable and was on the top of the world.

People can remember their grandparents, and parents fighting for survival after largely being uneducated immigrants coming to U.S. shores for a better life. Then they fought a war to maintain the status of an empire thrust upon them by a banking and geopolitical ruling class elite in the 1930s. The question must be asked, *"Is America really different than those empires that preceded us?"*

Historians such as Toynbee, Durant and others largely agree there are eight major stages to the rise and fall of empires. They are:

1. **BONDAGE** — The people are subject to an authority other than themselves.
2. **SPIRITUAL** — People develop a sense of identity through a faith in God and come to have a purpose.
3. **COURAGE** — They develop a sense of where they need to go to further themselves as a race. They venture out, breaking away from the shackles of their bondage.
4. **FREEDOM** — Manual work and a sense of fulfillment bring an identity. Laws are made to govern themselves.
5. **ABUNDANCE** — Work, identity, and accomplishment bear fruit. Risk over generations becomes worthwhile.
6. **SELFISHNESS** — Human nature forgets it is God who grants favors due to fidelity. There is a lack of cooperation of not helping others less fortunate. Creature comforts are now generally sought.
7. **APATHY** — A cynical approach sets in for many as the effort seems worthless. In abundance there is no spiritual advancement, thus they lose their vision of the higher good. They have become a visionless godless wasteland.
8. **DEPENDENCE** — Laws cripple initiative and answers are looked for in all the wrong places. There is no sense of purpose in life as ease of lifestyle is sought. The people are back to bondage and don't even know it.

America has gone full circle. It has risen from humble origins to the pinnacle of empire. It is now in precipitous decline as it pursues the here and now, what gives the most pleasure and causes the least pain. Its spiritual rudder and compass are amiss.

As people focus on themselves they tend to banish God from their lives. What we are seeing in the world today is darkness and evil being exposed. Precisely because of that, as a merciful God, many are experiencing what Catholic mystics call *The Warning* or the *Illumination of Conscience*. Some call it a *"near death experience"* or "life review." It has happened now to many people as the world unravels. It will be the greatest act of mercy Heaven can offer the world.

Some people are seeing the state of their soul before God — and many in public. Many books have been written recently on near death and life reviews, and are best sellers. People are taking notice and acknowledging that these experiences are real. For some, the veil between Heaven and earth is beginning to lift. The Triumph of the Immaculate Heart will bring changes to the world never seen before and we might just be watching Heaven's process of bringing in a New Era — in real time. The Blessed Mother, appointed by the Most Holy Trinity as the New Dawn, is Heaven's chosen instrument

JESUS I TRUST IN YOU

The Final and Mother of All Battles

Playing out in many families in America is some sort of crisis, or at least a dysfunction. What we are witnessing today is the manifestation after several generations of Americans in which at least half the population pushed a world-view which voids the presence of God. The fruit of that thinking is what we are watching today in real time on television, school-rooms, and all forms of media. At the 2012 Democratic National Convention in Charlotte, North Carolina, when God was brought up as an element in the party platform, more than half of the capacity filled arena booed God off stage. Illinois Governor Bruce Rauner recently signed a bill legalizing medical marijuana on the grounds of elementary and middle schools. And it is now obvious the baby boomers have lived beyond their means with a Federal Reserve that prints money out of thin air enabling a lifestyle in its twilight.

One doesn't need to be a Ph.D. in sociology to see where this is headed. Common sense is not commonly found.

Everything seems to be percolating towards an event. Precisely what that is, no one seems to know for sure, but nonetheless, people are anxious. Liberals today are not historical progressive Democrats. They are now an insane dysfunctional group of ideologues who want traditional morals removed from our culture. They have a diabolical agenda to destroy anything of God. Once that is understood, it is easy to comprehend where they want to bring the country.

But the battle inside the family and what constitutes a family is larger than all other battles put together. Why? When a family loses its moral structure, everything important is lost. Sociologists and historians agree that an intact nuclear family is the glue of all societies. The rock of all civilization is a strong family. Studies have clearly shown that strong marriages create emotionally healthy motivated children who grow up to become well-adjusted adults who themselves marry and have strong families. If Satan would try to destroy all of mankind, it would make sense that he would go to the heart of God's creation.

Under the guidance of Saint John Paul II, the Church fought back with the establishment of the *Pontifical Institute for the Studies on Marriage and the Family*. Pope John Paul II said marriage was the bedrock of civilization, expressing these views from the beginning of his pontificate in his writings on *The Theology of the Body*. This was an area of theology which he had been developing since his canoe and camping trips with youth while a young priest in Poland. He named the future Cardinal of Bologna Carlo Caffara founding president of this new Institute. Cardinal Caffara wrote Sister Lucia of Fatima asking for her prayers for the Institute, and placed it under the patronage of Our Lady of Fatima.

Facing the difficulties of his task, Cardinal Caffara wrote Sister Lucia of Fatima asking for her prayers not really expecting an answer back. In 2008 what she said to Cardinal Caffara became known through the Institute archives and the correspondence he had with Sister Lucia. Sister Lucy wrote back, *"The final battle between the Lord and the reign of Satan will be about marriage and the family. Don't be afraid. Anyone who operates for the sanctity of marriage will always be contended and opposed in every way because this is the decisive issue. However, Our Lady has already crushed its head."*

Here Sister Lucy is speaking of what we read in the Book of Revelation, *"And a great portent appeared in Heaven, a woman clothed with the sun, with the moon under her feet, and on her head a crown of twelve stars; she was with child and she cried out in her pangs of birth, in anguish for delivery."* (12:1-2). It is the Blessed Mother who crushes the head of the serpent. Something immediately prior to Revelation 12:1 is Revelation 11:19. *"Then God's temple in Heaven was opened, and the ark of his covenant was seen within his temple; and there were flashes of lightening, loud noise, peals of thunder, an earthquake, and heavy hail."* Just prior to the woman clothed with the sun appearing there is chaos in the world.

As the Ark of the New Covenant, it will be the actions of Our Lady that crush the head of the serpent. Sister Lucy is saying it is a fait accompli — it is already done. The chaos we are seeing around us shows that Satan knows his time is short and is doing everything possible to disrupt God's creation. Even in previous pagan civilizations, homosexuality was never seen as normal behavior. However, we see an assault like never before through every social medium available to normalize this behavior. Looking back, *Humanae Vitae* was prophetic when one looks at the abuse to natural law and sexual depravity in the past 50 years.

A seasoned OB/GYN will tell you what happens before a birth. First, the woman just wants to birth the child and be done with it. After nine beautiful months, she is ready and wants to give birth. Second, the woman about to give birth is in extreme discomfort. The pain is excruciating with the birth pangs. The pain of delivery confirms the sin of Adam, whereby a *"woman will have pain in childbirth."* Third, while a woman is pushing and grunting, she may wonder if she could die. There is a fear of death that she may not be able to accomplish this. She is the only one who can see this through. There is often yelling, screaming, apprehension, and exhaustion.

However, when the child is born, it is as if the pain was never there. It is forgotten as she holds her newborn. In a moment, the agony turns to ecstasy.

We are presently witnessing the dawn and birth of a New Era, The New Times, The Fullness of Time, a New Jerusalem, or as Saint John Paul II said, a New Springtime, with the attendant pain prior to a birth of a child. The confusion and lack of discipline we see in the Church and culture today is systemic chaos. Before the child arrives is a time of uncertainty and normal human anxiety because the old and familiar is being swept away, and the new is on the horizon. Major prophecy and Church approved apparitions sites are pointing to this. Cardinal Raymond Burke and several other leading cardinals and bishops have said there are many events pointing to the fact that we may be living in the days spoken of in Scripture. The Blessed Mother is saying those proclaiming the Word of God are now the Apostles of the Last Times. Saint Louis de Montfort said it will be Marian lay people who will carry the Church through the challenges it faces. Has any battle ever been bigger?

Our times are unique. In 1976, then Cardinal Karol Wojtyla (Saint John Paul II) gave an address at the Eucharistic Congress in Philadelphia for the Bicentennial Celebration of the Unites States and said,

"We are now standing in the face of the greatest historical confrontation humanity has ever experienced. I do not think that the wide circle of the American society, or the wide circle of the Christian community realize this fully. We are now facing the final confrontation between the Church and the anti-church, between the gospel and the anti-gospel. The confrontation lies within the plans of Divine Providence. It is, therefore, in God's plan, and it must be a trial which the Church must take up, and face courageously."

This was said nearly forty-five years ago, and it appears the confluence of events has risen to a fever pitch with Satan knowing his time is short. Thus we see the pain around us. In the Church we see a "progressive" element seeking to change the words of Jesus on marriage and family based upon the Gospel narrative. Moses under pressure from the people softened and watered down marriage requirements while His chosen Hebrew people slowly marched into the land of milk and honey complaining about this teaching of Lord while in the desert. Jesus cleared this up in Matthew 19 and Mark 10. What was supposed to be an 11-day journey, took 40 years due to disobedience. Scripture is not gray on these subjects and all the spin and manipulation by Google analytics in the world cannot change the words of Jesus.

This is the battle of all battles in our midst — marriage and family. Sister Lucia of Fatima articulated her prophetic utterance on the battle we would be witnessing for these times — and she was correct.

I will end on a constructive note. If you are looking to turn things around, start with the most basic of all, by keeping the Sabbath Holy. Keep Sunday for worship, rest, family meals, and no manual labor if possible. The Sabbath was not designed by God as a day for running errands and the mindless rules of Little League or soccer coaches arranging games and practices on Sunday mornings.

JESUS I TRUST IN YOU

Is America Moving Towards Socialism or Communism?

There are many forms of civil government throughout history with differing points of view concerning execution and enforcement. There is Progressivism, Socialism, Democratic Socialism, Marxism, Stalinism, Leninism, Maoism, Communism, and so forth. All of these ideologies mean different things, but Maoism, Leninism, and Stalinism are very similar with the widespread death associated with the implementation of the philosophy. Marxism is about redistribution of assets. God can exist in Marxism, but not under communist rule. Communism as an ideology does not necessarily have to be violent, but usually is, because God must be removed by the state. Communism does not allow independent thinking other than what the state allows, and Christianity is historically the last remaining obstacle for communist rule.

When the state reaches the point of not allowing God in a discussion on civil or moral matters, it will resort to means to criminalize Christianity. Over several generations we have advanced so far in social engineering that Christian tenets and biblical values are now being codified as hate speech, and are increasingly not welcome in the public square. Belief in God is an enemy of the State, because it is in direct contrast to their view of how they wish to rule the world — accepting sin as normal behavior. It is a stated goal of the United Nations and the global elite in control of these types of entities, to bring the Catholic Church into conformity to its agenda of a godless state. Christianity has to be eradicated for communist goals to be implemented under a new international order.

The long-term agenda of socialism will lead to communism. Communism is a social doctrine without God, where the State is supreme. Socialism moving towards communism inevitably strips mankind of all human dignity. There is never a place for Christianity in a communist government. Socialism is the slow calculated movement to a godless form of governance. It creeps incrementally day-by-day, month-by-month, year-by-year, and decade after decade. The United States has been, and is now moving fast to a communist form of governance. Communism is socialism in a hurry. If one listens and watches the left, there is no longer ambiguity where they wish to bring to bring the country. The left's slow calculated actions over the last several generations of legislating a socialist agenda, have now culminated in open field warfare on Christian doctrine.

The groundwork has been laid for a complete takeover by a communist government. Many will not even know it happened, nor care. The state has been so supportive of government largesse in the form of free goods and services it will take civil disturbance to reverse it. Believers have lost the culture war — for now. All the while much of the populace was lulled to sleep with bread and circus. The circus being the wide spread pagan entertainment, and the bread easy credit. Many like the proverbial frog boiled to death in water not even knowing how it happened. There are however, believers who understand the grave situation we face.

Every day there is something that is carried in the news showing the profound difference of the ideologies in our culture. There are things happening around us now that were unthinkable years ago. As the country descends into more chaos, the more we will see the bizarre. The bizarre is becoming the norm on a daily basis.

When you see Governor Cuomo of New York State on the 46th anniversary of Roe vs. Wade, proudly legitimize infanticide and embedding the law into the State Constitution and expanding its scope, you know we have reached a new place. This is not paganism, which historically has been isolated and involves a small percent of the population. What we now have is barbarism on a much broader level where the killing of children is sanctioned by the State. This is a communist agenda. In jubilation of Cuomo's signature, the State of New York lit up the One World Trade Center and other buildings in New York that night in pink. Government sanctioned death until the day before birth with non-doctors able to perform the abortion is now the law. Few are aware this will lead to the harvesting of baby body parts of the victims in late term abortions. Planned Parenthood has boasted off the record how much money is to be made in sales. Virginia introduced a nearly identical bill the day after New York, but it didn't pass. Especially in the blue state legislatures laws promoting infanticide (child sacrifice) have a greater chance of passing in the near future. Next on the docket for New York with the backing of the state is assisted suicide. This is theoretical and practical atheism. It may be wrapped in 21st Century legislative language, but it is barbaric paganism.

The next agenda nationally is more state sanctioned marijuana sales so the state can fund public pensions. Marijuana is a principal gateway drug for more serious addictions. Once you reach the point of generally accepted sin over time, greater and more heinous sin is around the corner.

Communism and paganism/barbarism are not first cousins, but brother and sister. Because communism is not Christ-centered it will eventually lead to pagan practices. State sanctioned abortion is Satanism. It is the Baal and Moloch worship which demanded child sacrifice over 4,000 years ago. Judgment and chastisement await those regions of the United States that have violated the rights of the defenseless unborn. It is historical and scriptural, and arguing otherwise will make you a biblical definition of a fool. God will not be mocked.

The Two Principal Reasons For This Behavior in the United States

1. *Who is Your Authority?* At a personal level, this is the basic question confronting man, and it is not a new thought. Satan said, *'I will not serve.'* This is the first disconnect of man from God. *Who Do You Serve?* You either serve God, asking Him to take over and direct the affairs of your life, or you are doing it through your own self-reason. There really is no in between. Many are lukewarm, and we know what the Lord said about those people. Planned Parenthood represents the extreme example of self-reason unwilling to surrender a will to God. *"I've gotta be me"* is the daily mantra. Until a person surrenders one's will to God, he or she will never find peace of

soul. There will always be another "ism" to confront, and an agitation in their spirit.

At a corporate level, the socialist/communist is always trying to direct the affairs of others to his or her own world-view. Unbelievers seek vindication and acceptance for their sin by trying to normalize their behavior through state sanctioned programs. LGBTQ is just one ideology that does this. Many on the left are no longer Christian, nor believers, nor traditional American democrats of old, but communists because they want a world without God. If one considers the current state of civility, normalcy, and lack of virtue, the West is looking more like Rome under the brute emperors before it fell. We have a controlled and propagandized press presenting lewdness and corruption on a daily basis and minimizing the good that believers are doing. At the senior level it is the cabal of the deep state running the show. The reality is the left is in control of the public relations industry, press, and many influential positions in government.

2. What Exactly is The Role of Government in Our Lives? The daily fight at the food court or café and yes, in nearly every home, revolves around what exactly is the role of government in our lives. Think of the origin of the arguments. Many communists want a cradle to grave government approach. They want the social services and goods from the state distributed evenly EXCEPT for those who are on the top who portion them out. In short time, they become a ruling class of their own under totalitarian rules. For them, with the unbridled human nature that exists in the lower nature of man, it is about stealing as much as they can for themselves.

When a government continues to give away free goods for votes using invasion and mass migration to do so, that nation is hanging by a thread for survival. The appeal is to the senses as an inducement for change under an unrealistic and idealist agenda. Leaders who call themselves Catholics championing godless causes need to be feared as sheep in wolves clothing because they have abdicated their first responsibility to God. When elected officials ignore their conscience for the sake of legislating their public responsibilities they lead the nation to chaos.

Many leaders have operated under the adage of *"Tell a lie often enough and people will believe it."* Who would have ever thought the LGBTQ and Planned Parenthood agenda could have garnered so much momentum years ago? When the United States Supreme Court removed prayer and the bible from the classroom in 1962/63, did anyone see this coming? Did people speak up? Did the Church speak up? Some good people did speak up then, but there were too few. Many believers have consented with their silence. What else could the outcome have been? There are now thousands of examples like this in America. Halloween can be celebrated as well as Islam in public venues of all sorts, (not just public schools) but Christian based themes cannot. Try having an Easter or Christmas celebration in a public high school and watch the flurry of letters to the school board. That is totalitarian communism and an assault on Christianity.

On January 24, 2019, Governor Kate Brown of Oregon stated by the end of 2019 she wants to pass a bill which would require home visits by state officials to all households with newborn babies. The issue is control by the State from cradle to grave.

This is just another example of government looking to regulate families from birth, and it is another element of state control of families. Thousands of instances like this could be used to show the extent of state intrusion into the lives of citizens ultimately designed to make the entire family a ward of the state.

There are many now in Congress who have never taken a civics lesson, do not understand the roles of the branches of government, nor the beauty or the wisdom of the Constitution, and what makes them work—and they could care less. They are anarchists and communists, and they are now the single largest voting block in democratically controlled House of Representatives. Rome in the end was barbaric due to its vast territory with grotesque brutality. The Senate of Rome at the time of its downfall had the same pathological makeup as it citizenry.

One may see great hope and encouragement in the fact that the Lord has a plan, with an agenda for believers so they do not fall into anxiety or despair. At Garabandal, an apparition in Northern Spain from 1961-1965, the Blessed Mother said to the young visionary Conchita, that before the **Warning** through which everyone will be able to see interiorly how they stand before God, and then the **Great Miracle**, it would appear the world would be overtaken by communism. These two prophesied events will reveal **"the conscience of mankind,"** and will destroy the evil deception in the world. The veil will be lifted from our eyes. That is Heaven's promise, and we wait for it in joyful hope.

JESUS I TRUST IN YOU

The Pedophile Network—More to Come

Hollywood is the nearest thing to Sodom and Gomorrah on the face of this earth. Hollywood has been the largest and single most powerful entity promoting and distributing sex, filth, and corruption in every form of human existence since the first talkie was ever made. Even in the silent movies, they pushed the envelope on decency laws. No institution in the history of the world has had such a negative effect on what could be considered an assault on a moral code. The breakdown of our culture is a straight line to Southern California, and the malcontent souls that inhabit the land. Like a moth attracted to light, perverted minds and hearts have flocked to Hollywood for over 100 years. The floodgates are open because now exposed, they can't duck the facts about their behind the scenes code of silence and their reprobate lifestyle. Like leading clergy who were protecting sex-offenders, once exposed we see how they played the populace for dumb suckers.

The hypocrisy in Hollywood is now in the open. It is interesting to note that the Harvey Weinstein sex scandal broke wide open for the world to see on the Feast of Divine Mercy, October 5, and the 100-year anniversary of Fatima. The issues with

Harvey Weinstein are the tip of the iceberg with over three-dozen (as of this writing) allegations of rape and perverted sexual behavior. While he is one of the worst offenders, he is far from alone in an industry plagued by sexual excess and impropriety. This problem is not just about Hollywood, but has become a pandemic in our entire culture of immorality in all social strata. Unfortunately many actresses and aspiring actresses are unwilling to come forward because many of them decided that the casting couch was a viable option for fame and fortune. It is the nature of the trade.

Things are now about to change with the deeds of many being made known on a global basis. What the Weinstein scandal demonstrated is that the untouchable Hollywood and media giants who pandered their liberal ideologies and accuse conservatives as being sexists have all of a sudden been caught in a net of sexual predation and depravity against women.

Against this backdrop, you have people on the right and the left equally dug in on their opinions and ideologies. There is little room for openness and negotiation anymore on many subjects. The left has always abhorred and held the right in outright disdain. The left continued to push the right, which has historically been more tolerant. The left has resorted to all sorts of name-calling to those who disagree with them. If you disagree with the left, it is you they say are a trousered ape.

Things in our culture, however, are changing and the aroma of that change in the air is palpable. The right is no longer willing to give up ground as they have now said — enough is enough. With the internet and social media in every hand or on every desk in America, the knives are out. Twitter, Facebook, and hundreds of other media outlets are about to expose the homosexual agenda along with the perverted nature of Hollywood because they can no longer run and hide from the facts in front of them. Hollywood and other institutions like them are about to have their day of reckoning. Evil will turn on itself because the rats will run for cover.

People are naming names and the list will be long so that it will eventually reach to pedophile networks in all parts of society. Evil is about to be exposed in a grand fashion. The biggest and most popular HBO Program in history called *Game of Thrones* openly promotes rape, adultery, incest, violence, killing, and rampant sexual promiscuity. The best words to describe the program are barbaric and outright pagan. It is the rage not only of youth, but of the general public. *Game of Thrones* is the religion of the unprofessed raised with no ideology other than pleasure and self-gratification in a world void of God. The lead actor boasts that he can't believe he gets paid to rape on a routine basis as part of his job.

Judgment Begins First in the House of God

In the year 2000, judgment first came to the house of God in the Catholic Church with the homosexual agenda exposed in Boston under Cardinal Law. The issue had been festering and hidden below the surface for two generations, but it exploded on the world scene and spread like the black plague throughout the rest of America. Hollywood was ecstatic. The problem then spread to nearly every diocese in America costing the Church well over $4 billion to settle claims of the abused. Church doors were shuttered due to lack of funds as people voted with their wallets, and then their feet.

The movie *SPOTLIGHT* released in 2015 was about an undercover investigative team from the Boston Globe exposing the lies of the clergy in Boston covering up the homosexual agenda inside the Church. It was disgusting to watch because it was true. Hollywood which generally has contempt for the Church, had the opening it needed to expose the hypocrisy inside the Church, and they jumped on it. A friend of mine's son who had attended Catholic schools from elementary grades through high school said that he would never enter a Catholic Church again after seeing the movie. While it may have been an immature position to take, it continues to be the young man's position to this day.

In the Old Testament, the Lord always chastised and exposed the Levites (priests) on account of their sin before He made any form of judgment on His people. We see this in Ezekiel 44:10-14; Isaiah Chapters 6-10, Lev. 8-10, Numbers 16-17, and in many other places in Scripture. He would remind them of duties of obedience and fidelity to His statues and commands as leaders of His people. If they did not comply, the Lord would then ramp up the punishment for disobedience. In essence, the Lord doled out a Divine Spanking, or as some may say, a Divine Pruning, which is a merciful chastisement. The Lord held HIS LEADERS responsible for the actions of His people. In Scripture, it was the responsibility of the Levites (priests) to proclaim sin first and bring it to the open, because as priests that was their job. They would be judged more harshly if they did not. Judgment first comes to the House of God (1Peter 4:17).

After warning (or warnings) the priests, the Lord would then inform them of the consequences for disobedience. If there was compliance to His Law, the Lord showed mercy. If the people were still stiff necked and hard of heart, the Lord never suffered from any lack of imagination in ways to rein in His people. We see this trend all the way to banishment of the Jews to Babylonian captivity for seventy years in Jeremiah 25:11 to 29 for disobeying the observance of the Sabbath and in 2 Chronicles (36:21) something as seemingly innocuous and innocent as the lack of observance of the Sabbath could bring judgment. Time and again His chosen people had been warned, but they ignored what was required of them as leaders.

Saint Paul wrote in Romans (1:28) that the godless of his day were given over to *"depraved minds."* Other Scripture translations speak of *"reprobate"* lives and minds. All light to our hearts, minds, and souls comes from the inspiration of the Holy Spirit. Reasoning with a person who has little light or goodness is very difficult today. The culture in Hollywood is a morally toxic place akin to a cesspool. Lost people are generally attracted to Hollywood precisely for those reasons. It is where they go to feed their carnal appetites. So many Hollywood aspirants trying to break in the business barely graduated high school and are looking for the self-esteem there that they never received at home. Yet, they seem to have counsel for all America. A moral movie today is as rare as a stable family the actors came from. We have recently seen people like Angelina Jolie, Lady Gaga and others openly talk how they gave themselves over to Satan in ritualistic form to achieve fame and wealth.

Why should we be shocked by Harvey Weinstein and men like him?

However, Heaven always operates to give the world answers where political and news media pundits define the problems but offer no relief.

The Blessed Mother Provides Solutions

In Message 256 (h-k) to the Marian Movement of Priests the Blessed Mother on December 31, 1982 said,

Prayer of Reparation: because the cup of divine justice is full, very full; it is over-flowing! See how hatred and sin burst all bounds. Today the majority of mankind no longer observes the Ten Commandments of the Lord. Your God is publicly ignored, denied, offended, and blasphemed. The day of the Lord is more and more profaned.

Daily an attack is being made upon life. Each year throughout the world, by the tens of millions, innocent children are being slaughtered in their mother's womb, and the number of murders, robberies, and acts of violence and kidnappings are increasing.

Immorality is spreading like a flood of filth and is being propagated by the means of social communication, especially the cinema, the press and television. By means of this last mentioned, a subtle and diabolical tactic of seduction and corruption has found its way into every family. The most defenseless victims are children and youth, whom I look upon with the tender preoccupation of a mother.

Only the powerful force of prayer and reparative penance will be able to save the world from what the justice of God has prepared because of its obstinate refusal to accept every demand for repentance.

JESUS I TRUST IN YOU

They Were Given Over to Depraved Minds

Last Saturday night (April 2018), America and the world watched and listened to another nail in the moral coffin of a divided America. In what is supposed to be a night of light jabbing over political differences, the White House Correspondents Dinner showed the world just how fast the USA is sinking spiritually. The signs of that demise are now visible for the entire world to see once again. In this age of all forms of social media, the league of nations heard it all, the nineteen-minute routine of what was called **"comedy,"** will be heard by multiple hundreds of millions of America's friends and enemies on the world stage. The "league of nations" heard it all and further solidified its opinion on who we are as a people. The night after the event, a personal friend told me he had dinner with a Japanese trade delegation that was in town. He said they were in shock that this type of tasteless parody could even take place at all. Many feel that the one hundred year old event has run its course.

What was so off key? Over 3,000 of the most rich and powerful annually fight for a spot at a table to be seen in black tie and gowns sipping drinks with the Washington media and political elites. And through it all, the foul fetid noisome profanity laced monologue received laughs from the crowd.

Each year the chosen illumined souls of Hollywood, the press, and big business that cling to the D.C. revolving door, gather to rub elbows and then head to all the local gin mills to wax philosophically on the future of the country – and try to push things in their ideological direction for financial gain. There they may hopefully find their rightful place at the table of government largesse in the form of multi year contracts and remain swamp masters. Much of the left today are a nihilist cabal of death seeking individuals seeking devoid of any human decency and with a godless agenda. They no longer follow a logical thought process that comes to a workable solution for anyone. To not understand this, is to not understand the fight. As Saint Mother Teresa of Calcutta would frequently say in public speeches to the West, *"The fruit of abortion is nuclear war."* The gloves are off as the civility is gone between the parties.

For those who have followed the event over the years, the White House Correspondents Dinner is just one of similar soirees taking place. The Gridiron Club and Alfalfa Club are two more examples with the attendee list more exclusive. A motto of the Alfalfa Club is *"singe, don't burn."* The roots of the alfalfa seed go deep, and that is what the attendees are after—deep relationships for the promotion of agendas and careers.

This year however, the Correspondents Dinner was different for several reasons. To those who have watched the evolution of the event it has become more personal and tasteless each year. No one will argue that it shows the moral depravity that is generally accepted on the world stage. Generations ago it was the wit and wisdom of Will Rogers who was loved by all for expressing the truth in charity. It was light-hearted humor poking fun at the differences of the political parties. Then came people like Bob Hope doing the same in times of war and peace. These men were guests in the White House and well received for humor, and became beloved institutions. But then again, the issues didn't have the profound moral divide for policy implementation we see today. The differences of thinking then is nothing compared to what it is today – not by a long shot.

The evening "entertainment" also showed it is the mainstream press that is perennially running the event. The speakers and entertainers are now from the hard strident virulent Planned Parenthood left. The comedians (an oxymoron) are unable to write a witty joke because they are not gifted enough to write innuendo or find humor in the obvious truth without tearing flesh. The more vulgar, crass, and obscene, the more a career will go parabolic because somewhere there is an audience that wants it. The next day Michelle Wolf said Washington, D.C is thin skinned and can't take a roast. This is a far cry from the good-hearted popular roasts of Dean Martin still watched on television today. Shock sells and they know it. Did you ever hear the name Michelle Wolf until Sunday morning? The odds are today Michelle Wolf's bookings just quintupled at double the fee.

One joke (?) is when Wolf commented, *"Mike Pence is very anti-choice. He thinks abortion is murder, which, first of all, don't knock it till you try it. And when you try it, really knock it. You know, you've got to get that baby out of there. And yeah, sure, you can groan all you want. I know a lot of you are very anti-abortion, you know, unless it's the one you got from your secret mistress."*

The evening also showed how virulent things have become in relationships. People have dug in on what they believe and it is disrupting family unity like never before. People are now making a conscious choice to avoid or limit contact with those that disagree with their view of the world. This is not insignificant historically because it is a precursor to civil disobedience. Revolutions brew for generations before the steam pot creates a whistle.

After World War 1 and the Treaty of Versailles, the Germans were boxed in with harsh terms for debt repayment, and rebuilding their nation. Recovery was brutally arduous and lengthy. The National Socialist German Workers Party (Nazi) quickly sprouted from a small seed of insignificant and illogical thought at the beginning with a mad man paper-hanger by the name of Adolf Hitler. Writing a manual for the restoration to national greatness while in prison, his plan matured in less than fifteen years into the Third Reich. On January 30, 1933 President Paul von Hindenburg reluctantly appointed Adolf Hitler Chancellor of Germany because he had such a strong following. An entire **"educated"** nation followed suit and wholeheartedly embraced a godless agenda with gusto because of the vision of a man to take away the pain of suffering from the Great War, and the destitution of the Weimar Republic.

What we are watching today in real time is a strategic plan to transform the United States into a godless culture of sin that is promoted legislatively. Everything Hitler did was legal because laws were enacted that allowed him to act with the tacit approval of the courts. The voice of the people was overwhelmingly silent as they took the bread of man over God.

Today, you are either **"IN or OUT,"** depending on your view. Christian views are increasingly OUT of what has been recently legislated, as believers are battling a system against their views. No one thirty years ago could have thought this was remotely possible coming from the courts and government. Christians are now leaving California as they see the trend is one of persecution on the near horizon.

A new Rasmussen Poll found that democrats are more concerned about Muslims being mistreated in the U.S. than Christians being slaughtered abroad in Muslim nations. The day after the Correspondents Dinner, Trump met with the president of Nigeria at the White House. One topic of discussion was the widespread horrible persecution and slaughter of Christians in his country. There wasn't a word from the mainstream press about it.

Words have meaning. What is said today has consequences tomorrow. Ideologies good and bad form opinions. What may seem completely absurd and outrageous to one may be acceptable to another. This is why the divide is so great in the Church as well as what one thinks about President Trump. Few are neutral anymore. The debate of words heats up before disturbance, and the strong rhetoric of opinion today is a prelude to civil war. The tolerance level of one person toward another with a different view is shrinking by the day.

The Holy Spirit is the ultimate source of truth, love, justice, and light. That light is the source of wisdom. If one is not trying to conform their views to the light, it is in conflict with the Holy Spirit because God alone is light. To the degree that light is not penetrating the soul, one will not achieve the Will of God. Abraham Lincoln would often quote a passage from Scripture during the Civil War that said, *"Every-man did that what was right in his own eyes"* (Judges 21:25). As people turn away from God, a humanist agenda seeks to dig in further. Jesus said, *"My ways are not your ways,"* because that is the battle of the ages. Each year the sacraments are absent from a life, one is incrementally given over to a depraved mind and will look at the world strictly from a human view. Light is not penetrating the soul, and therefore, one will not achieve the Will of God.

We now know the progressive socialist agenda, because it is in the open for all to see. Being able to see the whites of their eyes enables one to know the agenda of the enemy that is no longer shielded behind the false view of commonality. This is positive because the left can no longer hide through intentionally vague and ambiguous language. They can no longer cry peace when what they really want is a moral war extinguishing Christian views. The war is now in the open, and we need to plead to God to restore America through supernatural events to the ideals it was founded upon. We were not made to live this way. As Jesus said, *"My kingdom is not of this world"* (John 18:36).

JESUS I TRUST IN YOU

The Acceleration of Evil

"Socialism is the philosophy of failure, the creed of ignorance, and the gospel of envy. Its inherent virtue is the equal sharing of misery."

Winston Churchill

L ast summer, my wife and I had the pleasure of meeting two elderly Polish women while on vacation in Canada. Although I never asked their age, I assumed based upon the conversation they were in their 70s. At a beautiful outdoor café in Quebec Province, they told us their story of how their parents fled communist Poland and settled in the Boston area. They made a new life in the U.S. rather than endure the yoke of the hammer and sickle of communism. They met while young girls at their local Church. They each married, raised families and prospered spiritually and socially. The families socialized together and bonded over shared values. They shared a similar view of the world and have remained life long friends. It was obvious in the course of the discussion that that they had a great respect for each other. Now, with their children grown, the two women nearly sixty years later were thinking that this may be the last vacation of its kind. What impressed me most about them was their sensibility about the reality of our day.

Looking out over the beautiful Saint Lawrence River, both women lamented the direction of the United States heading fast into what they once fled. They were clear that the signs were not ambiguous. They both felt that Canada had lost its faith foundation, and the speed of the loss of faith in the U.S. was accelerating. Both were steadfast that it was faith that allowed their families to have the courage to leave their home in Poland, and that faith would sustain them in the future. Faith was their rock, and their *raison d'être* (reason for being) for living. Both were visibly shaken as they were certain where America was headed if it continued to abandon faith as the bedrock of its culture. Neither felt that it could be reversed outside of some spiritually spectacular event that would bring it back to its senses. They prayed it would happen, but they didn't know how it would come about.

Soviet dissident Alexander Solzhenitsyn at the Harvard Commencement in 1978 gave an hour-long address that was called *A World Split Apart*. Shortly after that it was modified and in publications was called *The Exhausted West*. In 1983 he was awarded the Templeton Prize and on that occasion largely focused his talk on the intersection of state and faith, and the severe crippling affects of a nation that is not Christocentric in its governance. He died in Moscow in 2008 at the age of 90. As an acute observer of socialism, communism, and abusive state policies lacking any humanity of faith, Solzhenitsyn painted a bleak picture for a culture that advocates, endorses, and embraces a godless state. This is what was spoken about at the outdoor café on the Saint Lawrence without ever mentioning his name. Solzhenitsyn was a giant among men in this genre. As a prisoner of the gulag for over ten years, he saw what the system was like personally.

At the end of World War II, as the GIs came home and finished their education on the much deserved GI Bill, many a professor learned the hard way not to abuse the soldier who had known war and death of brothers, friends, and family. War wasn't just theory to battle scarred men and women, and they would not tolerate junk philosophy based on the theories of Karl Marx. Senator Bernie Sanders and that ilk embody that nonsense. Sanders is the biblical definition of a fool who never had a paid job until he was 53 years old (a public one) and has mooched his way on public funds his entire life. He spews a communist manifesto of *"free everything,"* while he has three homes and a luxurious sports car — all supported by the government dole. It reminds one of Lenin's comment on how people can be used as **"useful idiots,"** for the communist purpose.

Solzhenitsyn made the following comments at his Templeton address:

*"More than half a century ago, while I was still a child, I recall hearing a number of older people offer the following explanation for the great disasters that had befallen Russia: **Men have forgotten God; that's why all this has happened.***

Since then I have spent well-nigh fifty years working on the history of our

Revolution; in the process I have read hundreds of books, collected hundreds of personal testimonies, and have already contributed eight volumes of my own toward the effort of clearing away the rubble left by that upheaval. But if I were asked today to formulate as concisely as possible the main cause of the ruinous Revolution that swallowed up sixty million of our people, I could not put it more accurately than to repeat: **Men have forgotten God, that's why all this happened.**

What is more, the events of the Russian Revolution can only be understood now, at the end of the century, against the backdrop of what has since occurred in the rest of the world. What emerges here is a process of universal significance. And if I were called upon to identify briefly the principal trait of the ENTIRE twentieth century, here too, I would be unable to find anything more precise and pithy than to repeat once again: **Men have forgotten God.**

The failings of human consciousness, deprived of its divine dimension, have been a determining factor in all the major crimes of this century. The first of these was World War 1, and much of our present predicament can be traced back to it. It was a war (the memory of which seems to be fading) when Europe, bursting with health and abundance, fell into a rage of self-mutilation which could not but sap its strength for a century or more, and perhaps forever. The only possible explanation for this war is a mental eclipse among the leaders of Europe due to their lost awareness of a Supreme Power above them. Only a godless embitterment could have moved ostensibly Christian states to employ poison gas, a weapon so obviously beyond the limits of humanity..."

Solzhenitsyn spoke back in 1983 but issued a warning to the west based upon what he saw coming. *The West has yet to experience a communist invasion; religion here remains free. But the West's own historical evolution has been such that today it too is experiencing a drying up of religious consciousness. It too, has witnessed racking schisms, bloody religious wars, and rancor, to say nothing of the tide of secularism that, from the Middle Ages onward, has progressively inundated the West.* **This gradual sapping of strength from within is a threat to faith that is perhaps even more dangerous than any attempt to assault religion violently from without.**

The remainder of the speech is lengthy and insightful on the reasons for the moral decline of the West and the United States in particular. He was clear in articulating that the perverting of Christian teaching is far worse to a nation than a violent enemy from without. He said often that courage was the single most necessary virtue for the believer, lest the culture fall to a godless state. He felt that the single most dangerous issue for a nation state was an irresponsible and controlled press.

A few of his many sayings are the following:
- *A genius doesn't adjust his treatment of a theme to a tyrant's taste.*
- *Unlimited power in the hands of limited people always leads to cruelty.*
- *Talent is always conscious of its own abundance, and does not object to sharing.*
- *In our country the lie has become not just a moral category, but a pillar of the state.*
- *Man has set for himself the goal of conquering the world but in the process loses his soul.*
- *Every man has handy a dozen glib reasons why he is right not to sacrifice himself.*

• *All Communist Parties, upon attaining power, have become completely merciless. But at the stage before they achieve power, it is necessary to use disguises.*
• *The solemn pledge to abstain from telling the truth was called socialist realism.*
• *Untouched by the breath of God, unrestricted by human conscience, both capitalism and socialism are repulsive.*
• *The concept of good and evil have been ridiculed for several centuries; banished from common sense, they have been replaced by political or class considerations of short-lived value.*

In George Washington's first speech after his election as President, he had a call to prayer, stating that:

"It would be peculiarly improper to omit in this first official act, my fervent supplication to that Almighty Being who rules over the universe, who presides in the councils of nations, and whose providential aids can supply every human defect... No people can be bound to acknowledge and adore the invisible hand which conducts the affairs of men more than the people of the United States. The propitious (favorable) smiles of Heaven can never be expected on a nation that disregards the eternal rules of order and right which Heaven itself has ordained."

In Washington's Farewell Address leaving government service he warned:

"... Of all the dispositions and habits which lead to political prosperity, religion and morality are indispensable supports. In vain would that man claim the tribute of patriotism who should labor to subvert these great pillars of human happiness."

In all of sports, when the game is toward the end and the final score is close, there is a flurry of activity as teams go for broke to win the game. The increase in evil we see around us is due to the fact that satan knows his time is short, and his goal is to destroy all good by any means while he still can. The war again is because **WE HAVE FORGOTTEN GOD. THAT'S WHY ALL THIS HAS HAPPENED.**

JESUS I TRUST IN YOU

The Secret Weapon Few Utilize

"And He said to them, because of the littleness of your faith; for truly I say to you, if you have faith the size of a mustard seed, you will say to this mountain, move from here to there, and it will move and nothing will be impossible to you. But this kind does not go out except by prayer and fasting."

Matt. 17:19-20

"Nothing will be impossible to you."

I f we were to dwell on this phrase alone, it is a mighty big promise from the Lord Himself. Yet Jesus ties faith to prayer *and* fasting.

Fasting is a part of the biblical narrative from start to finish. There are hundreds of verses in the Old and New Testament that speak of fasting. Many of those verses revolve around epic stories of how Israel won battles where the circumstances were not in their favor. Queen Esther knew that her people were in trouble and could be destroyed through an evil authority figure, the King of Persia. Knowing that the threat to her people was very real, she became very determined and said, *"Go, gather all the Jews, to be found in Susa, and hold a fast on my behalf, and do not eat or drink for three days, night or day. I, and my young women, will also fast as you do. Then I will go to the king, though it is against the law, and if I perish, I perish"* (Esther 4:16). The Jews fasted as they were told. The Lord heard their cry, and the Jewish people were spared. Clearly the Lord has shown that through fasting, the destiny of a nation can change.

At the institution of the Old Covenant, while the Jewish people were slowly marching toward the land of milk and honey, *"The Lord said, Moses, put these words in writing, for they are the terms of the covenant I am making with you and Israel. He stayed there with the Lord for forty days and forty nights, **eating and drinking nothing**. He inscribed on the tablets the words of the Covenant — the Ten Commandments"* (Exodus 34:27-28).

Similarly, in the New Covenant, just before Jesus began His earthly ministry, He went into the desert to fast and prepare Himself for His public ministry. *"Then Jesus was led by the Spirit out into the wilderness to be tempted by the devil. He fasted for forty days and forty nights after which He was very hungry, and the tempter came to Him"* (Matt. 4:1-2). Think of how profound it was, that God Himself would do this.

Above are two of the most significant events in world history. The Lord was pre-scribing a Covenant for His people while wandering in the desert, a new way of living for His people that will last thousands of years. Some people follow that way of living until this very day. When God's New Covenant came through His Son Jesus Christ, fasting was prescribed as a fundamental action to purify the soul, and the instances of fasting in the Bible recorded. Moses and Jesus each fasted for forty days. When we do fast, it shows we are in serious prayer for an intention.

Fasting also has been a constant message throughout history at the authentic apparition sites of Our Lady. She is a powerful prophetess for love and mercy to the world through her messages, and prayer and fasting are always central. Fasting has been one of the most consistent messages at Medjugorje since Our Lady started appearing there in 1981. The list that follows has been compiled by a Friend of Med-jugorje and are just a few of the many references to fasting in Our Lady's messages:

1.   Fasting stops wars (7/21/82).
2.   Fasting can suspend the laws of nature (7/21/82).
3.   Fasting reduces punishments from God (11/16/82).
4.   Fasting is a weapon of significant power to defeat Satan with which atomic power does not compare. Atomic power has no strength to conquer Satan (6/25/92).
5.   Bread and water is the best fast (7/21/82).

6. Fasting to be powerful must be done with the heart (9/20/84).
7. Through fasting, the whole plan of Our Lady, which God Himself planned for the world's salvation during this special time, will be achieved (9/26/85).
8. By giving our fasting to Our Lady, Satan is unable to seduce us and it drives him away (9/4/85).
9. Fasting purifies our hearts from the sins of the past (12/4/86).
10. Fasting, coupled with prayer, will obtain everything you ask for (the exception is something illicit) (10/29/83).
11. Fasting sanctifies you to the Holy Spirit (11/4/83).
12. Humility is a fruit from fasting when coupled with prayer (2/10/84).
13. The present fasting in the Church is not adequate. Our Lady desires this to change. She said that fasting has been forgotten in the last quarter of this century in the Catholic Church (5/84).
14. Fasting is one element that keeps Satan from conquering us. Faith and prayer are the other two (6/25/92).
15. Satan is enraged against those who fast and convert (6/16/83).
16. Fasting for the sick can cure them with faith and prayer (11/26/81).
17. Fasting and prayer can stop arguments in the Holy Priesthood (1/21/82).
18. Fasting will bring the Kingdom of God among us (3/14/84).
19. Fasting makes Our Lady happy (8/5/84).
20. Fasting will make prayer more vigorous (1/25/84).
21. Our Lady will make the maximum good come from our fast. She wants us to give our fasts to her, which she disposes of "according to the will of God" (9/24/82).
22. Fasting, coupled with prayer, especially community prayer, will protect you from Satan's aggression in destroying marriages, creating division among priests, and will crush Satan in his plans for obsessions and murders in society (12/26/82).
23. We are to fast out of gratitude (9/20/84).
24. It is best you let no one know you are fasting (1/28/87).
25. Fast to prepare for the coming of Jesus (11/25/96).

Her messages show how important fasting is in the eyes of Heaven. Saint John Paul II in his 1994 encyclical *Evangelium Vitae* said, *"Jesus Himself has shown us by His own example that prayer and fasting are the first and most effective weapons against the forces of evil."*

"Nothing will be impossible to you."

So the question must be asked, why do we not fast more often? I think there are many answers to that question, but one conclusion is that we lack the discipline. Laziness, lack of belief, a busy schedule, headaches, fatigue, sloth, unwillingness to deny a simple pleasure to our body, not fervent enough to conquer a personal prayer request, not wanting something bad enough, seeing too big of an obstacle — these are all just a few reasons why we don't fast. But when the history of the entire Bible is viewed through the pages of Scripture, fasting is a key spiritual weapon for the salvation of nations and souls. Fasting is often spoken of, but done the least for effective spiritual warfare.

What is fasting and what does it accomplish spiritually? First and foremost, fasting requires discipline and reorienting priorities. If you were to search the internet for "fasting," hundreds of biblical citations pop up, and those verses are a very small part of the whole story being told. Saint Alphonsus de Liguori said, *"God has given us the goods of the earth, not only that we may enjoy them, but also that we may have the means of... showing Him our love by voluntary renunciation of His gifts, and by the oblation of them to His glory. To abandon, for God's sake, all worldly enjoyments, has always been the practice of holy souls."* It is the biblical and historical greats who have made it a part of their spiritual regimen to fast.

Why does a regimen of fasting lead to greater spirituality? Through fasting we renounce the body, and simultaneously we heighten our spiritual senses. We also become more cognizant of our speech and actions. Fasting is for protection. Fasting has spiritual and physical components that can prevent evil or impure thoughts. Fasting is a method to acquire purity of heart because it gives us the needed grace for prayer. St. John Chrysostom said that *"Prayer and fasting are like two wings that carry a person to the heights of God."* Fasting helps us to become free from what prevents our growth when we have become stagnant and are not growing spiritually.

There are numerous Scripture passages that indicate fasting is a sign of repentance. Fasting is a sign of humility. Fasting is also a sign of expectation. We are in active supplication and petition asking in faith and in expectation for an answer due to our action because we are trusting God for the outcome. Fasting is an outward sign that we are serious about having our prayer answered. We have in essence thrown up our hands saying, "Lord I am at my wits end and it is time for Your glory to be manifested as this event is too big for me to do. You alone can change it." We face many of these difficulties in our lives on a daily basis, yet we fail to fast or pray hoping that we can affect change on our own merit alone.

The single greatest discourse of length where Jesus gave instructions on spiritual conduct for the believer in the world was the Sermon on the Mount. His instructions on fasting demonstrate repentance, humility, and expectation. *"When you fast do not put on a gloomy look as the hypocrites do; they pull long faces to let men know they are fasting. I tell you solemnly, they have had their reward. But when you fast, put oil on your head and wash your face. So that no one will know you are fasting except your Father who sees all that is done in secret; and your Father who sees all that is done in secret will reward you"* (Matt. 6: 16-18).

For those who are unable to fast for physical reasons, there are other ways of mortification. The Lord is not a bureaucrat requiring ritualistic formulas constricting the work of the Holy Spirit. He alone knows our heart when we fast for the correct reasons. He alone is judge. Ascetical reasons alone are not good enough, as many people use fasting as a form of dieting. You will know if you are on the right path if you are exhibiting kindness and mercy as a result of fasting. It will curb the sin of Adam and as Saint Peter Chrysologus wrote, *"Fasting is the soul of prayer, mercy is the lifeblood of fasting.... So if you pray, fast; if you fast, show mercy; if you want your petition to be heard, hear the petition of others. If you do not close your ear to others, you open God's ear to yourself."* (Sermo 43: PL 52, 320, 322)

"Nothing will be impossible to you."

Throughout all of biblical history, fasting has been a staple of an individual or a nation that wants to turn the tide of current events. Today, it is a highly neglected spiritual practice among even the most faithful. The fact that fasting could alter the destiny of all mankind defies all modern era reasoning. If we talked less and fasted more, we would see more answers to our prayers. Through our actions we would be saying to the Lord, you take over, it is bigger than me. My faith is in You Jesus to cast this mountain into the sea.

JESUS I TRUST IN YOU

Who is the Real Enemy of the Catholic Church?

"It is an act of charity to cry out against the wolf when he is among the sheep."

Saint Francis de Sales, *Introduction to the Devout Life*, Part III, Chap. 29

"In the Third Secret (of Fatima) it is foretold, among other things, that the great apostasy in the Church will begin at the top."

Cardinal Luigi Ciappi

A friend of mine is a believer and follows world events very closely. If you ask him his thoughts on a political subject, he can penetrate to what is being said, and what is going on behind the scenes, from an erudite standpoint based on history and modern political philosophy. He sees the divide among people is getting more intense, and feels like many, that violence is coming to the streets of America at some point in the future. Recently, I asked him who is the real enemy? Who is the wizard behind the curtain pulling the strings? He gave me a blank stare, stood back a step, and said, *"That is a really good question."* He ventured a guess to satisfy the question and said, *"the Democrats."* I said no, there is a malevolent dark force behind the curtain of humanity that people do not see. This is the real enemy of the Catholic Church and by extension, all of humanity.

The Enemy Fights to Win

In order to better understand the seriousness of the enemy, it first will be helpful to briefly review the seriousness of warfare. The ancient Chinese philosopher Sun Tzu wrote a book approximately in the year 500 BC called **The Art of War.** It may not have had a subtitle then, but has one now called **The Most Influential Book of Strategy in the World.** The book has been used in councils of elders and war colleges for nearly 2,500 years, and, as it concerns military and social strategy, is probably the most quoted book on war, peace, and combat in the history of the world.

A definition of the book can be described in three sentences: *"Know when to fight and when not to fight: avoid what is strong and strike at what is weak. Know how to deceive the enemy: appear weak when you are strong, and strong when you are weak. Know your strengths and weaknesses: know the enemy and know yourself, and you need not fear the result of a hundred battles."*

The pithy sayings dotted throughout the book are folklore to many, and deathly real to nations who have sought the book's principles to maintain their relevance or supremacy in the world. There is no book like it. It is a book about deception, which is not a laudatory practice for a person who professes a personal belief in Jesus Christ. But, for a nation state it is a book about survival of the fittest. Weak nations are invaded first. A few sayings include:

• All warfare is based upon deception.

• There are five essentials for victory: He will win who knows how to fight and when not to fight. He will win who knows how to handle both superior and inferior forces. He will win whose army is animated by the same spirit throughout all its ranks. He will win who prepared himself, waits to take the enemy unprepared. He will win who has military capacity and is not interfered with by the sovereign.

• There is no instance of a country having benefitted from a prolonged war.

• Appear weak when you are strong, and strong when you are weak.

• If he is superior in strength, evade him.

• The worst strategy of all is to besiege walled cities.

Infiltration and Operating in Stealth

Sun Tzu provides a blueprint for aggressive nations to conquer, and for those less able to maintain their own status quo until ready for combat. The historical reality of Sun Tzu's book of strategy is unmatched. Does this have relevance to the Roman Catholic Church and those looking to subvert its truth? The answer to the above question is yes, and it is relevant to discern who the real enemy of the Catholic Church is.

The enemy of the Church is Freemasonry. For the last several centuries, Masons have applied these principles of infiltrating and operating in stealth against the Church, hiding in the weeds, as well as in plain sight. To the casual observer, Masonry is an innocuous group of people. The men are Masons, the women have the Eastern Star, and youth are members of DeMolay. Masonry is designed by its framers to hide the truth. The barbarian is inside the gates. They have had enormous influence without the general population even knowing their plans, and with clergy thinking they are some sort of boys' club driving go-karts for sick children and wearing funny looking hats. A profound lack of understanding spiritual warfare and knowing how to fight your enemy enables them to operate so efficiently. Masonry roots run far, wide, and deep, and it is deceptively portrayed as just a fraternal organization doing good works.

As a young priest studying in Rome in 1917, St. Maximilian Kolbe saw the Masons marching in the streets saying they would control the Vatican in 100 years. He immediately founded the Militia Immaculata (MI) that very day putting the protection of the Church under the mantle of the Blessed Mother. Enlightened by the Holy Spirit, he instinctively saw a serious threat that has become an aggressive cancer to the world and the Church.

If one is intellectually and emotionally honest, they would have to ask, how did this apostasy in the Church happen? What is its origin? Was there an agenda? Is it a conspiracy theory? Is this the thinking of a disordered mind who believes this, or worse, one who perpetrates a deceptive agenda like this on an unsuspecting public? It is a topic worthy of consideration. It is not heavily talked about for two main reasons. First, ignorance of its existence, and secondly, fear of retribution. Social, political, and/or industrial marginalization are certain for the one who cries out against the wolf.

Find Out if It Is Organized

Under the guise of a novel, Father Malachi Martin treats the reality of Freemasonry in the Church through his work of historical fiction, *Windswept House.* He tells the story of an unsuspecting priest by the name of Gladstone who is summoned to the Vatican. Father Gladstone is an amalgam of a man from a wealthy Galveston, Texas home. He is a man's man, well bred, traveled, educated, and with enormous personal and intellectual gifts. If he were at a cocktail party or dinner, Gladstone by virtue of his presence and savoir-faire would command the room. He is the type of person who can walk by a friendly game of chess, look at the board for a second or two, and tell the friend to move the rook and take the knight, freezing the king. Checkmate.

He is now in Rome meeting with the pope. Passing pleasantries, the pope then tells him the reason for the meeting is to find out the intentions of these one world order people, the titans running the global show of power that the pope knows is anti-church. The pontiff knows they are evil men doing diabolical things. He then asks Father Gladstone the penetrating question, **"Is it organized?"** Gladstone is commissioned to find the answer.

Father Malachi Martin clearly understood the battle way in advance of others, and while alive, he was arguably the most controversial priest in the world. He already had seen the Vatican corruption and had the courage to speak about it. When Father Martin died, that title then went to Father Gruner who wrote on all things Fatima and the diabolical forces in the world looking to undermine the Church. Both had many things in common. They both intimately understood Fatima and the extreme relevance of the Third Secret, and the necessity of the Consecration of Russia to the Immaculate Heart of Mary, as the Blessed Mother asked at Fatima. Both Fathers Martin and Gruner died believing the Consecration of Russia was not done by the Church, as it was asked by the Blessed Mother, in unison with all the bishops of the world — **specifically mentioning Russia by name, as Our Lady asked. Not the consecration of the world, but Russia.**

Both priests were intimately aware of the hidden agenda of diabolical Masonry:

widespread apostasy, atheistic communism, and corrupt political institutions and governments. But both knew above all, how Masonry had infiltrated inside the Church and was blocking what Heaven was asking of mankind. They knew intensely the battle inside the Church and its Masonic influence, even having their own Lodge in Rome called Propaganda Due (The P2 Lodge). Because of this, Fathers Martin and Gruner were vilified by many, and understood by few. Most, due to a naïve understanding of how the corridors of power actually work, thought their views extreme. Their harshest critics came from inside the Church because they were so close to the truth of the Vatican intrigue surrounding why certain things are not being done as Heaven has asked.

Powerful and bright men knew they could not take the Church head on because it was too big, too wealthy, too organized, too centralized, and with a long tradition of too many faithful followers who would openly fight to preserve it. They needed another strategy rather than an unwinnable fight against a walled wealthy city. Following Sun Tzu's proven strategy, they found another way, and they found the best way: a Trojan Horse approach using infiltration to change the narrative. You can be the judge on its success.

Powerful Positions and Easy Careers

Masonry is often spoken of as the Deep State or the Shadow Government. It is a cabal of like-minded and ideologically similar people networking and promoting each other to fashion a world they want to see. Its utopian fantasy goes all the way back to Plato's belief that an ideal world government should have a ruling class, a working class, and a military class, best suiting the needs of citizenry. That is best accomplished in placing people in strategic positions in government, industry, and law enforcement. It is organized under Secret Societies that attract people looking for easy careers. These people are placed in powerful positions that give them privilege they could never attain on their own. To better understand, it is simply men going along, to get along, for financial and career prosperity.

If one were to research the list of Masons, you will find some of the most prominent people in the last 250 years on the list. There is a heavy concentration of industrial, banking, and political members with an overt intent to have control. No matter which party controls Congress and the White House, the same entities are in the most influential positions in government. Benjamin Disraeli, Prime Minister of Great Britain in 1844 states, *"So you see... the world is governed by very different personages from what is imagined by those who are not behind the scenes."* (All quotes in this article on the New World Order and its structure are from the book *Hope of the Wicked* by said author.)

Its modern day philosophical roots were birthed by Adam Weishaupt of Bavaria in 1776 for the New World Order or the Novus Ordo Seclorum. Weishaupt was a professor of Canon Law who adopted Masonic thinking for a new structure of the world. The word "illuminati" is thought to have come from him — an enlightened group of self-appointed men to rule the world. *"Illumined souls"* know what is best above all the rest, for a better mankind. Under their control, Secret Societies, and specifically

Masonry, blossomed at this time in Europe as the young colonies across the ocean were just being formed. They saw an opportunity and took it to mold the new world to their views.

The elite (illumined souls) believed the young colonies that comprised the new world could become the new Atlantis under their control. The French trappers and the Dutch mariners showed the British the potential of the New World, and they decided to control its destiny by providing a plan under men like Francis Bacon, a leading Mason in England. Benjamin Franklin, who worked in England before achieving prominence in the early colonial period, was asked who the founder of America was, and he said, *"Francis Bacon."* What we are witnessing today in Church and state is centralized power over a long period of time with people placed in very strategic positions doing the bidding and allegiance for the *illumined ones.*

The term *"New World Order"* has been used innumerable times in this century by high-powered proponents of federalized world government. For years, leaders in education, media, and banking have promoted political leaders with the same worldview as their own. On May 4, 1993, Council of Foreign Relations (CFR) president Leslie Gelb said on the Charlie Rose Show, *"You had me on before to talk about the New World Order. I talk about it all the time. It's one world now. The Council on Foreign Relations can find, nurture, and begin to put people in kinds of jobs this country needs. And that is going to be one of the major enterprises of the Council under me."* Former CFR chairman John J. McCloy (1953-1970) said, *"They have been doing this before the 1940s."*

Prior to the Federal Reserve Act of 1913, President Woodrow Wilson published *The New Freedom,* in which he revealed, *"Since I entered politics, I have chiefly had men's views confided to me privately, some of the biggest men in the United States, in the fields of commerce and manufacturing, are afraid of somebody, are afraid of something. They know that there is a power somewhere so organized, so subtle, so watchful, so interlocked, so complete, so pervasive that they had better not speak above their breath when they speak in condemnation of it."* One should be reminded that Wilson was president of Princeton, and Governor of New Jersey before he was elected president, and was the useful idiot that Lenin spoke about who did the dirty work for powerful people often without knowing it. When President Wilson was told by Edward Mandel House about the Federal Reserve Act of 1913, the bill Wilson had signed into law giving control of the U.S. Treasury to private bankers, Wilson wept.

The Rhodes Scholars were established in 1902 by Cecil Rhodes to create a new ruling class, looking for a modern day Utopia. A Utopia on earth will never exist unless it is under the sovereignty of God. As long as there is Original Sin, and people who seek power, it is an illusion of the financial and political elite. That is its Achilles heel. It is an ideal way to look at the world, but sovereign nations must be done away with to achieve its purpose, thus the role of immigration/migration to reduce man to a robotic state of compliance with statism.

As a result, the United States is experiencing a modern-day coup d'état. The elites utilize the administrative legal power of the executive branch of government with Gestapo tactics. Presently in the U.S., five media companies govern ninety percent of the narrative in the news, and a free press is an illusion. Multiple dozens of entities are under each of the major media corporations. Yes, the Deep State is organized, and controlling the narrative of the press is essential. Remember, all Hitler did prior to World War II was sanctioned by the German legal system that permitted his activities and endorsed by the media.

Prior to the election of Donald Trump to the presidency, there were a total of seventeen candidates battling it out on stage and the stump to be the GOP nominee. While the field was still full, former speaker of the House Newt Gingrich made a startling statement on the Bill O'Reilly Show on the chances of Donald J. Trump being the nominee, let alone president. I was so startled what he said on live television, I had to play it back several times to make sure I heard it correctly. Gingich said, **"Well because he's an outsider. He's not them. He's not part of the club. He's uncontrollable. He hasn't been through the initiation rites. He didn't belong to The Secret Society."**

It was a loaded truth rarely spoken in public. He said the word *"initiated," "member of the establishment,"* and *"THE Secret Society,"* which is Freemasonry. Not **A** secret society, but **THE**. This is the fight we see daily in the media, and it is intense because people with power do not give it up easily. This is a fight between the powers of darkness and light in the spiritual realm, and it is a white-knuckle fight to the last man standing. Well over a century of concentrated power in the halls of both sides of the aisle of the U.S. Congress will not capitulate without a fight. It is not about Democrats or Republicans, but those in secret societies working on the same agenda giving the appearance they are separate and distinct. There may be nuances like pro-life and other social issues, but not when it comes to control through banking and finance.

The agenda is being carried out using age-old principles of Sun Tzu in the modern era of the 20th and 21st centuries with an interconnected and smaller world of high speed everything. It is the digital age using social engineering to control the masses by controlling the message. It is the manipulation behind the scenes of masses of people without them even knowing about it, much less discerning their tactics. Yes, as our fictitious Father Gladstone found out, and the whispers of Woodrow Wilson attest, it is highly organized in Masonic halls throughout the world. With the rot and stench reaching a crisis, Our Lady is now exposing their evil agenda, as actively as she was in dismantling the evil of Soviet Russia in the early 1990s.

In the Name of Mary

Heaven historically has a lot to say about Masonry. In one of the most famous messages from the Marian Movement of Priests, Our Blessed Mother in Message 456 titled, **In the Name of Mary** (c-e), says,

"In the name of your Heavenly Mother, yes, in the name of Mary, the Turks were defeated, when they laid siege to the city of Vienna, and threatened to invade and destroy the whole Christian world. They were far superior in strength, in numbers and in weapons, and they felt that their victory was assured. But I was publicly invoked and called upon; my name was inscribed upon their banners and shouted out by the soldiers, and thus through my intercession, there took place the miracle

*of this victory which saved the Christian world from its destruction. It is for this reason that the Pope instituted, on this day, **the Feast of the Name of Mary.***

In the name of Mary, Marxist communism, which for decades had been exercising its rule and holding so many of my poor children in oppressive and bloody slavery, has been defeated in these countries. Not because of political movements, or persons, but through my personal intervention, has your liberation finally come about.

*It will again be in The Name of Mary that I will bring to completion my work with the **defeat of Masonry,** of every diabolical force, of materialism, and of practical atheism, so that all humanity will be able to attain its encounter with the Lord, and be thus purified and completely renewed, with the triumph of my Immaculate Heart in the world."*

Based upon the Blessed Mother's above role as Co-Redemptrix, Mediatrix, and Advocate, it is clear major events are happening in the world through her intercession. As the prophetess of our age, appointed by the Most Holy Trinity, she is doing major cleaning, caring for her children. Heaven is flushing out evil from where it hides and exposing it to the light. In the Old Testament, judgment first begins in the house of God. This is what we have been witnessing for the last twenty years as the hypocrisy of the hierarchy is being seen by all. At present, in a very unstable world, there could be numerous things that come to mind for the Blessed Mother to move, but she says her next target is Masonry. It is like a termite infested dwelling on borrowed time ready to topple from foundational rot. Just as her intercession brought victory at Lepanto, Vienna, and the former USSR, Masonry is now biding time. A new building will then be erected to replace the old one.

Masonic Forces vs. the Marian Movement

As the saying goes, *"You only take flak when you are above the target."* If you get too close to the unholy grail of Masonry, you will be attacked. You become an immediate threat to the establishment, and they will go to any extreme to discredit you. The Marian Movement of Priests (MMP), and Fathers Gruner and Martin had controversy around them for the simple reason they exposed Masonry hidden in the Church. When they got too close to the truth, the enemies of the Church discredited them with a vengeance. In particular, the Masonic forces in the Vatican have sought to discredit the MMP messages from the outset, saying they were prayerful thoughts, musings, meditations, and prayers of the MMP, but not Heavenly locutions given by the Blessed Mother as an encouragement to mankind. The MMP drove a dagger into the heart of Masonry calling *Secular Freemasonry, "the Beast Like a Leopard," and Ecclesiastical Freemasonry, "the Beast Like a Lamb."* The MMP flies above the target in majestic truth with language like no other. No one can articulate the truth clearer than the Blessed Mother, other than Her Son.

Many approved apparition sites in the world validate Masonry's authenticity as a supreme enemy of the Church. Our Lady of Good Success in Quito Ecuador, Blessed Ann Katherine Emmerick, the Devotion to the Holy Face, and a myriad of mystics attest to it. A document called *The Permanent Instruction of the Alta Vendita* lays out the plot of Masons to subvert and undermine the orthodoxy of the Church. Pope Pius IX in 1861 guaranteed the authenticity in a letter of approbation of the document, and asked that it be published. Below is an important part of the Alta Vendita:

> *"Our ultimate end is that of Voltaire and of the French Revolution — the final destruction of Catholicism, and even of the Christian idea.... The pope, whoever he is, will never come to the secret societies: it is up to the secret societies to take the first step towards the Church, with the aim of conquering both of them. The task that we are going to undertake is not the work of a day, or of a month, or of a year; it may last several years, perhaps a century; but in our ranks the soldier dies and the struggle goes on."*

Dozens of papal bulls and statements could be provided here from the Church over the last several centuries on the evils of Masonry. Presented below will be a lengthy exposition of both the MMP messages on secular and ecclesiastical Freemasonry, because frankly nothing else is so true, pure, and enlightening in the world on why we have the current state in the Church and the world. We'll let the Blessed Mother have her say, which will enlighten and bring you intellectually and spiritually to a new understanding of the enemy intentionally hiding beneath the surface — *The Art of War* at its finest.

The Beast Like a Leopard, #405 (c-v, C-D, F), MMP, Secular Freemasonry

> *"In this terrible struggle, there comes up from the sea, to the aid of the Dragon, a beast like a leopard.*
>
> *If the Red Dragon is Marxist atheism, the Black Beast is Freemasonry. The Dragon manifests himself in the force of his power; the Black Beast, on the other hand, acts in the shadow, keeps out of sight and hides himself in such a way as to enter in everywhere. He has the claws of a bear and the mouth of a lion, because he works everywhere with cunning and with the means of social communication, that is to say, through propaganda. The seven heads indicate the various Masonic lodges, which act everywhere in a subtle and dangerous way.*
>
> *This Black Beast has ten horns and, on the horns, ten crowns, which are signs of dominion and royalty. Masonry rules and governs throughout the whole world by means of the ten horns. The horn, in the biblical world, has always been an instrument of amplification, a way of making one's voice better heard, a strong means of communication.*
>
> *For this reason, God communicated His Will to his people by means of ten horns which made his Law known: the Ten Commandments. The one who accepts them and observes them walks in life along the road of the divine Will, of joy and peace....*
>
> *The grace of the redemption is communicated by means of the seven sacraments....*
>
> *The task of the Black Beast, namely Masonry, is that of fighting, in a subtle way, but tenaciously, to obstruct souls from traveling along this way, pointed out by the Father and the Son and lighted up by the gifts of the Spirit. In fact if the Red Dragon works to bring all humanity to do without God, to the denial of God, and therefore spreads the error of atheism, the aim of Masonry is not to deny God, but to blaspheme Him. The beast opens his mouth to utter blasphemies against God, to blaspheme His name and*

dwelling place, and against all those who dwell in Heaven. The greatest blasphemy is that of denying the worship due to God alone by giving it to creatures and to Satan himself. That is why in these times, behind the perverse action of Freemasonry, there are being spread everywhere black masses and the satanic cult. Moreover Masonry acts, by every means, to prevent souls from being saved, and thus it endeavors to bring to nothing the redemption accomplished by Christ.

If the Lord has communicated his Law with the Ten Commandments, Freemasonry spreads everywhere, through the power of its ten horns, a law which is completely opposed to that of God.

To the commandment of the Lord: 'You shall not have any other gods but me,' (cf. Exodus 20:3) it builds other false idols, before which many today prostrate themselves in adoration.

To the commandment: 'You shall not take the name of God in vain,' (Ex. 20:7) it sets itself up in opposition by blaspheming God and His Christ, in many subtle and diabolical ways, even to reducing his name indecorously to the level of a brand-name of an object of sale and producing sacrilegious films concerning his life and his divine Person.

To the commandment: 'Remember to keep holy the Sabbath Day,' (Ex. 20:8) it transforms the Sunday into a weekend, into a day of sports, of competitions and entertainments.

To the commandment: 'Honor your father and your mother,' (Ex. 20:12) it opposes a new model of family based on cohabitation, even between homosexuals.

To the commandment: 'You shall not kill,' (Ex. 20:13) it has succeeded in making abortion legal everywhere, in making euthanasia acceptable, and in causing respect due to the value of human life all but disappear.

To the commandment: 'You shall not commit impure acts,' (cf. Ex. 20:14) it justifies, exalts and propagates every form of impurity, even to the justification of acts against nature.

To the commandment: 'Thou shall not steal,' (Ex. 20:15) it works to the end that theft, violence, kidnapping and robbery spread more and more.

To the commandment: 'You shall not bear false witness,' (Ex. 20:16) it acts in such a way as the law of deceit, lying and duplicity becomes more and more propagated.

To the commandment: 'You shall not covet the goods and the wife of another,' (Ex. 20:17) it works to corrupt in the depths of the conscience, betraying the mind and the heart of man.

In this way souls become driven along the perverse and wicked road of disobedience of the laws of the Lord, become submerged in sin and are thus prevented from receiving the gift of grace and the life of God.

To the seven theological and cardinal virtues, which are the fruit of living in the grace of God, Freemasonry counters with the diffusion of the seven capital vices, which are the fruit of living habitually in the state of sin. To faith it opposes pride; to hope, lust; to charity, avarice; to prudence, anger; to fortitude, sloth; to justice, envy; to temperance, gluttony.

Whoever becomes a victim of the seven capital vices is gradually led to take away the worship that is due to God alone, in order to give it to false divinities, who are the very personification of all these vices. And in this consists the greatest and most horrible blasphemy. That is why on every head of the Beast there is written a blasphemous name. Each Masonic lodge has the task of making a different divinity adored....

The task of the Masonic lodges is that of working today, with great astuteness, to bring humanity everywhere to disdain the holy Law of God, to work in open opposition to the Ten Commandments, and to take away the worship due to God alone in order to offer it to certain false idols which become extolled and adored by an ever increasing number of people: reason, flesh, money, discord, domination, violence, pleasure. Thus souls are precipitated into the dark slavery of evil, of vice and of sin, and, at the moment of death and of the judgment of God, into the pool of eternal fire which is Hell.

Now you understand how, in these times, against the terrible and insidious attack of the Black Beast, namely of Masonry, my Immaculate Heart becomes your refuge and the sure road which brings you to God. In my Immaculate Heart there is delineated the tactic made use of by your Heavenly Mother, to fight back against and to defeat the subtle plot made use of by the Black Beast....

Thus I am making use of you, my little children who have consecrated yourselves to me, to unmask all these subtle snares, which the Black Beast sets for you and to make futile in the end the great attack which Masonry has launched today against Christ and his Church. And in the end, especially in his greatest defeat, there will appear in all its splendor, the triumph of my Immaculate Heart in the world."

Heaven is making it very clear there are opposing forces in the world. For all virtue, there is an equally powerful vice. For obedience to the Ten Commandments, there are also powerful forces in the world working diligently to counter the intent of Heaven. According to the words of the Blessed Mother, it is organized inside Mason lodges throughout the world.

Where the Beast like a Leopard is secular, the Beast Like a Lamb is ecclesial. The Blessed Mother, through the Marian Movement of Priests, gives a message to the world about Freemasonry inside the Church.

The Beast Like a Lamb, #406, MMP, Ecclesiastical Freemasonry

"I also foretold to you the subtle and dark work, carried out by Freemasonry with the purpose of separating you from the observance of the Law of God and thus making you victims of sins and vices.

Above all, as Mother, I have wanted to warn you of the grave dangers which threaten the Church today, because of the many and diabolical attacks which are being carried out against it to destroy it.

To attain this end, there comes out of the earth, by way of aid to the Black Beast which arises out of the sea, a beast which has two horns like those of a lamb.

The lamb, in Holy Scripture, has always been a symbol of sacrifice....

The beast has on its head two horns like those of a lamb. To the symbol of the sacrifice, there is intimately connected that of the priesthood: the two horns. The high priest of the Old Testament wore a headpiece with two horns. The bishops of the Church wear the mitre with two horns to indicate the fullness of their priesthood.

The black beast like a leopard indicates Freemasonry; the beast with the two horns like a lamb, indicates Freemasonry infiltrated into the interior of the Church, that is to say **ecclesiastical Masonry, which has spread especially among the hierarchy.** *This Masonic infiltration, in the interior of the Church was already foretold to you by me at Fatima, when I announced to you that Satan would enter in even to the summit of the Church. If the task of Masonry is to lead souls to perdition, bringing them to the worship of false divinities, the task of ecclesiastical Masonry on the other hand is that of destroying the Christ and his Church, building a new idol, namely a false christ and a false church....*

And so **ecclesiastical Masonry** *works to obscure His divine word, by means of natural and rational interpretations and, in the attempt to make it more understandable and acceptable, empties it of all its supernatural content. Thus errors are spread in every part of the Catholic Church itself. Because of the spread of these errors, many are moving away today from the true faith, bringing to fulfillment the prophecy which was given to you by me at Fatima: 'The times will come when many will lose the true faith.' The loss of faith is apostasy....*

Jesus is the Life because He gives grace. The aim of **ecclesiastical Masonry** *is that of justifying sin, of presenting it no longer as an evil but as something good and of value. Thus one is advised to do this as a way of satisfying the exigencies of one's own nature, destroying the root from which repentance could be born, and is told that it is no longer necessary to confess it. The pernicious fruit of this accursed cancer, which has spread throughout the whole Church, is the disappearance everywhere of individual confession. Souls are led to live in sin, rejecting the gift of life, which Jesus has offered us.*

Jesus is the way which leads to the Father, by means of the Gospel. **Ecclesiastical Masonry** *favors those forms of exegesis which give it a rationalistic and natural interpretation, by means of the application of the various literary genres, in such a way that it becomes torn to pieces in all its parts. In the end, one arrives at denying the historical reality of miracles and of the resurrection and places in doubt the very divinity of Jesus and his salvific mission.*

After having destroyed the historical Christ, the beast with two horns like a lamb seeks to destroy the mystical Christ which is the Church. The Church instituted by Christ is one, and one alone: it is the one, holy, catholic and apostolic Church, founded on Peter. As is Jesus, so too is the Church founded by Him which forms the Mystical Body, truth, life and way....

Ecclesiastical Masonry seeks to destroy this reality through **false ecumenism,** *which leads to the acceptance of all Christian Churches, asserting that each one of them has become part of the truth. It develops the plan of founding a universal ecumenical church, formed by the fusion of all the Christian confessions, among which, the Catholic Church....*

In the Eucharist, Jesus Christ is truly present with his glorified Body and his Divinity. And so **ecclesiastical Masonry,** *in many and subtle ways, seeks to attack the ecclesial devotion towards the sacrament of the Eucharist. It gives value only to the meal aspect, tends to minimize its sacrificial value, seeks to deny the real and personal presence of Jesus in the consecrated Host. In this way there are gradually suppressed all the* *external signs which are indicative of faith in the real presence of Jesus in the Eucharist, such as genuflections, hours of public adoration and the holy custom of surrounding the tabernacle with lights and flowers.*

The Church is the way because it leads to the Father, through the Son, in the Holy Spirit, along the way of perfect unity....

*Beloved children, I have urged you to consecrate yourselves to my Immaculate heart and to enter into this, my motherly refuge, above all in order to be preserved and defended against this terrible snare. In this way, through the act of consecration of my Movement, I have urged you to renounce every aspiration of building up a career. Thus you will be able to remove yourselves from the strongest and most dangerous snare, made use of by Masonry in order to associate in its **secret sects** so many of my beloved children. I bring you to a great love for Jesus-Truth, making you courageous witnesses of the faith; to Jesus-Life, leading you to great holiness; to Jesus-Way, asking you to be in life the Gospel alone, lived out and proclaimed to the letter.*

Then I lead you to the greatest love for the Church.

I bring you to love the Church-truth, making of you strong proclaimers of all the truths of the Catholic faith, as you set yourselves in opposition, with strength and courage, to all errors.

*I make you ministers of the Church-life, helping you to be faithful and holy priests. Be always available to the needs of souls, lend yourselves, with general abnegation, to the ministry of Reconciliation, **and the burning flames of love and of zeal for Jesus present in the Eucharist. In your churches may you once again hold frequent hours of public adoration and reparation to the Most Holy Sacrament of the altar....***

*Thus to the dark force of which **ecclesiastical Masonry** is today exercising to destroy Christ and His Church I am opposing the powerful splendor of my priestly and faithful army, so that Christ may be loved, listened to and followed by all, and that His Church may be more and more loved, defended and sanctified.*

In this there shines forth above all the victory of the Woman Clothed with the Sun, and my Immaculate Heart attains its most luminous triumph."

The above needs to be read several times to understand how profound the concepts are that the Blessed Mother is saying—better than anyone else can say. Only a portion of the total message was provided, and when read in its totality, it is even more powerful.

Our Lady Will Destroy Masonry

No less than Our Mother has cried out to warn us against the wolf. She diagnoses the problem and gives an immediate solution to turn around the negative cycle we see around us. So goes the Church, so goes the world. The home is designed by God to be a domestic Church. If the priests were fulfilling their role and vocation as asked by God, and by virtue of being a victim priest, the culture would heal. But, she is making it very clear many in the hierarchy are complicit with plans to destroy the Church from within, by opposing the Gospel. Some clergy compromise by seeking a career, rather than being a victim soul, another Christ. *"The great apostasy in the Church will begin at the top."*

There is encouraging news, and as we wait in joyful hope for things to change, we are told to continue seeking the truth no matter the chaos around us. To the MMP, Our Lady said, *"Since by their consecration they have allowed themselves to be possessed by me, I will manifest myself in them, and through them I will act to strike at the heart of my enemy and to crush his head with my heel"* (25f).

It is through the cohort of believers Heaven will bring victory as scripture promises, but we must first be the agents of change. When was the last time you spent an hour before the Eucharist in Adoration? (cf. MMP #29q).

And most encouraging of all, do not walk the streets with slumped shoulders and neck at a 45-degree angle in spiritual defeat. The Blessed Mother gives very encouraging words that we win in the end. She says to the MMP (#29g), *"[A]t the very moment when Satan will be enthroned as lord of the world and will think himself now the sure victor, I myself will snatch the prey from his hands. In a trice [means quickly] he will find himself empty handed, and in the end the victory will be exclusively my Son's and mine. This will be the triumph of the Immaculate Heart in the world."*

JESUS I TRUST IN YOU

44 Herods for Today

"A nation can survive its fools, and even the ambitious.
But it cannot survive treason from within. An enemy at the gates is less formidable,
for he is known and carries his banner openly. But the traitor moves amongst
those within the gate freely; his sly whispers rustling through all the alleys,
heard in the very halls of government itself. For the traitor appears not a traitor.
He speaks in accents familiar to his victims, and he wears their face
and their arguments, he appeals to the baseness that lies in the hearts of all men.
He rots the soul of a nation. He works secretly and unknown in the night to undermine
the pillars of the city. He infects the body politic so that it can no longer resist.
A murderer is less to fear."

Cicero 106 BC to 43 BC

On February 25, 2019, the United States Senate voted on a piece of legislation that puts the country on a par with the most heinous transgressors of moral and scriptural law in the history of the world. There is a strong argument that the United States is worse than all previous morally offending empires, because we are a people who vote legislators into office with free will in a constitutional republic. In previous generations and empires, it was largely a totally illiterate class of people under a king or some despotic ruler, inhibiting rights to its citizenry, precluding a free election. Votes do matter today, albeit in many instances one could rightfully question the legitimacy of the process.

On that cold winter night at the U.S. Capitol, forty-four United States Senators voted against bringing the *Born-Alive Abortion Survivors Protection Act* to a procedural floor vote. Under Senate rules, sixty votes were needed for consideration of the bill on the floor of that legislative body. The bill would punish any doctor who fails to provide medical care after a child is born alive after a botched abortion. The bill was voted down 53-44 with three democrats abstaining. Senate Leader Mitch McConnell (R-KY) had an agenda to let the constituents of every state know where their senators stood on the issue of life.

This came after the comments of Virginia Governor Ralph Northam (D-VA), and his now famous radio interview saying that infanticide after birth was permissible. Again, the vote was forty-four people (all democrats) of the highest elected office (other than President) in the land voted for infanticide. Rome under the brutes and the likes of emperors Nero and Caligula has nothing on the morals of the democratic U.S. Senators, and millions of people who think like them. You need to think about that vote and let it sink in to understand the spiritually bankrupt state of our country — and emotionally comprehend the moral slide over the last several generations.

To stand against the killing of the innocent is paramount, because if people get that wrong, they won't get anything else right that matters. The hedge of God's protection is due to obeying His laws — and for some time, the USA has been outside that boundary. We know a playing field by its boundaries. The lack of fruit now in our culture is seen nightly on the news. The policies of extreme abortion under the democrats and the Obama Administration have become normalized in the courts, and mainstream in the culture, and the democrats presently are a party that has little respect for human decency.

If one wants to read a single chapter of Scripture that explains the blessing and the cursing of a nation, read Chapter 28 of Deuteronomy. The "deutero" means the law. When we have leaders of the nation sitting in U.S. Senate seats voting as the democratic 44, it is time to realize that we are in a new place of radical barbaric criminal insanity, akin to Rome prior to its fall. If you are not fully aware of this, you are putting you and your family in a dangerous place in the coming years. The assault on Christian values is daily and it has been a gradual creep. California Assemblyman Jessie Gabriel recently introduced bill AB 624 making it mandatory that every Student ID in the state include the phone number for Planned Parenthood for all students ages 12-24. If one looks at the trajectory of the vice coming from California over the last several generations, don't bet it won't pass on to the rest of the country at some point. We are now dealing with very darkened intellects.

Something that has always confused me is the lack of passion from believers to proclaim the truth. It is the nonbeliever singing off key, not the believer. Yet, often there is fear to speak out when truth, goodness, and virtue are on their side. Often believers want to be *"the church of nice"* as we decay from within, even though they may not have the foresight to see it clearly. A believer has history, human nature,

Scripture, theology, philosophy, and common sense on their side. Unbelievers leave a trail of chaos, deceit, corruption, and confusion around them. People live in a world of fantasy and outright stupidity ignoring the potential cruelty of human nature if God is absent in their life. Their thinking is nothing but a mass of contradictions. The believer will give in self donation, while the unbelievers often leave nothing but failed agendas because their plans are not under the Lordship of Heaven. Their plans are built on shifting sands rather than on a firm foundation.

Poet W. B. Yeats speaks of this in his poem **The Second Coming** saying that *"the best lack all conviction —"*

> *Turning and turning in the widening gyre*
> *The falcon cannot hear the falconer;*
> *Things fall apart; the center cannot hold;*
> *Mere anarchy is loosed upon the world,*
> *The blood-dimmed tide is loosed, and everywhere*
> *The ceremony of innocence is drowned;*
> *The best lack all conviction, while the worst*
> *Are full of passionate intensity...*

"The falcon cannot hear the falconer" is the cry of the ages. We are in this predicament today because believers have remained silent when they should have proclaimed truth. They are afraid of being marginalized from a peer group for being viewed as excessively radical if they do speak up. Well......44 U.S Senators voting for infanticide is radical, yet there has not been a peep from the hierarchy across the land. W.B. Yeats articulated the emotional constitution of *"the church of nice"* and their lack of passion. This was a near constant theme of Archbishop Fulton J. Sheen from the1950s until his death.

Author Flannery O'Connor in *Mystery and Manners* (1969) also spoke about what she called *"tenderness"* that could also be called *sentimentality or softness,* or *the church of nice.* It is clear where a lack of discipline and fortitude leads us. A more modern word for sappy sentimentality could be **snowflakes, buttercups, or cupcakes,** with the present generation offended by truth that has endured for millennia. This is resulting from the general lack of awareness what man is capable when deprived of the ease of living and creature comforts — something deficit spending by government has enabled generations of Americans to enjoy since World War II, to possess with no consequence for indulgence. As Leo Tolstoy once said, *"Man is what he is when stripped of his finery."* O'Connor wrote:

If other ages felt less, they saw more, even though they saw with the blind, prophetical, unsentimental eye of acceptance, which is to say, of faith. In the absence of this faith now, we govern by tenderness. It is a tenderness which long cut off from the person of Christ, is wrapped in theory. When tenderness is detached from the source of tenderness its logical outcome is terror. It ends in forced-labor camps and in the fumes of the gas chamber.

Words and policy have a life span. Starting with the birth control pill in the late 1960s, we have evolved into a perverted culture. This just didn't happen overnight.

Lax moral standards have allowed us to appease the base nature of man. Now, with the U.S. Supreme Court assuring legal abortion as a constitutional right, with homosexuals acquiring rights not even thought possible years ago, and transgender identity generally becoming normalized, the next step in the progression of sin could very well be the acceptance of pedophilia as a right. If infanticide doesn't change your view of America, the question must be asked, what will it take to for you to speak up, and be active turning around the mess we find ourselves in? Relentlessly shaving a point off your golf handicap seems to be a mindless endeavor when the city is on fire, and the salvation of the next generation is at stake.

John the Baptist spoke truth to power when he confronted King Herod Antipas for adultery with his brother's wife. Jesus said about John, "*He was the greatest man ever born of woman.*" Yes, speaking the truth may cost you, but at least at this point it won't cost you your head. That may happen in the future if the present trend continues — as your silence is consent.

JESUS I TRUST IN YOU

When Our Lady Speaks

There are a few things in Catholic circles and well beyond as controversial as the Blessed Mother's apparitions in world history. C.S. Lewis once remarked that he left the Blessed Mother out of *Mere Christianity* because she was such a divisive subject. What are people afraid of if they listen to her or openly talk about her? What do they have to lose? Why are they hostile or ambivalent? Is she to be admired or venerated, but nothing more?

There are approved apparitions in Catholic history as well as those that have been disapproved and those which are somewhere in the middle still subject to review. We should steer clear of those that have been disapproved and be cautious or judicious as to those for which the verdict is still out. That is the Church's prudence. Time will always weed out those that are bogus. However, we should not be immediately skeptical of an apparition until we have known and studied the facts. There are ongoing apparitions like Medjugorje in Bosnia-Hercegovina where the Blessed Mother has been appearing since June of 1981. The Vatican has recently given approval of the first seven apparitions. Some apparitions, like those at Fatima in 1917 are approved in Rome after consideration by the Congregation for the Doctrine of the Faith. Then there are others that have been approved by the local Bishop like Our Lady of Kibeho in Rwanda, Our Lady of All Nations in Amsterdam, Our Lady of Betania in Venezuela, Our Lady of America in Ohio and many others. In authentic Marian messages there is always a plea to an amendment of life and its contents are not contrary to the Church's deposit of faith and morals in any way. So why are some people skittish when speaking about Our Lady's messages?

Many Catholics are highly guarded or worse when it comes to these phenomena. Sometimes persons who express an opinion believing in a particular apparition are often pegged as a bit odd. Minimally many may just pay lip service with respect to a particular apparition, but won't go too far out on a limb regarding whatever messages Our Lady has communicated because there is potentially a social price to pay if they do. Whether folks are incredulous, or skeptical of the fact that apparitions and supernatural phenomena do occur even in our midst, the fact is they often ostracize those who do believe, keeping them and those expressing similar views at a distance, lest they become tainted by association. The contents of messages communicated in an authentic apparition is a timeless message often repeated: pray the Rosary as a daily exercise, make Mass the center of one's life, read Scripture, go to confession regularly, adhere to the Sacraments, and follow the timeless message of the Gospel, *"Do whatever He tells you."* I can't find a radical message in any of this that is contrary to the Gospel.

Yet, woe and behold if one brings these issues up in many circles. Sadly the most virulent reactions tend to come from those who are most conservative and traditional within the Church. These people will often venerate Our Lady on her feast days, pray for her intercession and yet have serious misgivings about anything that Mary may be communicating in real time. As long as she doesn't speak, things are fine and it is business as usual. Their attitude is nonsensical, even illogical. Many of those same conservatives can articulate profound social and moral problems in our midst, but here a solution is being given by the Blessed Mother, and they reject it. They are often unaware that Our Lady has been appointed by the Most Holy Trinity to a very special role in these times. She is bringing many people back to her Son, Jesus Christ.

Why is there often such negativity and abhorrence to what the Queen of Heaven and Earth is saying when the message is only meant to help humanity? What mother would not speak up if she saw her children in danger? We will name just a few of the apparition sites where what was foretold happened as had been communicated by Our Lady. Dozens more could easily be mentioned.

At Fatima in 1917 (approved), the Blessed Mother appeared to three young illiterate shepherd children and gave the most prescient message of the 20th Century. She said that if we did not amend our lives, then *"Russia would spread her errors throughout the world."* On the other hand, if mankind complied there would be peace in the world. She also asked that Russia be consecrated to her Immaculate Heart and that it be done in a certain manner. However, if that Consecration was not done, the world would not find peace. Most know about the connection between Fatima and Russian Communism. However, few know that one of those errors was the Russian promotion of abortion globally starting in 1921. Our Lady's request for the Consecration was specific, yet there was a lack of compliance by Church leaders to consecrate Russia by name. The results of not complying are felt in every living room of the world to this day. Fatima was the cornerstone of apparitions for the 20th Century.

The Blessed Mother promised peace if her requests were made. Some 70,000 people witnessed the Miracle of Sun on October 13, 1917, yet people still doubted the authenticity of the messages immediately after the event. It was asked at Fatima *"Why was the Blessed Mother here?"* Her response was *"So people would believe."* The question must be asked, *Do we have peace in the world?* Mankind had everything to gain and nothing to lose by complying with her requests.

In Rwanda (approved) the Blessed Mother appeared to young children in April of 1981, just two months before the apparitions of Medjugorje. Her message was again the same to a new group of people this time in Africa. Our Lady requested that they live the Sacraments, repent, go to confession and attend Mass. Again, there was nothing too radical in her messages to cause an average Catholic concern. She asked for fidelity to her Son. She said that *"Rwanda would become a river of blood"* unless the people heeded her messages. During the Rwanda genocide in1994, approximately 800,000 Rwandans were hacked to death and approximately two million refugees were displaced in a period of about 100 days. The Rwandan genocide was a tribal retribution for a similar mass killing that had occurred back in the 1950s when millions fled for their lives into the jungles of the Congo. Neighbors from different tribes who lived side by side for two generations hacked each other to death over previous grievances and disputes. After the events, many Rwandans said, "If only we had listened." Time and Newsweek magazine covers showed the same photo of a river of blood with dead corpses floating downstream. There was and is a price to pay for not listening.

At Akita, Japan in 1973, (approved), the Blessed Mother said that in the future Church there would be *"cardinal opposing cardinal, bishop against bishop, priest against priest...."* If you are watching the news, the *Dubia* issued by four Cardinals is reflective of the fact that there is dissention within the Church and that it is serious. As they watch the disintegration of doctrine, many clergy in the rank and file are angry yet largely silent due to potential pushback from their bishop if they go public with their views.

We could go on and discuss many more authentic apparitions, but the larger issue is why are there such obstructionists? Why do negative attitudes toward authentic apparitions come from those who say they pledge fidelity to the Church?

So why are the laity and clergy alike so apprehensive in acknowledging and shouting from the rooftops the messages deemed authentic? We'll look at just several reasons.

Lack of faith

Unfortunately there are many Catholics today whose faith is weak or worse. This includes both lay folks and clerics. For many it has been reduced to a political discourse. Those in this category doubt the true presence of Christ in the Eucharist, the role of the Blessed Mother, Scripture, Tradition, and even have doubts about God in general. They may give the appearance of belief saying answers are in politics, philosophy, and social justice, but are not willing to amend their lives according to the Gospel message or obey the Magisterium of the Church. For those whose lack of faith emanates from lack of proper catechesis, the answer is simple. Learn the faith. For those who are obstinate in their unbelief as an exercise of their will, the answer is also simple. John the Baptist, the *"greatest man ever born of women,"* had only one message — Repent.

Denial of the supernatural

When Jesus turned the water into wine, it was recognized by all at the wedding feast as an actual event, not an allegorical story. It was an historical and supernatural fact. It was the same when Jesus restored the sight of the blind man by adding spittle to dirt and applying it on the man's eyes. However, in a world that searches for answers in reason and solely based on intellect, there is wholesale denial of the supernatural. Human beings are a combination of the finite natural and the infinite supernatural. One cannot attempt to find God by reason alone. One needs to leave room for the Holy Spirit to work on our soul. When St. Thomas Aquinas encountered the living God, he never wrote again. He said, *"All I have written is mere straw."* This supernatural manifestation could not be explained rationally by Aquinas, thus he never tried to explain God again in print. Similarly, Edith Stein experienced her own supernatural manifestation. After searching for God in philosophy, she started reading the autobiography of St. Teresa of Avila. Reading throughout the night she said in the morning, *"That is the truth."* She encountered a personal God that penetrated the soul, not just the intellect. When we refuse to accept the supernatural operations of the spiritual world of Heaven, we unnecessarily block the manifestations of our Heavenly Mother.

Fear

The Blessed Mother *"reveals the hearts of men."* (Luke 2:35) When we give our hearts over to the Blessed Mother we become exposed without our finery. To give ourselves to her is to be childlike, humble and meek as she is. Many fear a loss of self, or being labeled by the world as weak. It is a degree of sanctity and abandonment to the Divine Will. The Holy Spirit and Our Lady are one. St. Louis de Montfort said that the apostles of the end days would be Marian devotees. There are signs of this in our midst.

Marginalization

People have a fear of being marginalized if they get too close to Marian themes. For some reason, the study of Mary is not thought of by some as a serious intellectual pursuit. But, much to the contrary of many when devotion to Her is the greatest, the Church thrives. The Blessed Mother spoke very little as recorded in the New Testament. Yet when she speaks in abundance presently and has done so in the past, many are uncomfortable with that. It is not uncommon to find that many seminarians and priests today have been touched at Medjugorje, and the experience helped them to discern their vocation. Yet, when they enter seminary, they often speak in hushed tones regarding their experience and feel somewhat embarrassed by it when asked by those less knowledgeable on the subject. However, often it was the single greatest grace that propelled them into religious life. If the world is in a place of diabolical disorientation what do we have to lose when nothing but good can come from submitting to Our Lady's requests? Why not pay attention to what Our Lady says when there is nothing to lose and everything to gain for **our** welfare, **our** family, and **our** way of living?

In approved apparitions in Ohio dating back to the 1950s, the Blessed Mother told Sister Mary Ephrem that if the statue of Our Lady of America is processed and placed in the Shrine of the Immaculate Conception in Washington, D.C by the U.S. Bishops, America would be restored to purity. Why would it not be done? With the destruction and free fall of the U.S. political system in conjunction with the moral obliteration of the family, what do we have to lose to by processing and placing the statue as she asked? The question is, why do people doubt her words, thus her promises? We have seen in hindsight the destruction and confusion for a century of not abiding by the request made at Fatima for the Consecration of Russia. There are powerful evil forces at work here. Let us pray that Our Lady's plan for peace is fulfilled.

JESUS I TRUST IN YOU

A Place Like No Other

I was in bed with my girlfriend,
  smoking pot and watching TV.
I taught scuba diving in the summers
  in Hawaii, and skied in the Swiss
  Alps all winter.
I was independently wealthy living
  the life of a playboy.

— José, Spain

Married, committed adultery for years,
  divorced.
Married again, committed adultery for
  years, divorced.
Married for a third time in a helicopter,
  didn't really respect marriage that
  much.
At 20 years old my daughter was twice
  divorced with a baby.

— Patrick, British Columbia, Canada

My world was science being an MD,
  and married to an MD.
Science was my life with no faith.
I had everything I wanted in life with
  a home over the Pacific Ocean and
  three young boys.
I lost a child at nine months due to
  a genetic disorder and was helpless
  to do anything. My girl died in
  my arms.
Pregnant again, and had a miscarriage.
Pregnant again, and had another child
  who died at 21 months due to the
  same genetic disorder.

— Cyndi, California,
author of *Waiting For a Miracle.*

This was what I heard in my first 24 hours in Medjugorje, Bosnia. If I wrote about the rest of my ten days there and the stories I heard, it could fill a book.

Every person has a story. José in the circumstances of smoking pot felt a blanket of love come over him so great he knew it was God, and then it changed his life. He knew instinctively his lifestyle was wrong, but it was the love of the Blessed Mother that drew him to Medjugorje. When I met him in early November, he had driven from Madrid, Spain to spend a month in Medjugorje to grow spiritually. He said he felt that he was drawn to Medjugorje by a magnet.

Patrick had made money selling cars in Canada, and read a line in a book on messages from Medjugorje that said, "*This is your last chance to convert.*" He knew after a life time of serious sin this applied to him. His life was radically changed. He sold his business and moved to Medjugorje and says with humor, "*I wanted to be the Blessed Mother's neighbor.*"

Cyndi, as many successful people, was in charge of her own destiny, or so she thought. Having achieved the American Dream of a beautiful family, material and job success, she now found herself no longer in charge. She found out about Medjugorje, and found her faith and meaning in life. Her first trip was in 2001 as she sought a healing for her baby with Father Jozo Zovko. In the next few months and ensuing years, she found something few do — faith to face life's obstacles and challenges for peace of soul, and bringing others to the love of God.

By design, I went alone to Medjugorje to truly understand and absorb the spirituality of what is happening there. On other trips I had made there since 1990, there were always people around, with the excitement of new relationships and the dinners at the Dubrovnik and Columbo's restaurant drowned out what I came to hear. In the noise of previous visits, the Holy Spirit was not heard as well as I would have liked. So, I went on my own, and took a room in early November. The crowds of the summer were gone. However, seeing the November 2 appearance of the Blessed Mother to Mirjana was a first for me, and contemplating Our Lady in another dimension was an inspiration.

I had many thoughts on Medjugorje then, and have more now. I looked; I heard; and I wandered alone. I walked everywhere and walked a lot, miles every day observing. I saw the water oozing from the leg of the Cross of the Risen Christ. I saw the past suffering of the "Iron Curtain" Church as I read its history with 66 Franciscans killed in World War II, and 16 dying in the war from 1991 to 1995. I heard of the exponential growth of Islam in Sarajevo and Mostar, and how Medjugorje grew so fast in the early years with the fall of the Berlin Wall. I wandered the land of genocide in the Serbian War. Bosnia had the most victims with an estimated 150,000 dying with heavy religious and ethnic generational hatred.

I thought how truly catholic (universal) was the charism of Medjugorje. The restaurant menu at Viktor's was in fourteen languages. There were thirty two Croatian confessionals, with twenty seven in many languages of the world and with people fifteen and twenty deep waiting for hours. This does not account for events like the Medjugorje Youth Festival during which 300 cardinals, bishops, and priests from all over the world concelebrated on the altar and then sat in chairs in open spaces hearing confessions at all times of the day.

I spent five hours with the unofficial town historian and archivist who grew up directly next door to Marija Pavlovic'-Lunetti one of the visionaries, and is still a close friend of all the visionaries. I had always wondered about the count of visitors and she admitted no one really knows. She did provide an interesting piece of data that explains Medjugorje even as a bigger light to the world. Since the beginning of the apparitions, Saint James Church has distributed sixty million hosts at Masses! Churches and dioceses keep count of those numbers. This would account for all of the Croatian and Bosnian pilgrims who do daily round trips from nearby cities and towns as well as parishoners who come to Mass there daily or weekly. If one accounts for the fact that few knew of and journeyed to Medjugorje until the mid to late 1980's, and the war in the early 1990s it is not a stretch to reach 35 million out of country pilgrims as many say.

Medjugorje is the most important apparition in world history, and clearly builds on the message of Fatima. The number of apparitions there is unprecedented. According to messages received, it is the last apparition to the world. The Blessed Mother said very early, *"I have a great plan for the salvation of mankind."* There is a sense of urgency and transcendence associated with the messages. It is the fulfillment, completion, and as Mirjana says, *"the fusion"* of Fatima with Medjugorje. The attempted assassination attempt on Pope John Paul II was May 13, 1981.

While there, I could not help but think of the Poem by Emma Lazarus called *The New Colossus* inscribed on the pedestal of the Statue of Liberty in New York that says,

"...*A mighty woman with a torch, whose flame is the imprisoned lightening, and her name the Mother of Exiles. From her beacon-hand glows world wide welcome; her mild eyes command the air bridged harbor that twin cities frame... Cries she with silent lips, give me your tired, your poor, your huddled masses yearning to breathe free, the wretched refuse of your teeming shore. Send these, the homeless, tempest-tost to me...*"

Medjugorje is for the world. It is Heaven's agenda, not just addressed to one country. When the Blessed Mother speaks, she says, *"My children."* I saw Romanians, Bulgarians, Poles, Czechs, Slovenians, Serbians, Croatians, Germans, Ukrainians, Spanish, Italian, French, Irish, Americans, and many more nationalities.

It is a place of unheralded grace where people unburden their sorrow, their guilt, and their sins like nowhere else on earth. Saint John Paul II called it, *"the world's confessional."*

Medjugorje is principally about one thing. Grace. Grace that is freely given, and freely accepted. As the rays of light came from the fingers of the Blessed Mother at Rue du Bac in 1830, we were told by Saint Catherine Laboure they were the graces available to the souls who ask for them. A place where people journey who are devout as daily communicants searching for more from God, and those who are the lost sheep. A place where the shepherd leaves the ninety-nine sheep to find the one that is lost. Medjugorje covers the entire spectrum of the Body of Christ converging to know more about God and asking for grace in the trials and obstacles that confront them. A place of redemption to start again with a clean slate, and do as God asks. The Divine Mercy of rescuing someone who is lost. The Good Shepherd loves his flock and they hear His voice.

Everyone has a story and they are drawn and invited to Medjugorje by grace and the love of the Queen of Peace — The Blessed Mother — The Advocate of God — The Mediatrix of Grace. Since 1981 the Blessed Mother has been appearing there to six individuals, all well past middle age now, and several approaching their mid 50s. Some appearances are still daily, while others less frequent, and others only on special occasions. Ivanka, one of the visionaries, has said that she has been told the future of the world, as well as the future of the Catholic Church. It is unlike any apparition in world history, and when it ends, it will be the last on earth.

Despite many trials, the visionaries are living joyful and peaceful lives producing fruit on a daily basis. As Jesus said to His apostles in the midst of a storm, *"Fear not, it is I."*

Heaven has a plan.
Don't look right.
Don't look left.
Look upward.

JESUS I TRUST IN YOU

She Spoke Not a Word, But I Understood All

One of the greatest conversion stories of all time is that of Alphonse Ratisbonne of France. It is arguably one of the most miraculous since Saul of Tarsus became Saint Paul. It is profound, yet simple when the Holy Spirit plucks a person and decides to reorient the thinking of the individual.

Alphonse Ratisbonne was a young Jewish man born in 1814 in the area of Strasbourg, France, and was the eleventh of thirteen children. He was from a socially and financially prominent banking family with ties to the Rothschild Family, the wealthiest banking family in all of Europe. Having finished his studies and securing a law degree, he set out for a little adventure in Italy and environs before marrying his niece, who was also Jewish. After travel, his plans were to write a book on all he saw and seek his fortune in the family business of banking.

Ratisbonne, not being a practicing Jew, had a particular venomous distaste for the Roman Catholic Church and was not bashful about expressing his views. While in Rome, he took in the sights and sounds of a man with no particular agenda other than seeing the city as a tourist. Calling on an old school friend by the name of Gustave de Bussieres, he also met his brother Baron Theodore de Bussieres, a recent convert to Catholicism. Since Alphonse knew that once he returned to France and marry, he may not get another chance to see Rome again, he decided to stay a few extra days. As fate would have it, Gustave's brother Theodore volunteered to show him the city.

After seeing Saint Peter's Basilica, Theodore asked Alphonse to accept a Miraculous Medal, and instructed him in the words of the Memorare. Rather than showing the inner contempt he felt for such a bold affront as a Jew and an unbeliever, he accepted the medal of his gracious travel host and put the medal in his vest pocket. Here is where eternity intersected time, and history was altered. Baron de Bussieres had asked a friend to pray for Alphonse the night before, and the man promised he would. The man prayed the Memorare one hundred times for Alphonse's conversion.

On January 20, 1842, Ratisbonne accompanied Baron de Brussieres to a church by the name of St. Andrea della Fratte, as the Baron was making arrangements for a funeral the next day. Alphonse decided to tour the church while his friend was occupied with funeral details. Returning to the interior of the church, Theodore saw Ratisbonne on his knees in front of the Chapel of Saint Michael. Tapping Ratisbonne on the shoulder, he saw his face drenched in tears, and Ratisbonne said, *"Oh, how this gentleman has prayed for me."* Baron de Brussieres saw the altered state Ratisbonne was in and almost had to carry him out of the church.

Asking what happened to him, Ratisbonne drew from his vest pocket smothering the Miraculous Medal with kisses and sobs while saying, *"Oh, what bliss is mine! How good is the Lord! What a fullness of grace and of happiness! How pitiable the lot of those who know not!"* He would then say in front of a priest the same day:

"I had been but a few moments in the church when I was suddenly seized with an unutterable agitation of mind. I raised my eyes, the building had disappeared from before me; one single chapel had, so to speak, gathered and concentrated all the light; and in the midst of this radiance I saw standing on the altar, clothed with splendors, full of majesty and of sweetness, the Virgin Mary, just as she is represented on my medal.

An irresistible force drew me towards her; the Virgin made me a sign with her hand that I should kneel down; and then she seemed to say, 'That will do!' SHE SPOKE NOT A WORD BUT I UNDERSTOOD ALL."

Giving thanks for all that happened to him, Ratisbonne first went to the Church of St. Maria Maggiore where he spoke of the Real Presence as if he had intimately understood it for a lifetime. Ratisbonne had seen the Blessed Mother as a three dimensional person as anyone would see another. Her hands were outstretched as depicted on the Miraculous Medal with the luminous rays of grace being extended to the world. He would describe what happened further:

"I who but half an hour before was blaspheming still! I who felt a hatred so deadly of the Catholic religion! But all who know me know well enough that, humanely speaking, I have the strongest reasons for remaining a Jew. My family is Jewish, my betrothed is a Jewess, my uncle is a Jew...In becoming a Catholic, I sacrifice all the interests and all the hopes I have on earth; and yet, I am not mad — everyone knows that I am not mad, that I have never been mad! Surely they must receive my testimony."

Ratisbonne's older brother had also become a Catholic, and then a priest, and he too, was ostracized by his family for accepting the Catholic faith. He wrote the following:

> *"My brother, two hours after his conversion, was seen by Cardinal Mezzofanti, who was ready to throw himself on his knees in adoration to God. Nothing was known of my brother at Rome, and at first, great apprehensions were entertained as to what his character may turn out to be. He had never read two pages of the Bible, never received any religious instruction whatever, was altogether of a light and superficial character. The Blessed Virgin appeared to him as close as I am to you; she made a motion to him that he should remain quiet under divine influence. On rising out of his ecstasy, he had received intuitively the knowledge of the Christian faith... I believe that he has more than once received a repetition of the grace he had at Rome, but I have never asked him on the subject... My uncle is worth from six to seven millions of francs; he has disinherited my brother, who has renounced everything"* (M.L'Abbe' Theodore Ratisbonne, Allies' Journal in France, p. 44).

Eleven days after the miracle of conversion, the Cardinal Vicar was present at his baptism, confirmation, and first Holy Communion. He then became known as Marie Alphonse Ratisbonne. Pope Gregory XVI said that this was indeed a miracle. The apparition of Alphonse Ratisbonne was approved by the Holy See on June 3, 1842.

In six short years from the date of his conversion, he was ordained a Jesuit. With the permission of the Superior General of the Jesuit order and the blessing of Pope St. Pius IX, he left to join his brother in the *Order of the Peres de Sion* in Paris. For the remainder of his life he set up monasteries and several orphanages for boys and girls in Israel.

Ratisbonne would say later about this eventful day in 1842:

> *"All I can say about the moment when the Blessed Virgin made a sign with her hand, the veil fell from my eyes; not one veil only, but all the veils which were wrapped around me disappeared, just as snow melts beneath the rays of the sun... All that I know is that when I entered the church, I was profoundly ignorant of everything, and that when I came out I saw everything clearly and distinctly."*

Several things are very important in this story. First, there was prayer by several people for the conversion of Ratisbonne. He would credit this to his conversion. Second, the Blessed Mother acted nearly immediately on those requests. Third, he received the preternatural gift of **infused knowledge** much in the same way St. Catherine of Siena had during her dialogues with the Lord, yet she had no formal religious education.

Another earlier incident had a profound impact on him for the rest of his life. Ratisbonne had seen a cross in his sleep prior to his apparition and he didn't know how to interpret this. In his instruction of baptism and confirmation it was impressed upon him, "You must bear your own cross." The cross with a corpus was understood to be his salvation. A Bible verse was opened by a friend to the second chapter of Sirach which read:

"Son when thou comest to the service of God, stand in justice and in fear, and prepare thy soul for temptation. Humble thy heart and endure: incline thy ear, and receive the words of understanding: and make not haste in the time of clouds. Wait on God with patience; join thyself to God, and endure, that thy life may be increased in the latter end. Take all that shall be brought upon thee; and in they sorrow endure, and in thy humiliation keep patience. For gold and silver are tried in the fire, but acceptable men in the furnace of humiliation. Believe God, and he will recover thee; and direct thy way, and trust in Him. Keep His fear, and grow old therein" (Sirach 2:1-6).

When the Blessed Mother is involved in a person's life, there is a special preternatural grace that accompanies the believer's walk. There are storehouses of graces that come to persons when they consecrate themselves to the Immaculate Heart, which has no human explanation. It is a spiritual gift. Think of a person who wants to go to the top floor of a tall building. One way up is the elevator, the other is walking up the stairs. The Blessed Mother is the elevator. It takes less effort and it is quicker to the top with Her. No matter the academic background, family pedigree, or theological/philosophical training, there are extra graces bestowed when one asks for her intercession. The person matures much more rapidly when a Consecration or devotion takes place. As St. Louis de Montfort said, *"She is the shortcut to the Heart of God."* **She spoke not a word, but I understood all.**

JESUS I TRUST IN YOU

Heaven, Hell, & Purgatory
What Some Saints and Others Have Said
Who Have Visited Them

"My sheep hear my voice, and I know them, and they follow Me: and I give unto them eternal life; and they shall never perish, neither shall any man pluck them out of My hand."

John 10: 27-28

If one were to search the internet for "Purgatory," what is Heaven like, "Hell, "near death experiences" (NDEs), "life after death" and similar subjects, you will find those categories get millions of hits. Subjects like NDEs have been a topic of fascination for over thirty years. Yet we rarely hear **about Heaven, Hell, Purgatory or the Four Last Things — Death, Judgment, Heaven, or Hell taught in the Church.** Is there a connection between not hearing the most fundamental of truths that were taught for nearly 2,000 years and the sugar water we hear so much today from ecclesiastical and political leaders as we watch in real time the destruction of our culture?

The data is clear that people are very interested in this genre of spirituality given that they research and read about these subjects. Many books on these subjects are best sellers. Jesus addressed Heaven and Hell in the Gospels, and He was not ambiguous as to their reality. A person could possibly go to Church for a lifetime and never hear a sermon on Purgatory or Hell. A priest might be considered too extreme or negative by many as the talk may offend someone. To deny the devil is to deny sin, and as a result of not being taught about these most basic truths, people have become desensitized to sin, and therefore, deny sin as a reality along with its repercussions. Sin has virtually drenched our culture and become normalized.

In the same vein, people today know something is very wrong in our culture. Society is talking and operating on the extremes, with a festering civil disturbance on the horizon. Based on many conversations, we can tell immediately if someone we meet is on the same political and spiritual wavelength as a believer. It is obvious to everyone now as the divide is so great. It doesn't take long to find out if one has a starkly contrary view from your own.

It has only been in the last generation with the ubiquitous and viral form of social media, that people have recognized the events around near death experiences are very similar worldwide. There is speculation in the Near Death Experience community, that their experiences are the norm, and not the exception for hundreds of thousands who do not tell their story in public. Information is traded much more openly and freely without censorship or detractors on the internet, thus there are so many similar stories. What is most interesting is that many who experience a life review, see their lives in slow motion for major events in their lives; areas of their life that hurt people, the long term impact of sin, sins of omission and commission, not forgiving someone harming themselves and others, and sins against the commandments. If there is a profound lesson to be learned, it is that sin has consequences, much in the same way as an act of love has consequences. As a stone is thrown on a still pond, sin ripples for great distances. It is God's justice that determines one's fate. The Lord said, *"My thoughts are not your thoughts, and My ways are not your ways"* (Isaiah 55:8). If the justice of God is thought to be odd to you, the Lord views our lives through a different prism.

It would be a safe bet that most readers have not heard the words "**Mortal Sin**," "**Hell**" or "**Purgatory**" from the pulpit for a long time — if at all. Generations of the past were more spiritually and Scripturally literate, and had a more sober view of life after death for millennia based upon teachings of the Catholic Church. Now, if one attends a funeral, it is often mentioned that the deceased is *"now lovingly looking down upon us from on high."* However, the Church has taught that few go directly upon death into the presence of God.

The Church has deemed Heaven, Hell, and Purgatory real, and there are considerable Scriptural passages where all of these places are addressed. I will rely primarily on what the saints said about them as the Church has laid hands on these people as authentic. The Church heavily scrutinizes an individual before sainthood is granted, and this is prudent and wise. Testing them over time to assure their validity for the benefit of the mystical body of Christ now and in the future, is the approach of the Church. It is not abnormal for people in previous times as well as today to be taken to Heaven, Hell, and Purgatory, and come back to tell their story. For those operating in the spiritual realm, it is normal to know and speak of such things. To someone not versed in spirituality, it is considered an abnormality, or something not real.

The Apocalypse means the *"Unveiling."* As evil is being exposed in every sphere of the human condition, and being brought to light, we just might be watching the seeds of the Triumph of the Immaculate Heart that was promised at Fatima, taking on a new acceleration or quickening. The Triumph is when we enter a new dimension, a New Era. Sin is being exposed that has operated in stealth for generations, and the *"Unveiling"* is taking place. The body can't heal until a disease is exposed and excised. Removing the cancerous growth and the pus of disease is unpleasant, but necessary if the body is to heal. This is the painful time we are witnessing for the ecclesiastical profession, and it is necessary to clean the rot.

Some of the stories were written several hundred years ago in the vernacular of the day, and not in the conversation of the modern era. The words have not been altered to maintain as they were either dictated or written, albeit, some of the language is not the way we speak today. For capitalization and punctuation, the same applies.

Saint Faustina (1905-1938) on Heaven

After Holy Communion, I was carried in spirit before the throne of God. There I saw the Heavenly Powers which incessantly praise God. Beyond the throne I saw a brightness inaccessible to creatures, and there only the Incarnate Word enters as Mediator (Diary 85).

I learned in the Heart of Jesus that in Heaven itself there is a Heaven to which not all, but only chosen souls, have access. Incomprehensible is the happiness in which the soul will be immersed. O my God, oh, that I could describe this, even in some little degree. Souls are penetrated by His divinity and pass from brightness to brightness, an unchanging light but never monotonous, always new though never changing. O Holy Trinity, make Yourself known to souls! (Diary 592).

Today I was in Heaven, in spirit, and I saw its inconceivable beauties and the happiness that awaits us after death. I saw how all creatures give ceaseless praise and glory to God. I saw how great is happiness in God, which spreads to all creatures, making them happy: and then all the glory and praise which springs from this happiness returns to its source: and they enter into the depths of God, contemplating the inner life of God, the Father, the Son, and the Holy Spirit, whom they will never comprehend or fathom.

This source of happiness is unchanging in its essence, but it is always new, gushing forth happiness for all creatures. Now I understand St. Paul, who said, eye has not seen, nor has ear heard, nor has it entered into the heart of man what God has prepared for those who love Him (Diary 777).

The sight of this great majesty of God, which I came to understand more profoundly and which is worshipped by the Heavenly spirit, according to their degree of grace and the hierarchies to which they are divided, did not cause my soul to be stricken with terror or fear; no, no, not at all! My soul was filled with peace and love, and the more I come to know the greatness of God, the more joyful I become that He is as He is. And I rejoice immensely in His greatness and am delighted that I am so little because, since I am little, he carries me in His arms and holds me close, to His Heart (Diary 779).

O my God, how I pity those people who do not believe in eternal life: how I pray for them that a ray of mercy would envelop them too, and that God would clasp them to His fatherly bosom (*Diary 780*).

A vivid presence of God suddenly swept over me, and I was caught up in spirit before the majesty of God. I saw how the angels and the saints of the Lord gave glory to God. The glory of God is so great that I dare not try to describe it, because I would not be able to do so, and souls might think that all I have written is all there is... And all that has come forth from God returns to Him in the same way and gives Him perfect glory (Diary 1604).

Saint Faustina on Purgatory

... [The next night] I saw my Guardian Angel, who ordered me to follow him. In a moment I was in a misty place full of fire in which there was a great crowd of suffering souls. They were praying fervently, but to no avail, for themselves; only we can come to their aid. The flames which were burning them did not touch me at all. My Guardian Angel did not leave me for an instant. I asked these souls what their greatest suffering was. They answered me in one voice that their greatest torment was longing for God. I saw Our Lady visiting the souls in Purgatory. The souls call her "The Star of the Sea." She brings them refreshment. I wanted to talk with them some more, but my Guardian Angel beckoned me to leave. We went out of that prison of suffering. [I heard an interior voice] which said, My mercy does not want this, but justice demands it. Since that time, I am in closer communion with the suffering souls (Diary 20).

Once I was summoned to the judgment [seat] of God. I stood alone before the Lord. Jesus appeared just as we know Him during His Passion. After a moment, His wounds disappeared except for the five, those in His hands, His feet, and His side. Suddenly I saw the complete condition of my soul as God sees it. I could clearly see all that is displeasing to God. I did not know that even the smallest transgressions will have to be accounted for. What a moment! Who can describe it? To stand before the Thrice-Holy God! Jesus asked me, Who are you? I answered, "I am your servant, Lord." You are guilty of one day of fire in purgatory. I wanted to throw myself immediately into the flames of purgatory, but Jesus stopped me and said, which do you prefer, suffering now for one day in purgatory or for a short while on earth? I replied, "Jesus, I want to suffer in purgatory, and I want to suffer also the greatest pains on earth even if it were to the end of the world." Jesus said, One [of the two] is enough; you will go back to earth, and there you will suffer much, but not for long; you will accomplish My will and My desires, and a faithful servant of Mine will help you to do this. Now, rest your head on My bosom, on My Heart, and draw from it strength and power for these sufferings because you will find neither relief nor help nor comfort anywhere else. Know that you will have much, much to suffer, but don't let this frighten you, I am with you." (Diary 36)

One evening, one of the deceased sisters, who had already visited me a few times, appeared to me. The first time I had seen her, she had been in great suffering, and then gradually these sufferings had diminished; this time she was radiant with happiness, and she told me she was already in Heaven... And further, as a sign that she only now was in Heaven, God would bless our house. Then she came closer to me, embraced me sincerely, and said, "I must go now." I understand how closely the three stages of a soul's life are bound together; that is to say, life on earth, in purgatory, and in Heaven [the Communion of Saints] (Diary 594).

After Vespers today, there was a procession to the cemetery. I could not go, because I was on duty at the gate. But that did not stop me at all from praying for the souls. As the procession was returning from the cemetery to the chapel, my soul felt the presence of many other souls. I understood the great justice of God, how much each one had to pay off the debt to the last cent (Diary 1375).

Saint Faustina on Hell

"Most of the souls there are those who disbelieved that there is a Hell."

Today I was led by an Angel to the chasms of Hell. It is a place of great torture; how awesomely large and extensive it is! The kinds of torture I saw: the first torture that constitutes Hell is the loss of God; the second is perpetual remorse of conscience; the third is that one's condition will never change; the fourth is the fire that will penetrate the soul without destroying it — a terrible suffering, since it is purely a spiritual fire, lit by God's anger; the fifth torture is continual darkness and a terrible suffocating smell, and, despite the darkness the devils and the souls of the damned see each other and all the evil, both others and their own; the sixth torture is the constant company of Satan; the seventh torture is horrible despair, hatred of God, vile words, curses and blasphemies. These are the tortures suffered by all the damned together, but that is not the end of the sufferings.

There are special tortures destined for particular souls. These are the torments of the senses. Each soul undergoes terrible and indescribable sufferings, related to the manner in which it has sinned. There are caverns and pits of torture where one form of agony differs from another. I would have died at the very sight of these tortures if the omnipotence of God had not supported me. Let the sinner know that he will be tortured throughout all eternity, in those senses which he made use of to sin. I am writing this at the command of God, so that no soul may find an excuse by saying there is no Hell, or that nobody has ever been there, and so no one can say what it is like.

*I, Sister Faustina, by the order of God, have visited the abyss of Hell so that I might tell souls about it and testify to its existence. I cannot speak about it now; but I have received a command from God to leave it in writing. The devils were full of hatred for me, but they had to obey me at the command of God. What I have written is but a pale shadow of the things I saw. **But I noticed one thing: that most of the souls there are those who disbelieved that there is a Hell.** When I came to, I could hardly recover from the fright. How terribly souls suffer there! Consequently, I pray even more fervently for the conversion of sinners. I incessantly plead God's mercy upon them. O my Jesus, I* *would rather be in agony until the end of the world, amidst the greatest sufferings, than offend You by the least sin* (Diary 741).

Saint Faustina recorded an image of what she saw as one road to Heaven, and the other to Hell. Few people in the history of the Church can match her writings since it was Jesus Himself who gave her instruction on the splendor of Heaven, and the torments of Hell.

The Repercussions Of The Choices We Make

"One day, I saw two roads. One was broad, covered with sand and flowers, full of joy, music and all sorts of pleasures. People walked along it, dancing and enjoying themselves. They reached the end without realizing it. And at the end of the road there was a horrible precipice; that is, the abyss of Hell. The souls fell blindly into it; as they walked, so they fell. And their number was so great that it was impossible to count them. And I saw the other road, or rather, a path, for it was narrow and strewn with thorns and rocks; and the people who walked along it had tears in their eyes, and all kinds of sufferings befell them. Some fell down upon the rocks, but stood up immediately and went on. At the end of the road there was a magnificent garden filled with all sorts of happiness, and all these souls entered there. At the very first instant they forgot all their sufferings (Diary 153).

The Location of Purgatory—St. Frances of Rome (1385-1440).

It has pleased God to show in spirit the gloomy abodes of Purgatory to show some privileged souls, who were to reveal the sorrowful mysteries thereof for the edification of the faithful. Of this number was the illustrious St. Frances, foundress of the Oblates, who died in Rome in 1440. God favored her with great lights concerning the state of souls in the other life. She saw Hell and its horrible torments: she saw also the interior of Purgatory, and the mysterious order — I had almost said hierarchy of expiations — which reigns in this portion of the Church of Jesus Christ.

*In obedience to her supporters, who thought themselves bound to impose this obligation upon her, she made known all that God had manifested to her; and her visions, written at the request of the venerable Canon Matteotti, her spiritual director, have all the authenticity that can be desired in such matters. Now, the servant of God declared that, after having endured with unspeakable horror that vision of **Hell**, she came out of the abyss and was considered by her celestial guide into the regions of **Purgatory**. There reigned horror nor disorder, nor despair nor eternal darkness; there divine hope diffused its light, and she was told that this place of purification was called also **sojourn of hope**. She saw there souls which suffer cruelly, but angels visited and assisted them in their sufferings.*

Purgatory, she said, is divided into three distinct parts, which are as the three large provinces of that kingdom of suffering. They are situated the one beneath the other, and occupied by souls, of different orders. These souls are buried more, deeply in proportion as they are more defiled and farther removed from the time of their deliverance.

The lowest region is filled with a fierce fire, but which is not dark like that of Hell; it is a vast burning sea, throwing forth immense flames. Innumerable souls are plunged into its depths: they are those who have rendered themselves guilty of mortal sin, which they have duly confessed, but not sufficiently expiated during life... Although the souls are enveloped in the same flames, their sufferings are not the same; they differ according to the number and nature of their former sins.

In this lower Purgatory the saint beheld laics (one of the laity) and persons conse-crated to God. The laics were those who, after a life of sin, had had the happiness of being sincerely converted; the persons consecrated to God were those who had not lived according to the sanctity of their state. At that same moment she saw descend the soul of a priest whom she knew, but whose name she does not reveal. She remarked that he had his face covered with a veil which concealed a stain. Although he had lead an edifying life, this priest had not always observed strict temperance, and had sought too eagerly the satisfaction of the table.

The saint was then conducted into the intermediate Purgatory, destined for souls which had deserved less rigorous chastisements. It had three distinct compartments; one resembled an immense dungeon of ice, the cold of which is indescribably intense; the second, on the contrary, was like a huge caldron of boiling oil and pitch; the third had the appearance of a pond of liquid metal resembling molten gold or silver.

The upper Purgatory, which the saint does not describe, is the temporary abode of souls which suffer little, except the pain of loss, and approach the happy moment of their deliverance. Such, in substance, is the vision of St. Frances relative to Purgatory.

St. Magdalen de Pazzi (1566-1607), Her Vision of Purgatory

The following is an account of St. Magdalen de Pazzi, a Florentine Carmelite, as related in her life by Father Cepari. It gives more of a picture of Purgatory, while the preceding vision traces its outlines.

Some time before her death, which took place in 1607, the servant of God, Magdalen de Pazzi, being one evening with several other Religious in in the garden of the convent, was ravished in ecstasy, and saw Purgatory open before her. At the same time, as she made known later, a voice invited her to visit all the persons of Divine Justice, and to see how truly worthy of compassion are the souls detained there.

At this moment she was heard to say, "Yes, I will go." She consented to undertake this painful journey. In fact, she walked for two hours round the garden, which was very large, pausing from time to time. Each time she interrupted her walk, she contemplated the sufferings which were shown to her. She was then seen to wring her hands in com-passion, her face became pale, her body bent under the weight of suffering, in presence of the terrible spectacle with which she was confronted.

She began to cry aloud in lamentation, "Mercy my God, mercy!"

Descend, O Precious Blood, and deliver these souls from their prison. Poor souls! you suffer so cruelly, and yet you are content and cheerful. The dungeons of the martyrs in comparison with these were gardens of light. Nevertheless, there are others still deeper. How happy should I esteem myself were I not obliged to go down into them.

She did descend, however, for she was forced to continue her way. But then she had taken a few steps, she stopped terror-stricken, and sighing deeply she cried, "What! Religious also in this dismal abode! Good God! how they are tormented! Ah, Lord!" She does not explain the nature of their sufferings; but the horror which she manifested in contemplating them caused her to sigh at each step. She passed from thence into less gloomy places. These were the dungeons of simple souls, and of children in whom ignorance and lack of reason extenuated many faults. Their torments appeared to her much more endurable than those of the others. Nothing but ice and fire were there. She noticed that these souls had their angel guardians with them, who fortified them greatly by their presence; but she saw also demons whose dreadful forms increased their sufferings.

Souls of Hypocrisy

Advancing a few places, she saw souls still more unfortunate, and she was heard to cry out, "Oh! how horrible is this place; it is full of hideous demons and incredible torments! Who, O my God, are the victims of these cruel tortures? Alas! They are being pierced with sharp swords, they are being cut into pieces. "She was answered that they were the souls whose conduct had been tainted with hypocrisy."

Advancing a little, she saw a great multitude of souls who were bruised, as it were, and crushed under a press; and she understood that they were those souls who had been addicted to impatience and disobedience during their life. Whilst contemplating them, her looks, her sighs, her whole attitude betokened compassion and terror.

A moment later her agitation increased, and she uttered a dreadful cry. It was the dungeon of lies that now lay open before her. After having attentively considered it, she cried aloud, "Liars are confined in a place in the vicinity of Hell, and their sufferings are exceedingly great. Molten lead is poured into their mouths; I see them burn, and at the same time tremble with cold."

She then went to the prison of those souls who had sinned through weakness, and she was heard to exclaim, "Alas! I had thought to find you among those who have sinned through ignorance, but I am mistaken; you burn with an intenser fire."

Further on, she perceived souls who had been too much attached to the goods of this world, and had sinned by avarice.

"What blindness" said she, "thus eagerly to seek a perishable fortune!" Those whom riches could not easily satiate, are here gorged with torments. They are smelted like metal in a furnace.

From thence she passed into the place whose souls which were imprisoned which had formerly been stained with impurity. She saw them in so filthy and pestilential a dungeon that the sight produced nausea. She turned away quickly from that loathsome spectacle. Seeing the ambitious and the proud, she said, Behold those who wished to shine before men; now they are condemned to live in this frightful obscurity.

She was then shown those souls which had been guilty of ingratitude towards God. They were a prey to unutterable torments, and, as it were, drowned in a lake of molten lead, for having by their ingratitude dried up the source of piety.

Finally, in the last dungeon, she was shown souls that had been given to any particular vice, but which, through lack of proper vigilance over themselves, had committed all kinds of trivial faults. She remarked that these souls had a share in the chastisements of all vices, in a moderate degree, because those faults committed only from time to time rendered them less guilty than those committed through habit.

After this last station the saint left the garden, begging God never again to make her witness of so heartrending a spectacle; she felt that she had not strength to endure it. Her ecstasy still continued, and, conversing with Jesus, she said to Him, "Tell me Lord, what was Your design in discovering to me those terrible prisons, of which I knew so little, and comprehended still less? Ah! I now see; You wished to give me the knowledge of Your infinite sanctity, and to make me detest more and more the least stain of sin, which is so abominable in Your eyes."

Dr. Gloria Polo, Bogota, Columbia, Sees the Afterlife.

On May 5, 1995, Gloria Polo a dentist from Bogota, Columbia was struck by lightning and had either a near death, or life after death experience. She was judged and came back to life. She was taken to Heaven, Hell, and Purgatory. Her book ***Struck by Lightning*** has been a best seller. Dr. Polo has been an inspiration to hundreds of thousands of people at speaking events around the world on the necessity of repentance and confession and the reality of an afterlife. This article is based on her book, a speech she gave at the Shrine of the Immaculate Conception in Washington, D.C for the International Week of Prayer and Fasting, and a three hour personal interview in 2011. Her story is so powerful we have done four articles on her testimony over two years for this magazine, **Signs and Wonders.** The story is told in her words as a native Spanish speaker. I watched an audience sit in rapt attention not moving a muscle when she spoke.

Gloria was walking with her husband, and her twenty three year old cousin who was also a dentist, when she and her cousin were both struck by lightning. Her cousin immediately died (giving off smoke for some time after being struck), and Gloria lived to tell the story. Her husband was unharmed. The lightning bolt struck her cousin from behind on the shoulder and came out his feet and carbonized his body.

She says, *"As for me, the lightning bolt entered my shoulder, burning terribly the whole body, inside and out; in short my flesh disappeared including my breasts, especially the left one, leaving a hole. It caused to disappear the flesh of my abdomen, of my legs, of the ribs; it carbonized the liver, it greatly burned the kidneys, the lungs, the ovaries... and came out through the right foot."*

For my contraceptive, I was using a spiral (an intrauterine device in the form of a T), and because of the material with which it is made (copper) it is a good conductor of electricity, the lightning bolt carbonized and pulverized also the ovaries which became like two raisins. I remained in cardiac arrest, just about without life, with the body that was jumping due to the electricity that was still present in that place.

But, this is only the physical part... The good part is that, while my body lay there carbonized, in that same moment I found myself inside a beautiful white tunnel of light, a wonderful light, which made me feel a joy, a peace, a happiness, that I do not have words to describe the greatness of that moment. It was a true ecstasy. I looked, and in the end of that tunnel I saw a white light, like a sun, a beautiful light... I say white to tell you a color, but we are talking about colors, that cannot be compared to those that exist on the earth. It was a splendid light; I felt from it a source of peace, of love, of light...

When I went up in this tunnel toward the light, I said to myself: "Caramba, I'm dead!"

So I thought about my children and I sighed: "Woe is me my God, my little children! What will my children say? This mother so occupied, that she never had time for them..." In fact, I left early every morning, and I did not return before eleven at night.

*And so I saw the reality of my life, and I felt much sadness. I had left my home determined to conquer the world, but at what price? Putting in second place my home and my children! In that moment of emptiness, due to the absence of my children, without feeling any more of my body, nor of the dimension of time or of space, **I looked, and I saw something very beautiful: I saw all of the people of my life... In one single moment in the same moment, all of the people, those living and those dead. I was able to embrace my great grandparents, grandparents, parents (who were dead)... everyone!***

In an instant I heard the voice of my husband. He laments and cries with a profound sentiment, and cries, "Gloria!!! Gloria! Please, do no leave me! Look at your children, your children need you. Gloria, go back! Do not be a coward, return!"

*I heard everything, and I saw him cry with such pain. **Alas, in that moment our Lord granted me to leave. But I did not want to return! That peace, that peace in which I was wrapped, fascinated me! But, slowly, I began again to descend toward my body, which I found without life. I saw it lifeless on a stretcher at the National Nursing University. I saw the doctors who were giving me electric shocks to my body, to pull me out of cardiac arrest. I and my cousin, remained more than two hours laid on the ground, because our bodies were giving off electric discharges, and they could not be touched. Only when the electric charge was completely discharged, could they help us. And then they began the attempts to revive me.***

Gloria goes on to speak at length about the physical manifestations of dying by a lightning strike. Gloria is very honest that she was a worldly woman seeking financial success with adulation from an admiring world. As a physical fitness fanatic she focused primarily on accentuating the beauty of her legs and breasts. In the moment of the lightning strike, her breasts were torn off, and her legs were left severely deformed. In a flash, vanity had been stripped from her, and all that she most cherished was taken from her. Up until that point in her life, she had no interest in spirituality other than the cultural events that were fun activities. She explains,

It was a terrible suffering, I felt the intense pain of my burned flesh, the body totally burned caused an indescribable pain, it was blazing terribly and gave off smoke and vapor. I heard the doctors cry out; "She is coming back! She is coming back!"

They were very happy, but my suffering was indescribable! My legs were frightfully black, there was live flesh on the body, and on the arms! The problem of the legs was complicated when they considered the possibility of amputating them.

I Was A Slave To My Body, Beauty, and Fashion

But, there was another terrible pain; the vanity of a worldly woman, intellectual, the student... Slave to the body, to beauty, to fashion. I dedicated four hours every day to aerobics; enslaved to having a beautiful body. I underwent massages, diets, and injections. Basically everything you can imagine. This was my life, a routine of slavery in order to have a beautiful body. I used to say: If I have two beautiful breasts, they are there to show them, so why hide them? I said the same thing about my legs. Because I knew I had spectacular legs, nice abdominal muscles...

But in an instant, I saw the horror how my whole life had been only a continual and useless care of the body. Because this was the center of my life: love for my body. And now, I no longer had a body! I had startling holes where my breasts were, especially the left one, which was practically gone. The legs were a sight to be seen, like fragments, but without flesh, and black as coal. The parts of the body that I held in highest esteem were the most completely burned and literally without flesh.

Gloria describes her life as a Catholic. In a nutshell she really could have cared less about spiritual matters. She considered herself an atheist, but went to Mass to cover the bases and to ease the sense of guilt. She specifically found a Mass where she could get in and out in twenty-five minutes or less. Adultery never bothered her, as she knew her father had been an adulterer by the time she was fourteen years of age. Once hearing a sermon that Hell does not exist, she decided anything goes. So she decided, *"if everyone goes to Heaven, what is there to fear?"* She says, *"What makes me most sad now, and I confess to you with great shame, is that the only tie that held me in the Church, was the fear of the devil. When I heard that Hell does not exist, I immediately said: 'very good, if we all go to Heaven it is not important what we are or what we do.'"*

I no longer had any fear of sin, and I began to ruin my relationship with God. I began to say to everyone that demons do not exist, that they are the inventions of the priests, that they are the manipulations on the part of the Church, and finally... I arrive to the point of saying to my colleagues at the University that God does not exist, that we were products of evolution, etc., succeeding in influencing many people.

No one can blame anyone for the bad decisions they make but themselves. But, there are influences in our lives that do have profound affects with our ideological perspective which shapes our outlook on life. For a priest to say there is no Hell, shows the dramatic impact in a negative way for bad catechesis. Here is a perfect example of someone being taught incorrectly and manifesting their lifestyle in an unfavorable and immoral life.

While being worked on by surgeons immediately after being struck by lightning, and had been taken to Hell and Purgatory, she speaks of her descent into darkness, and how she was shown the impact of her sins of commission and omission.

She says, *"And, I ever more terrified, continued to descend, seeking to get out of there, while the light was going away diminishing... I carried on roaming in those tunnels in a frightening darkness, until I arrived to an obscurity that cannot be compared to anything else... I can only say that, in comparison, the darkest obscurity on earth is not even comparable to the full sunlight at midday. Down there, that same obscurity generates pain, horror, shame, and stinks terribly. It is a living obscurity, yes, it is alive: there the mind is dead or inert."*

Even though I was an atheist, but there I began to cry out: "Souls of Purgatory! Please, pull me out of here! I beg you, help me!" While I was crying out, I began to hear crying thousands and thousands of persons, youth... Yes, above all youth, with so much suffering! I perceived that there, in that horrible place, in that quagmire of hate and suffering, they were gnashing their teeth, with screams and laments that filled me with compassion and that I will never be able to forget. Already ten years have passed, but I still cry and suffer, when I remember the suffering of all those persons.

Do you know what is the greatest torment? It is to see how one's own parents, or relatives who are alive, are crying and suffering with a tremendous sense of guilt: if I would have punished, or if I would not have punished, if I had said to him, or not have said to him, If I had done this or that... In the end, these regrets so terrible — a true Hell for those who love them and remain in this life — they are what makes them suffer the most. It is the greatest torment for them, and it is here that the demons rage.

Gloria Sees The Evil She Has Done

Jesus showed me how I was in no way grateful in regard to Him, and in the laziness I had in going to Mass. When I still lived with my parents, and my mother obliged me to go, I said to her, "But mom, if God is everywhere, what need do I have to go to Mass?" Clearly for me it was very convenient for me to talk like this. And Jesus showed this to me. I had the Lord twenty-four hours a day for me, all my life God took care of me, and I was so lazy to dedicate to Him a little time on Sunday, to show him my gratitude, my love for Him. But the worst thing was to know that, to frequent the Church meant to nourish my soul. I instead, dedicated myself totally to the care of my body, I became a slave to my flesh, and forgot that I had a soul. And never did I take care of it.

Regarding the Word of God, I even said, imprudently, that the one who read the bible a lot became crazy. I arrived at the point to be a blasphemer, and the incoherence of my life brought me to say, "But what Most Holy? And God would be present there? In the ciborium and in the chalice? The priest should add brandy to give it flavor.

To what point did I arrive to degrading my relationship with God? I left my souls without nourishment, and if that were not enough, the only thing I did was to criticize the priests. If you knew brothers, how bad I felt about this before Jesus. The Lord showed me how my soul was reduced due to all of these criticisms. Beyond everything else, consider the fact I declared a priest to be a homosexual, and the whole community came to know this. You cannot imagine the evil I did to that priest. No, you cannot imagine it. I tell you that one word has the power to kill or destroy souls. Now I saw all the evil I had done.

And then, who says that adultery does not kill? Moreover, how many abortions are done due to adultery? For example, how many women who had been unfaithful became pregnant, have had recourse to abortion so their husband may not discover

it? They kill an innocent one that is not able to speak, nor defend himself! And this is only some examples. Adultery kills in so many ways and diverse forms. Then, we still have the courage to protest against God when things do not go well, when we have problems, when sicknesses arrive; while it is we who procured these things with our sins, drawing evil on our life.

She was taken to Heaven by Jesus, and when she looked down she saw the map of the world in darkness with many white lights. She saw that North America had the most twinkling lights. Our Lord told her this was the place that had the most Eucharistic Souls feeding on Him.

She Saw Her Parents in Purgatory

She was in a deep coma and in agony while in Purgatory. She saw her father who had died five years before she was struck by lightning, and he was at the entrance of the abyss due to his continued adultery. He had a little bit of light, near the lowest level of Purgatory. She saw her mother who was in a higher level of Purgatory closer to Heaven. She was shown how her father's unfaithfulness was a grievous sin that afflicted his relationship with God, his wife, and his children. He used to brag about his other women and Gloria's mother would cry. Gloria also admits she had a hyper critical spirit of everything and everyone, and its root was envy. Our Lord showed her the greatest sin is abortion. Gloria said, *"every time that the blood of a baby is shed, it is a holocaust to Satan, who acquires still more power."* She was also shown how **resentment** limits our growth in God by taking us away from God, and others.

Maria Simma is Visited by the Souls in Purgatory.

In a book called, Get Us Out of Here, Maria Simma Responds to This Call From the Poor Souls in Purgatory, by Nicky Eltz, and approved by her (1915-2004). The book explains how the souls in Purgatory come and visit, and tell her what Purgatory is like. She was a very simple and humble woman who was born and died in the same village in Austria. Many souls would come and tell her their stories of the sins they committed and how they ended up in Purgatory. Maria's book was released in 2002, and had gone through ten printings through March of 2013, and had sold half a million copies by that date. Since my copy is a 2013 edition, it is unknown how many more have been printed, but an estimate would be well over a million as it has gained traction worldwide with each printing. The total page count in the book is 340 pages, and I am only presenting here a tiny vignette on an important subject. I have chosen Divorce because it has been so devastating to families. The total chapter on **Marriage, Family, and Children** is fifteen pages and I have only presented a little over two pages of that chapter. There is a heavy emphasis in the chapter on the devastation of divorce to families. She is asked questions and answers them.

In a marriage where the wife must suffer a lot at the hands of the husband or vice versa, is it all right for one to leave the other?

They may, but it is certainly better that they do not. They should offer it all up. But the line one ought to be drawn if physical suffering occurs.

What have the poor Souls said about divorce?

They have said that it is one of the greatest of all sins against God Himself. It hurts everyone tremendously and, of course, the innocent ones the most. It is NOTHING LESS than spiritual, mental, and emotional murder committed upon God's greatest gift to us, that being our ability to participate in the creation of life and its fruit — our children. No child of divorce will ever grow to the fullness God had planned for it. In this century, millions of times more than ever before, Satan is ripping into the families and wombs of women, poisoning and cutting to pieces the Holy threads that keep families in His plan, poisoning and cutting to pieces the babies God has given to them. It is reparation for these two sins that the souls say is coming soon and will be earth shattering. And in the countries like the USA where more than 50% of marriages now break up, God will soon arrange for these matters to change quickly. He will step in for the humble, the innocent, prayerful and loving people and will punish the others for the never ending insults against love. The industries, the organizations, the attorneys, the cults, the physicians, and psychologists who lie, confuse, collude, make profits, and thereby distort the truth to keep this most horrid of wars going will soon experience God's wrath as it has NEVER been experienced before! God have mercy on the ones who know what they are doing! And we have the duty to inform the unknowing ones of what they are doing.

Have the Poor Souls ever told you anything about annulments in the Church?

Yes, they have told me that the Church grants far too many annulments today. Such matters must be examined far more thoroughly today. I am afraid it is true to some degree that the well connected and well endowed have easier access to annulments and that is hardly God's wish. Of course there are cases where coercion, emotional limitations of other situations in place at the time did invalidate the marriage to begin with, but these are serious matters that must be handled very lovingly but thoroughly as well.

What else can you think of that the Poor Souls communicate to their families?

They can ask a family member to make something good that the soul itself had done badly or unfairly while here. And by following the instruction the living ones will be assisting the soul to go on its way. They can warn them to avoid this or that. They protect them, guide them, and convey love and security in various ways.

Have the Poor Souls said anything about the women's movement?

No, not in those terms, except that no women should be around the altar. In the secular world it is quite all right that they compete with men on an equal basis. Having their own careers is fine but ONLY as long as the family is not in any way ignored. Here too, both women and men commit many great sins today. If either the children or the spouse are in any way neglected, the other one will have to suffer a lot for it later. This is most definitely a serious and most divisive sin.

What in the spiritual realm might happen more between a couple married in the Church and a couple not married in the Church, or a couple not married at all?

God's Blessing, the marriage Vows, which are after all Vows before God, the Marriage Mass and the support of all family members are all such powerful protective graces that the lack of any one or several of these will seriously weaken its needed strength and unity. In calling on God and His Church's Blessing, things certainly unfold far stronger and thus happier than without them.

Things do happen that are similar to what I see when the Poor Souls come to visit me, and among the living we would call it bilocation. Or it also happens that an angel takes on the appearance of the one spouse to bring the other a message. He or she would then hear, or both see and hear the other, and thereby receive protective or guiding words. This happens often and must be seen as a wonderful gift from God for a holy couple. It certainly will not happen when people live together in sin. In those cases there is far less protection from outside of this world. I would caution them very urgently to step away from that and to come back to God's protection.

It is also common that a deceased spouse would come close to accompany the still living one through the death process. What a tremendous joy this must be for both to experience! True, giving a holy love never, never dies. Yet it is only this when God has blessed the marriage and is always near to them in prayer and in their acts of selfless love.

What should parents do to form the consciences of their children?

A good example is the most important thing. Then by praying a lot for them and also with them. Also, by blessing them often; that too is worth a lot. And then a good education and the most important one is before they go off to regular school. Jesus told us to bring His children to Him and not to block them.

JESUS I TRUST IN YOU

The above information on the stories were taken directly from:

Saint Faustina's Diary, *Divine Mercy in My Soul,* Based upon the contents of her diary from 1934 until her death in 1938.

Purgatory: Explained by the Lives and Legends of the Saints, by Fr. F.X. Schouppe, S.J., Imprimatur, 1893, translated from the French.

Struck by Lightning, Death, Judgment, & Conversion by Dr. Gloria Polo, 2009

Get Us Out of Here, Maria Simma Responds to This Call from the Poor Souls in Purgatory, Maria Simma Speaks with Nicky Eltz, 2002

The Wisdom of the Founding Fathers Understanding the Origins of What Made America Unique

The Story of Young George Washington

A young man by the name of George Washington was a surveyor, first starting out in the Virginia countryside, and then venturing further north and east in what is now the New York and Pennsylvania area. Washington eventually became a member of the American militia fighting with the British against the French and the Indians, beginning what became an illustrious military and political career. In 1755 approximately 1,300 British and American soldiers were heading into what is now Pittsburgh, when they were ambushed by the French and Indians using the tactic of hiding behind trees, not the British tactic of open field combat that we saw all the way through the U.S. Civil War.

The French and the Indians massacred the British and the American troops killing seven hundred and fourteen men. There were eighty-six British and American officers, and **all but one was killed**. Casualties on the French and Indian side were minimal. The only officer that was not killed was George Washington, then a twenty-three year old. Washington after the battle wrote his mother saying,

"By all the powerful dispensations of Providence (God), I have been protected beyond all human probability or expectation for I had four bullet holes passed through my coat and two horses shot out under me, yet I escaped unhurt, although death was leveling my companions on every side of me..."

Fifteen years after that event in 1770, the Indian chief that was in the battle arranged to meet George Washington when he was passing though the area. Over a camp fire the Indian chief said to Washington,

"You don't know me. Fifteen years ago you and I were in these woods together. I was the chief in charge of the Indians. We saw you riding and knew you were one of the leaders and if we could kill you, we could scatter your men. So I told my braves to single you out and fire at you. I personally shot at you seventeen different times. When we saw the bullets were having no effect on you, I told my braves to stop shooting at you. I came all this way to meet the man God would not let die in battle."

In George Washington's first speech after his election as President, he had a call to prayer:

"It would be peculiarly improper to omit in this first official act, my fervent supplication to that Almighty Being who rules over the universe, who presides in the councils of nations, and whose providential aids can supply every human defect... No people can be bound to acknowledge and adore the invisible hand which conducts the affairs of men more than the people of the United States. The propitious (favorable) smiles of

Heaven can never be expected on a nation that disregards the eternal rules of order and right which Heaven itself has ordained."

In Washington's Farewell Address leaving government service he warned:

"...of all the dispositions and habits which lead to political prosperity, religion and morality are indispensable supports. In vain would that man claim the tribute of patriotism who should labor to subvert these great pillars of human happiness."

From the very earliest days of the formation of the American colonies, Heaven had a plan for what became the United States of America. It was a Divine Plan for a new country with vast resources and a commitment to God. For one to doubt the anointing the United States was given from its earliest formation by Almighty God, would render that soul oblivious to early American history.

The Early Education Model in the Colonies

The country's roots first started with a Christian formation in faith. Here is American excellence — reliance and belief in the providence of Almighty God. In 1606 a charter for the earliest settlers establishing a colony in Virginia read as such, making it clear the motivation for those risking life and limb to make the arduous and risky journey to an unknown land, knowing they would need to endure extreme hardship:

"To make a habitation... and to deduce a colony of sundry of our people into that part of America commonly called Virginia... in propagating of Christian religion to such people as yet live in darkness."

In 1609 it read further: *"The principal effect which we can desire or expect of this action is the conversion... of the people in those parts unto the true worship of God and Christian religion."*

The Mayflower set sail for Virginia, but was blown far north due to a storm, and arrived on the shores of Plymouth, Massachusetts just before winter in 1620. Those early settlers called Pilgrims, drafted what was known as the **Mayflower Compact**, and it said in part,

"Having undertaken for the glory of God and advancement of the Christian faith... we combine ourselves together into a civil body politic for...furtherance of the ends aforesaid."

William Bradford a leader among the group made it clear why they came to these shores when he said,

"...a great hope and inward zeal they had of laying some good foundation, or at least to make some way thereunto, for the propagating and advancing the gospel of the kingdom of Christ, in those remote parts of the world."

Another leader came along about a decade later by the name of John Winthrop and was a member of the new group called the Puritans. He was more missionary than sea going traveler or farmer when he wrote,

"We are a company professing ourselves fellow-members of Christ... knit together by this bond of love...We are entered into covenant with Him for this work... For we must

consider that we shall be as a city upon a hill, the eyes of all people are upon us; so that if we shall deal falsely with our God in this work we have undertaken and so cause Him to withdraw His present help from us, we shall be made a story and a byword through the world."

Word had come from the French trappers, Spanish Conquistadors, and possibly Vikings how vast this new world was for settlement. There was a desire for freedom and self-rule, with a new virgin world where they could grow and prosper. All this would be away from the oppressive crown of England that crippled initiative due to constriction of class. In addition, the greatest motivator would have been the preaching of the gospel into foreign lands fulfilling the commandment of Jesus in the Great Commission, *"Go therefore and make disciples of all nations, baptizing them in the name of the Father, and the Son, and the Holy Spirit, teaching them to observe all that I have commanded you. Behold I am with you always, to the end of the age..."* (Matt. 28: 19-20, among several other places).

The expansion of the gospel was a strong force to risk death due to hardship. Pilgrims, Puritans, Quakers, Catholics, Jews and others came to what became the early colonies. The Carolinas, Virginia, Rhode Island, Massachusetts, Delaware, Pennsylvania, and other territories sought the largesse of the land, and all the new world had to offer — especially freedom to worship as they saw fit. All documents civilly and spiritually indicate Christ the King was to be the rock on which their foundations would lie.

The Bedrock of Education Was the Lordship of Christ

The early framers from all states and faiths understood and implemented laws to protect people from tyrants that they had seen and known in Old Europe. They knew an illiterate population not schooled in Sacred Scripture could be more easily manipulated and abused than an educated population. This thinking immediately moved to the Lordship of Christ in education when they wrote:

"In being one chief project of that old deluder, Satan, to keep men from the knowledge of the Scriptures, as in former time.... it is therefore ordered... that after the Lord hath increased the settlement to the number of fifty householders, they shall then forthwith appoint one within their town, to teach all such children as shall resort to him, to write and read... And it is further ordered, where any town shall increase to the number of one hundred families or householders, they shall set up a grammar school, to instruct youths, so far as they may be fitted for the university."

An educated class of people through public schools was thus conceived in the earliest days of the settlements, setting America apart from all previous civilizations wanting to educate its citizens for the general welfare of its people. This thinking on education became the bedrock of an emerging nation evolving under the Lordship of Jesus Christ contrary to previous civilizations looking to suppress education. Tyrants and kings alike knew it was easier to control a populace that is illiterate than one that is educated. Education in Scripture is many steps beyond a good civic education, because a follower of Scripture will need less instruction than one without.

In 1690 Connecticut wrote:

"This legislature observing that... there are many persons unable to read the English tongue and thereby incapable to read the holy Word of God or the good laws of this colony... it is ordered that all parents and masters shall cause their respective children and servants, as they are capable, to be taught to read distinctively the English tongue."

Harvard First Founded as a Divinity School

In other words, if you can't read the English tongue, you can't read Sacred Scripture to know what God is asking of you to be truly civic minded. This thinking continued with the first theological school in the new colony of Massachusetts by the name of Harvard. The 1636 rules of Harvard said:

"Let every student be plainly instructed and earnestly pressed to consider well the main end of his life and studies is to know God and Jesus Christ which is eternal life (John 17:3) and therefore to lay Christ in the bottom as the only foundation of all sound knowledge and learning. And seeing the Lord only gives wisdom, let everyone seriously set himself by prayer in secret to seek it of Him (Prov. 2:1-3). Everyone shall so exercise himself in reading Sacred Scriptures twice a day that he shall be ready to give such an account of his proficiency therein."

Harvard was first a Divinity School that then became a college. In 1790, there was still little changed in thinking how important Christianity was to the new colonies and the experiment of self-rule as a Constitutional Republic. The Harvard administration wrote:

*"All persons of what degree forever residing at the College, and all undergraduates... **shall constantly and reasonably attend the worship of God in the chapel, morning and evening...** All the scholars shall, at sunset in the evening preceding the Lord's Day, lay aside all their diversions and... it is enjoined every scholar carefully to apply himself to the duties of religion of said day."*

Harvard was so committed to this thinking, at this time the twin mottos were, **For the Glory of Christ**, and **For Christ and the Church**. Over a dozen Founding Fathers coming from Harvard with this thinking were signers of the Declaration of Independence, and then went on to forge the United States Constitution.

Yale and Princeton Founded as Divinity Schools

Many of the Massachusetts students felt that Harvard was becoming too liberal so Yale was founded by ten ministers as a Divinity School in 1699. When the first day of school began in 1701, Yale required, *"The Scriptures... morning and evening are to be read by the student at the times of prayer in the school... studiously endeavoring in the education of said students to promote the power and purity of religion."*

This thinking continued well into the future when in 1720 Yale encouraged students, *"Seeing God is the giver of all wisdom, every scholar, besides private or secret prayer, wherein we are all bound to ask wisdom, shall be present morning and evening at public prayer in the hall at the accustomed hour."* In 1743 and 1745 the admonition of faith continued at Yale, *"Above all have an eye to the great end of all your studies,* which is to obtain the clearest conceptions of divine things and to lead you to a saving knowledge of God in His son Jesus Christ."

Then, later on in time, many felt that Yale was becoming too liberal. Therefore, Princeton was initially founded principally as a Divinity School, in 1746, with a mandate, *"To plant and under the Divine Blessing, to propagate in this wilderness the blessed reformed Protestant religion."* Originally founded by Presbyterians, and then with continued governance with Presbyterian ministers, as presidents for decades with men such as Aaron Burr Senior, Jonathan Edwards, Samuel Davies, and Samuel Finley who were members of the Great Awakening or Great Revival.

Princeton requirements read, *"Every student shall attend worship in the college hall morning and evening at the hours appointed and shall behave with gravity and reverence during the whole service. Every student shall attend public worship on the Sabbath ... Besides the public exercises of religious worship on the Sabbath, there shall be assigned to each class certain exercises for their religious instruction suited to the age and standing of the pupils ... and no student belonging to any class shall neglect them."*

Some of the early great patriots, intellects, and participants in the early formation of American documents were men of Christian moral principles that came from these classrooms. James Madison, Richard Stockton, Benjamin Rush and numerous other prominent founding Fathers graduated from Princeton Seminary, a training ground for ministers.

Dartmouth and Columbia Founded on Christian Principles

Then in 1754, Dartmouth College in New Hampshire was founded by Reverend Eleazar Wheelock with a clear charter to, *"Whereas ... the Reverend Eleazar Wheelock ... educated a number of the children of the Indian natives with a view to their carrying the Gospel in their own language and spreading the knowledge of the great Redeemer among the savage tribes. And ... the design became reputable among the Indians insomuch that a larger number desired the education of their children in said school ... Therefore Dartmouth College is established for the education of youths ... in reading, writing and all parts of learning which shall appear necessary and expedient for civilizing and Christianizing the children."*

Also, in 1754 Kings College was founded, which became Columbia University with the name change in 1787. Its first president was Constitution signer William Samuel Johnson who was appointed its first president. Columbia's admission requirement read as such, *"No candidate shall be admitted into the College unless he shall be able to render into English ...the Gospels from the Greek ... it is also expected that all students attend public worship on Sundays."*

If anyone were to doubt the view of Christian principles and the role of education, part of Johnson's commencement speech reads,

"You this day, gentlemen ... have ... received a public education, the purpose whereof, hath been to qualify you the better to serve your Creator and your country ... Your first duties, you are sensible, are those you owe to Heaven, to your Creator and Redeemer. Let these be ever present to your minds and exemplified in your lives and conduct. Imprint deep upon your minds the principles of piety toward God and a reverence and fear

of His holy name. The fear of God is the beginning of wisdom." The remainder of the speech sounds like a sermon.

One year after the Declaration of Independence was signed, the English embargo of goods was considerable. One of the things in short supply was bibles. On July 7, 1777, Congress approved the purchase of 20,000 bibles to be imported. The request to Congress read, *"That the use of the Bible is so universal, and its importance so great... your Committee recommend that Congress will order the Committee of Commerce to import 20,000 Bibles from Holland, Scotland, or elsewhere, into the different ports of the States of the Union."*

On November 1, 1777 leading Congressional members approved a National Day of Prayer, *"Forasmuch as it is the indispensable duty of all men to adore the superintending providence of Almighty God; to acknowledge with gratitude their obligation to Him for benefits received and to implore such farther blessings as they stand in need of... to offer humble and earnest supplication that it may please God, through the merits of Jesus Christ, mercifully to forgive and blot our sins out of remembrance...and to prosper the means of religion for the promotion and enlargement of that kingdom which consisteth in righteous, peace, and joy in the Holy Ghost."*

The early framers understood the sensitive and tenuous issues that come with a Constitutional Republic. On December 15, 1777, John Adams wrote to his wife Abigail that the frequent intervention of God was evident to most Americans:

"I have had many opportunities in the course of this journey to observe how deeply rooted our righteousness cause is in the minds of the people... One evening as I sat in one room, I overheard a company of the common sort of people in another [room] conversing upon serious subjects... At lengths I heard these words, 'It appears to me the eternal Son of God is operating powerfully against the British nation for their treating lightly serious things.'"

(Note: The quotes and some narrative in the above section of this article are taken directly from David Barton's book, *Original Intent, The Courts, the Constitution, and Religion,* 544 pages, 2000. In my estimation Barton is the premier writer of our age on the role of the early thinking of the Founding Fathers and the development of Christian thinking for the United States). Barton, as any Christian writer today, has his detractors. The above schools became the de facto standard for academic excellence in faith, morals, and the teachings of Sacred Scripture. This classroom education then filtered throughout the entire colonies and beyond for generations.

President John Adams was aware a nation can only attempt to have civilized self-rule if there is an authority greater than the individual, through voluntary compliance with the law. It is a tenet of Christian principles. In the Constitutions of all fifty of the United States, there are references to the Almighty God of the Universe. The framers of the Constitution of the United States knew it was only a belief in God that could make America a great nation.

The Role of Christianity in the Early Formation of America

There are thousands upon thousands of books written on the early formation of the colonies, and the role of education in an emerging country. To truly understand the thought process behind the statements and quotes of the Founding Fathers, one would need to know the origin of their education. The role of Christianity was central to the men who forged the documents of democracy and self rule at a critical time in the early growth of the country. Many of the best and brightest early college graduates' primary focus was bringing Christ to the world. By serving Christ first, their fellow man would be best served.

Dozens of schools began to sprout where a Christian education was the focus of the entire curricula of the student. Around this time in the earliest part of the 19th century we also see the advent of the Catholic parochial education with St. Elizabeth Ann Seton (1774-1821) in Emmitsburg, Maryland operating under the Baltimore Diocese. She founded the religious order, the Sisters of Charity, with a Catholic Christian identity supplementing the early framers mentality of Christian orthodoxy.

It was considered the highest honor and privilege of the early graduates in the colonies to serve their Creator and go into public ministry. The same was true for the graduates of Oxford and Cambridge in England. The mentality of mandatory chapel had come from England and was considered the single most important part of early American education. It was for this reason there was such a heavy emphasis in studying classics, theology, and philosophy. Scripture study was paramount to be a well-rounded educated individual. If one were to lack knowledge of Scripture, they were not considered to be educated. At that point in history, it was considered a most noble profession to be an educator of youth, or a missionary.

The founders, and early framers of the Declaration of Independence, the Constitution, and the Bill of Rights, were some of the brightest minds to ever inhabit the earth. Their infused wisdom and knowledge came directly from Almighty God with this new land called America, and the early writers and founders had lightning in their brains infused by the blessings of God. The experiment of a philosophical ideal for self-governance was based upon natural law, scripture study, and the knowledge and understanding of history. There also was an acute awareness of what man is capable of being when human nature is left without a system of checks and balances, and without a belief in God and the Ten Commandments. The United States had three primary foundations in its early formation of documents: Greek Logic, Roman Law, and Christian Principles (Scripture).

Belief in God and Sacred Scripture Were Key to a Republic

The framers were clear it was a belief in God and the tenets of Scripture that made America work. Benjamin Rush, a signer of the Declaration of Independence, was considered one of the brightest minds of his time as an essayist, educator, a theologian, doctor, historian, and an early founder of public education for the masses. Rush said, *"The only foundation for a useful education in a republic is to be laid in religion. Without this there can be no virtue, and without virtue there can be no liberty, and liberty is the object and life of all republican governments ... Without religion, I believe learning does much mischief to the morals and principles of mankind."*

Benjamin Franklin has often been misunderstood by historians for various reasons, however, few would say he was a saint. Some were unaware his diplomatic art was for the success of the Revolution, albeit he is considered a rascal by many. Needing to draw the French on the side of the youthful colonies for victory, Franklin knew his clients were the French aristocrats, and he had to win them over. Although not religious in a formal or ritualistic sense, Franklin said as an elder statesman at the Constitutional Convention,

"In the beginning of the contest with Britain, when we were sensible of danger, we had daily prayers in this room for Divine protection. Our prayers, sir, were heard, and they were graciously answered. All of us who were engaged in the struggle must have observed frequent instances of a superintending Providence in our favor... And have we now forgotten this powerful Friend? Or do we imagine we no longer need His assistance? I have lived, sir, a long time, and the longer I live, the more convincing proofs I see of this truth: **that God governs in the affairs of men.** *And if a sparrow cannot fall to the ground without His notice, is it probable that an empire can rise without His aid?*

"We have been assured in the Sacred Writings that except the Lord build the house they labor in vain that build it. I firmly believe this. I also believe without His concurring aid, we shall succeed in the political building no better than the builders of Babel; we shall be divided by our little partial interests; our projects will be confounded; and we ourselves shall become a reproach and a byword down to future ages. And what is worse, mankind may hereafter, from this unfortunate instance despair of establishing government by human wisdom and leave it to chance, war, or conquest. I therefore to beg leave henceforth, **prayers imploring the assistance of Heaven and its blessings on our deliberation be held in this assembly every morning before we proceed to business."**

In Noah Webster's 1790 essay, ***On the Education of Youth in America,*** he wrote,

"Every child in America should be acquainted with his own country. He should read books that furnish him with ideas that will be useful to him in life and practice. As soon as he opens his lips, he should rehearse the history of his own country; he should lisp the praise of liberty, and of those illustrious heroes and statesmen, who have wrought a revolution in her favor. A selection of essays, respecting the settlement and geography of America; the history of the late revolution and of the most remarkable characters and events that distinguished it; a compendium of the principles of the federal and provincial governments, should be the principal schoolbook in the United States. These are understanding objects to every man; they call home the minds of youth and fix them upon the interests of their own country, and they assist in forming attachments to it, as well in enlarging the understanding."

One can see just how profound this Christian teaching was on the fabric of all American culture at the time. There is a story of what Alexis de Tocqueville saw when he came to America under the sponsorship of the French government to find what made America unique. As America's first social biographer, he published a four volume treatise in 1835 called *Democracy in America,* and he observed and wrote about what he saw as he traveled throughout America. In short he wrote,

"I looked to find what made America great in her cities and did not find it; I looked in her countryside to find what made America great and did not find it; I looked in her

factories to find what made America great and did not find it; I looked on her farms and did not find it; I looked in her homes to find what made America great, and did not find it; but when I looked in her churches I found what made America great."

As Tocqueville roamed a young America, and saw the vibrancy of her people, he recognized **it was America's faith and thus churches that made it different.**

Tocqueville as well as Thomas Jefferson wrote the greatest threat to a democracy would be a strong centralized government that would in time become corrupt usurping individual rights.

What is the Role of Faith and Government in Our Lives Today?

Since our country's founding, it has had a run similar to great civilizations before us. See the sequence of stages for the rise and the decline of an empire as articulated by Scottish philosopher Alexander Tytler of the University of Edinburg in 1887.

Tytler wrote, *"A democracy is always temporary in nature; it simply cannot exist as a permanent form of government. A democracy will continue to exist up to the time the voters discover that they can vote for themselves generous gifts from the public treasury. From that moment on, the majority always votes for the candidates who promise the most benefits from the public treasury, with the result that every democracy will finally collapse over loose fiscal policy, which is always followed by a dictatorship."*

The hottest issue of our times now is what exactly is the role of the state or government in our lives. Embedded inside that, is the hot spot of the Second Amendment and gun rights. The Founding Fathers had seen the abuses of the British Empire at home in Scotland, Ireland, and England. Many of the early immigrants came to U.S. shores from the British Isles, and were second or third generation Americans. So, they devised a Bill of Rights that would best assure them of a peaceful existence in their new country. They based their new system of government of what was considered acceptable and workable governance, based upon study of previous civilizations. They melded a blend of many civilizations and empires and took the very best from them. A system designed on Greek logic and norms, Roman law, the Magna Carta, and Christianity. No easy task for a fledgling nation and a brand new experiment of self-rule.

A democracy exists because the people obey the law voluntarily for the good of the individual, the family, and the public good. Not because of a government mandate, but because it is principled self-governance based on individual virtue that preserves freedom and liberty.

Over the last thirty plus years we have seen an accelerated decline in morals than in previous generations. If the decline once galloped, it is now a full- fledged horse race to the abyss. Words are often incorrectly used when discussing political views. Language manipulation is used as a tool to disguise the intended purpose of legislation. There are many terms used to discuss a political philosophy.

Sister Lucia of Fatima said the last assault of the devil would be on **marriage and the family**. Looking at the bold onslaught of an immoral one world agenda in every area, it is now happening at a ferocious pace. **Years before Sister Lucia died in 2003,** she said the world was experiencing *"diabolical disorientation."*

Taking children from the home is being done in several countries for teaching a biblical view and this is communism at its finest. The homosexual community is moving forward with its agenda, now often sanctioned by many churches of all denominations. One can now expect law on top of law legitimizing this behavior culminating in more of a general acceptance through resignation and acquiescence.

We fail to realize the treasure of our faith that brings peace and serenity in our homes, neighborhoods, and society. Many believers are culpable for not speaking up. Jewelers get used to fine stones. Likewise, democracy without boundaries and constraints breeds fascism. Democracy in excess breeds a lawless society to contain the abuses of the rule of law. It is for this reason the framers of the U.S. Constitution said democracy can only exist within a Christian culture. Christianity has a belief system where one primarily chooses obedience to God.

We obey the law because it is what is best for us and God asks it. Once the law breaks down, democracy ceases to work. It will take a totalitarian governmental regime to enforce a democracy out of control. That is what we are seeing evolve. We are in severe moral decline as a nation. Law on top of law, and regulation upon regulation is making us unable to govern. Today our government is not working, and is not accountable to its citizens because we have abandoned God. The wholesale breakdown in our culture is because faith and morality are not at the center of our laws — thus we are failing miserably.

The Ten Commandments are about seventy-two words depending on what version you read. They seem pretty clear to most people and easy to understand, but obedience is an entirely different matter. It is sin that clouds the mind where grace cannot penetrate unless there is confession. The longer one is in sin, the less clarity they possess. The Federal Register of laws fills hundreds of thousands of pages and grows every day.

In 1922, five years after the Bolshevik Revolution in Russia, an old Russian woman (loosely translated to Babushka) was asked in the streets of Moscow how it all happened? She gave the most profound and concise answer possible in three simple words. **"We forgot God."** For those who are not historians, they would at least know how fast it deteriorated from the film *Doctor Zhivago,* based on the book written by Boris Pasternak.

America and the Catholic Church are the Remaining Obstacles to a One World Government and a One World Church

With an ideology of the New World Order for One World Government, and a One World Religion, by a radical group of practical atheists, this form of previous thought, governance, and sovereign nationhood is increasingly extinct today in the public square. There is an intense battle to restore what has been lost. It has been a long time since Civics was taught in America's schools. We are at the point of needing God's divine intervention or America is headed to the ash heap of history.

The ideal of the nation state is an old world idea by progressives that has to be driven from education to achieve the goals of a cabal of men and governments

Hell bent on the destruction of the United States. As the 900-pound gorilla in the room, foreign nations must reduce the vote and authority of the United States in the United Nations General Assembly to any rogue government anywhere in the world. America and the Catholic Church must be destroyed for world government. The humanist, the godless, the socialist, and the communist have made great strides towards this goal of removing God everywhere possible.

There is a great battle to divide America and prevent her from God's destiny. Do you give up the fight? No. Never. But, the forces of Hell are nearing a culmination of evil never seen before. We don't call it the iron horse anymore (trains); the Model T is long ago; we have jet travel to cross the sea; the telegraph is now with a cell phone to anywhere in the world; we don't use typewriters anymore; we no longer use a pony express or stagecoach for the United States Mail Service; we use cars and planes, not horses for travel; and on and on... Change is the normal cycle of history. We are at a new place and we must recognize yesterday is gone.

The former American Empire is over, but the country of America will still exist. Greece brought the world a new way of thinking based on philosophy, civil government, and sea travel. Rome had its long dominant period with its mighty ruthless sword. England sailed the seas subjecting nations for commodities. Spain had its Armada knowing the world wasn't flat. France conquered under the sun kings to Napoleon. These countries still exist, however, they are just not empires as they were in ages past.

The world can only be saved by conforming to God's laws, statutes, and commands. Obedience to His commands brings civility, order, peace, and prosperity to a nation. Otherwise it descends into chaos. Faith is central for the survival and sustenance of a nation. That is the conclusion of history of why nations rise and fall.

As Jonah walked through Nineveh in sackcloth and ashes preaching repentance, he showed it is possible to move the heart of God. With all that is said above, yes, everything is possible with God. But there must be repentance first. Thus, we as a remnant must fulfill our duty to try to restore faith in education.

President John Adams, one of the chief framers of the U.S. Constitution, wrote about the experiment that the United States was going through attempting to live in a democracy. He said, *"Our Constitution was made only for a moral and religious people. It is wholly inadequate to the government of any other. We have no government armed with power capable of contending with human passions unbridled by morality and religion."*

"This book of the law shall not depart out of your mouth, but you shall meditate on it day and night, that you may be careful to do according to all that is written in it; for then you shall make your way prosperous and have good success."

Joshua 1:8

JESUS I TRUST IN YOU

The Future of the American Empire

President John Adams, one of the chief framers of the U.S. Constitution, wrote about the experiment that the United States was going through by attempting to live in a democracy. In a letter to the officers of the Massachusetts Militia, dated October 11, 1798, he said, *"We have no government armed with power capable of contending with human passions unbridled by... morality and religion... Our Constitution was made only for a moral and religious people. It is wholly inadequate to the government of any other."* Adams was clearly saying that a nation can only attempt to have civilized self-rule if there is an authority greater than the government to encourage voluntary compliance with the law. In the Constitutions of all 50 U.S. states, there are references to the Almighty God of the Universe. The framers of the Constitution of the United States knew it was a strong belief in God that would make America work.

As Christians, we obey the law because it is what is best for us and God asks it. However, once the law breaks down democracy ceases to work. The wholesale breakdown in our culture is because morality and spirituality are not at the center of our laws — thus we are failing miserably. It will take a totalitarian governmental regime to enforce a democracy out of control. That is what we are seeing evolve. We are in decline as a nation. Law on top of law is making us unable to govern. Today our government is not working and is not accountable to its citizens, and because we have abandoned God it has no chance of properly functioning.

When the legislators realize they can give themselves largesse from the treasury with no repercussions from the people, and when lawmakers continue to raid the public treasury to simply satisfy their constituents' demand for free goods and services, a democracy ceases to be sustainable. It becomes fiscally impossible to have civil self-rule. The system will collapse. From the time of ancient Greece and her philosophers to modern day empires, history demonstrates how this type of behavior ensues. The USA is the twenty-third great empire in world history, and our role as world leader is coming to an end. The ancient Greeks spoke of a democracy being capable of lasting only approximately 200 years. As the United States approaches its 250th year of existence, we are beyond our allotted time.

Since our country's founding, it has had a run similar to those great civilizations before us. See the sequence of stages for the rise and the decline of an empire as attributed to Scottish philosopher Alexander Tytler of the University of Edinburg in 1776.

1. From bondage to spiritual growth
2. From spiritual faith to great courage
3. From courage to liberty
4. From liberty to abundance
5. From abundance to selfishness
6. From selfishness to complacency
7. From complacency to apathy
8. From apathy to dependence
9. From dependence back to bondage

Tytler wrote, *"A democracy is always temporary in nature; it simply cannot exist as a permanent form of government. A democracy will continue to exist up to the time the voters discover that they can vote for themselves generous gifts from the public treasury. From that moment on, the majority always votes for the candidates who promise the most benefits from the public treasury, with the result that every democracy will finally collapse over loose fiscal policy, which is always followed by a dictatorship."*

Depending on your vantage point, you can decide what stage we are in, but a good guess would be somewhere near complacency to apathy. Some would say dependence because the only thing propping us up at the moment is the printing of fiat money by the trillions. With millions of free loaders taking advantage of the public dole, we are on the precipice of collapse. When the printing of fiat money is exhausted, it is anyone's guess where we will end up as a nation. From apathy, complacency, and dependence, it can spiral down very fast. The nation that is caught up in these last stages is so out of touch with reality that t doesn't even recognize it.

Trade imbalances show how unsustainable our business practices are with just one nation — China. The Chinese, like other nations of the Middle East and Far East have been less prone to adapt blithely the economics of John Maynard Keynes, that the notion that deficit spending leads a nation to prosperity. No nation can print trillions of fiat dollars and expect to survive for very long. The destruction of the United States from within has been intentional. In 2013, the U.S. spent over $2 trillion on entitlements and benefits from the Federal Government. Just one indicator of trade with China shows the general trend. U.S. yearly trade deficits with China have been increasing enormously for the last twenty-five years. In 1990 the annual deficit was $10 billion, and by 2013 it had grown to $318 billion — a year.

The overall strategy of think tank and public policy global elites in the United States has been to manufacture a crisis to bring about change. Every great crisis will have an equal or greater reaction in social change and new policy. In 1968, American sociologists and political activists at Columbia University devised the Cloward-Piven strategy to implement a crisis by overwhelming the U.S. Public Welfare System. This was done so government could gain control of the entire political and social welfare system through its default of financial obligations, and usher in a new aggressive socialist policy. Increase taxes and regulations of all sorts, and you only exacerbate the problem. Factor in the engineered language of social justice and equality and you have a formula few understand as the agenda of the global elites. This has been the model used to gain control. By overwhelming the system, there is a new crisis weekly that deserves attention by Congress and policymakers. However, with the constant onslaught of crisis situations thrust upon law-makers in Congress, nothing is able to get accomplished. When the problems are no longer even remotely manageable, legislation will come that will destroy our way of life and bring us to a place we have never been before. Social unrest will be the norm. Out of chaos will come a New Order — that is the agenda being deliberately and strategically being implemented.

But know this, God does not abandon His people and the woman clothed with the sun (Rev. 12) will play a key role. It is Our Lady who will end the present carnage we see going on in a mystical way, just like the Berlin Wall and the former Soviet Empire fell without a shot being fired. In Message (456) speaking from Slovakia to the Marian Movement of Priests titled, **In the Name of Mary** (c-e) she said:

"In the name of your Heavenly Mother, yes, in the name of Mary, the Turks were defeated, when they laid siege to the city of Vienna and threatened to invade and destroy the whole Christian world. They were far superior in strength, in number and weapons, and they felt that their victory was assured. But I was publicly invoked and called upon; my name was inscribed upon their banners and shouted out by the soldiers, and thus through my intercession, there took place the miracle of this victory which saved the Christian world from its destruction. It is for this reason that the Pope instituted, on this day, the feast of the Name of Mary. In the name of Mary, Marxist communism, which for decades has been exercising its rule and holding so many of my poor children in oppressive and bloody slavery, has been defeated in these countries. Not because of political movements or persons, but through my personal intervention, has your liberation finally come about. It will again be in the name of Mary that I will bring to completion my work with the defeat of Masonry, of every diabolical force, of materialism, and of practical atheism, so that all humanity will be able to attain its encounter with the Lord and be thus purified and completely renewed, with the triumph of my Immaculate Heart in the world."

"In the beginning was the Word, the Word was with God, the Word was God."

John 1:1

JESUS I TRUST IN YOU

They Hated Me....

I f one doubts the virulent alienating nature of sin, try expressing a biblical view at a public setting funded by government/public expenditures. Certain historians have said that the end of early Christianity happened when Constantine relaxed the edict on persecuting believers in 313 AD. However, at the time of Saint Ambrose (340-397 AD) in Milan, believers were still heavily persecuted. In 374, Ambrose was made Bishop and had enormous influence on a young man by the name of Augustine, who we now know as Saint Augustine of Hippo, an early doctor of the Church. Ambrose and Augustine worked tirelessly to legitimize this young ideology of belief called Christianity. Once persecution relaxed under Constantine, many historians have said that Christians no longer had to pay with their life for their Christian beliefs.

While that may seem like a radical thought today, the reality is that Christians have always been persecuted and continue to be persecuted today.

Throughout history, it has been the believer that has been the outsider. If you are willing to compromise belief, often personal and financial advancement is quickened. The believer today is increasingly feeling like an alien, a stranger, like a duck out of water not conforming to what the culture is promoting. Jesus Himself was clear when He said to Pilate, *"My kingdom is not of this world; if My kingdom were of this world, My men would have fought My being surrendered to the Jews. But, My kingdom is not of this kind"* (John 18:36). Jesus is saying clearly that a believer is being held to different criteria for living than the non-believer. Turning the other cheek was a novel idea no one had ever heard until Jesus presented this concept of love through self-sacrifice and self-donation.

Pilate asked what truth was, and Jesus said, *"I am truth."* No one had ever spoken like that. No man had ever said he would rise from the dead and then do it. Not Buddha, not Mohammed, not Confucius, not Socrates, not a Caesar expressing the divine right of kings. Truth had come in the form of a Man God called Jesus, not a Greek or Roman mythological deity.

The believer is different by believing in miracles, believing in forgiveness, believing in prayer, believing in a Most Holy Trinity, believing in a virgin birth, believing in the Incarnation, believing in a Resurrection, believing in scripture, and believing that unless your ego is in subjection to your flesh, you cannot bear fruit, nor inherit the Kingdom of God. Jesus was a contrarian with those He came in contact. He ruffled just about everyone's world-view in His time and few of influence came near Him for fear of being ostracized and losing human favor. And so it continues today, because *"Jesus Christ is the same yesterday, today, and forever"* (Hebrews 13:8).

When a man is about to die he will say only the most important things to those he loves. There will not be any fluff in what he is saying near death. At the Last Supper Jesus gave a very lengthy discourse on a world that will be hostile to the conduct of a follower of Jesus. Jesus told them their life will not be an easy one as they are walking into a culture that does not want Him. Jesus said: *"If the world hates you, remember that it hated me before it hated you. If you belonged to the world, the world would love you as its own; but because you do not belong to the world, because my choice withdrew you from the world, therefore the world hates you ... If they persecuted me, they will persecute you too ... But it will be on my account that they will do all this, because they do not know the one who sent me...Anyone who hates me hates my Father. If I had not performed such works among them as no one else has ever done, they would be blameless; but as it is, they have seen all this, and still they hate both me and my Father"* (John 15: 18-24).

The believer can expect to be an alien and a stranger in this world, because until there is a conversion to the thinking of God's worldview, the world WILL be hostile to you if you proclaim the truth. The light has no association with the darkness, (Eph. 5:11, 2 Cor. 6:14), therefore, most often this is the division when speaking with a non-believer. To be accepted into the mainstream thought and culture was not for Jesus, and it will not be, nor has it ever been, for us either. The believer is the light of the world that will bring salvation through Jesus to those in darkness, and the darkness hates Him for it. This is the formula the believer must walk in the market place.

Many people at some point have a touchstone moment when they have truly embraced their faith. It is called being *"born again."* However, many subsequently fall away after they realize the cost of what they are called to do. Often the decision to follow Christ occurs during an emotional or spiritual- high that is sincere. After they see the reality of their decision, they find that many of the old habits are hard to break. Friends, associations, activities and habits may need to go. Unless there is a formula for formation and discipleship where the seed falls on fertile ground, people will simply fall back into old ways and cease to grow. Because the seed never took root in a solid formation of faith, often they will come to the conclusion, *"This isn't for me."* They will fall away and not produce fruit because they never first counted the cost, which for them ultimately was too high.

The central part of that formula is a public expression of one's faith through words or action. Jesus again spoke of this when He said, *"I tell you, if anyone openly declares himself for me in the presence of men, the Son of Man will declare Himself for him in the presence of God's angels. But the man who disowns me in the presence of men, will be disowned in the presence of God's angels"* (Luke12:9). Saint John wrote: *"Those who prove victorious will be dressed, like these, in white robes; I shall not blot their names out of the book of life, but acknowledge their names in the presence of My Father and His angels"* (Rev. 3:5). John writing from Patmos was saying, that we must endure and fight the good fight to the end. The flesh is battling the spirit, and only if we adhere to the fundamental rubrics of the faith will we say as Saint Paul said at the end of his life, *"I have fought the good fight, I have finished the race, I have remained faithful"* (2 Tim. 4:7).

Saint Francis of Assisi would tell his young men as they went into the world to *"preach the Gospel and speak only if necessary."* Francis was being clear that actions speak louder than words, something the believer today often fails to grasp. Time will show us all if the seed took root and the profession of faith is real. Life is not a sprint, but a marathon. There is no winning a marathon without training.

Jesus Was Not Spared, Will We Be?

Jesus was the only man in the history of the world to come into the world with a mandate to die at an appointed time to save others. Saint Paul throughout his epistles speaks of being *"In Christ"* or *"Out of Christ"* (I Cor. 1). He makes it clear that there is a line of demarcation that one must make a choice in life to be *"sanctified in Christ"* (I Cor. 1-2). A theme in all of his writings is that we are either In or Out, and we will not have God's best being out. Life is to be lived **"In Christ."**

If the believer is feeling like an outcast, there are good historical precedents — Jesus and the apostles. Eleven of the twelve apostles died violent deaths. Peter was crucified upside down not thinking himself equal to the death of Jesus. The apostle John was probably pushed off the boat and had to wade into exile on Patmos, where he then wrote the Book of Revelation. The apostles and followers of Christ did not have an easy time being strangers in a strange land, which is the calling of being **In**

Christ. Neither will we. Our final destination place is not here. This is a way station before the eternal prize of Heaven. St. Therese of Lisieux would remind us that life is not the port but the boat. Pascal's Wager applied then as it does today, *"If there is no God, it doesn't matter, if there is a God, then nothing else does matter."*

Jesus came for the salvation of all mankind and lived in the form of a slave. After an unjust trial with unjust charges after doing nothing but good, He was condemned to death because He was a threat to the establishment. He did not arrive adorned in royal purple as the Jewish people perceived the new king to be. He was just the son of a carpenter born on the wrong side of the tracks. *"Can anything good come from Nazareth?"* (John 1:46).

If we think our circumstances have marginalized us we should consider the Gospel narrative of Luke 23: 35-43. *"The people stayed there watching Him, and as for the leaders, they jeered at Him. He saved others they said, let Him save Himself if He is the Christ of God, the Chosen One. The soldiers mocked Him too, and when they approached to offer Him vinegar they said, if you are the king of the Jews save yourself. Above Him there was an inscription: This is the King of the Jews."*

It continues. *"One of the criminals hanging there abused Him. Are you not the Christ he said? Save yourself and us as well. But the other spoke up and rebuked him. Have you no fear of God at all? He said, you got the same sentence as he did, but in our case we deserved it: we are paying for what we did. But this man has done nothing wrong. Jesus he said, remember me when you come into your kingdom. Indeed I promise you, He replied, today you will be with me in paradise."*

Here comes a man destined to change the course of history and He is being treated worse than a common criminal. The "sign of contradiction" has been sentenced to death for healing people, freeing them from bondage, restoring relationships, performing miracles on their behalf, and giving them a meaning and purpose in life, and He is treated unjustly and ultimately killed for it. While hanging on the cross Jesus was still being mocked. Condemned to death, as He died He forgave His enemies. Yet, one thief who was moments away from death himself still did not see who Jesus or His ministry was , while the other one did. One stole Heaven and was promised paradise by Christ Himself. The other through free choice rejected grace. Some accept Christ, while others reject Him. In Christ or Out of Christ. There has been nothing new from then to now. We are all without excuse, but some submit to the authority of Heaven while others do not. He is no fool who gives what he cannot keep, to gain what he cannot lose. We all make choices, some good, some not so good.

For those interested in this vein of thinking, consider reading the book by Archbishop Charles Chaput, OFM Cap. called *Strangers in a Strange Land.* With 267 pages it provides an historical analysis of how believers are to conduct their affairs and still be *"In the world, but not of it."* Archbishop Chaput has been a consistent thinker and writer on this subject for many years seeing the direction of the Church through the culture, the Church, and the intrusive nature of the state. Chaput quotes political scientist Robert Kraynak who noted that *"The strangeness of our day consists in a strong moral passion for the virtue of justice sitting alongside a loss of confidence in the very foundations of justice, and even an eagerness to undermine them. The crucial requirement for human equality is a conception of human dignity, which views human beings as having a special moral status in the universe, and individuals as having unique moral worth entailing claims of justice. What is so strange about our age is that demands for justice are increasing as the foundations for these demands are disappearing. In particular, beliefs in man as made in the image of God, or an animal with a rational soul, are being replaced by a scientific materialism that undermines what is noble and special about man, and by doctrines of relativism that deny the objective morality required to undergird human dignity"* (page 137).

Paraphrasing Kraynak, Archbishop Chaput continues, *"Secular thinkers live off the capital of religious beliefs they reject. Their faith is actually a convenient, parasitic laziness. It enables them to have respectable moral commitments while avoiding the hard work of actually establishing foundations for them, whether in the moral order of nature or the revealed knowledge of God."*

I see no group of people more guilty of this than the liberal, tenured, tweed jacketed professors who are overwhelmingly not just liberal, but hard-core socialist nihilists who profess babble wrapped in self-absorbent pride. They are able to expound such illicit thinking for something they never created because they are doing so on the sweat of others. They don't even try to preserve the original integrity of truth and goodness, but with intellectual depravity seek to destroy the generation coming up behind them. This is the parasite Kraynak points to. These people are sponges living off the welfare of the state, not producing anything but merely tearing down what previously worked with nothing to put in its place but anarchy. The moral order is obliterated under this type of thinking.

Archbishop Chaput has written previously on the subject. He is aware that believers will see a great marginalization or worse in the market place for their public views of belief. We are in an increasingly darkened world, where grave sin is not only accepted, but promoted and sanctioned by the state. He states the America of old is gone, and that the new paradigm today is a place the Founding Fathers would not recognize. History is dynamic, and moves forward—with or without us. As young Dorothy said in the Wizard of Oz, *"Toto, I don't think we're in Kansas anymore."*

Believers need to provide alternatives to the culture, not just letting the events take away our freedoms and liberties. The world lacks an answer, and so acts the way it does. We all need to start being a part of the solution, not part of the problem. Providing a formula for an alternative to the lifestyle of the world and being more active in our faith is the first place to start.

The fire of love is strongest when the way is dark. We should also be reminded of the words of Jesus when He told his apostles, *"I am sending you out like sheep among wolves; so be cunning as serpents and yet as harmless as doves"* (Matt. 10:16).

"Greater is He who is in you, than he who is in the world" (I John 4:4).

JESUS I TRUST IN YOU

A Joy Filled Life in the Midst of Adversity
Heaven's Prescription For Peace

In Chapters 2 & 3 in the book of Revelation, the Lord speaks to the seven Churches that have contemporaneous spirits that have endured through the ages. With each Church the Lord has something very positive to say as well as something negative, save one, the Church of Philadelphia—the Church of brotherly love. The seven Churches addressed are Ephesus, Smyrna, Pergamum, Thyatira, Sardis, Philadelphia, and Laodicea. Each Church satisfies the Lord for what it has done, and in the same manner there is something that displeases the Lord. For instance of Ephesus (Rev. 2: 2-4) the angel says to the scribe, the Apostle John, *"I know all about you: how hard you work and how much you have put up with. I know you cannot stand wicked men, and how you tested the imposters, who called themselves apostles and proved they were liars. I know, too, that you have patience, and have suffered for my name without growing tired. Nevertheless, I have this complaint to make; you have less love now than you used to."* In other words, you have left your first love.

The angel is saying that they have forgotten what is most important — love. They have been fighting to stay faithful, yet they have not been able to say as Saint Paul said at the end of his life, *"I have fought the good fight, and run the good race."* In the age of the American prosperity gospel, where the Lord is a type of cosmic bellhop, the world is changing at an unprecedented pace. People speak of a quickening of time where events of the day deluge our senses like never before. To make sense of it all requires a sequestering of data to properly order how we are to process it for a life of priorities. We must decide what matters most in an age of a constant bombardment all day long of useless trite and banal information.

As believers gather in groups large or small, there is lament that is heard in the din of the evening. It is, "I am weary." The distractions of the day sap the energy from the sinew of our bodies. From the time we wake up in the morning, to the moment our eyes close after a long day, there is a constant barrage of information invading our senses draining away the life of joy. With the direction of the world and all that it is throwing at us, the issue is, how are we to thrive in such an atmosphere of negativity. The social indices of well-being — health, employment, finances, home, care of children and parents, the direction of our faith, commuting, and all that a day entails, may well justify the believer into a state of near despair. How then are we to respond and live a meaningful joy-filled life in the times in which we live?

First we must understand that in this life we are not going to fully comprehend what the Lord is doing. He has a plan. It is just that we can't see it all in its totality. There is always an element of suffering in this life at some point whether it be physical, emotional, or spiritual. Suffering, if used properly, will bring us closer to the Immaculate and Sacred Hearts for our welfare. If we are high and mighty for too long it often brings pride. If the emotions are too low for an extended period of time, they can often bring depression or worse. The dark night of the soul is often a step to bring us to the realization that we can do nothing without Him. As Jesus said, *"without me you can do nothing"* (John 15:5). The Lord calibrates our needs accordingly; we often don't visualize at the moment that we are enduring the trial for our own spiritual good.

In the New World Order that has arrived in all its sordid policies, you will either be IN or OUT. You will either adhere to the philosophy of those in ungodly rule or you will not. A properly formed conscience will not allow one to participate in the political and social agenda being thrust upon us. As time moves on, it will be difficult to straddle the fence without making a commitment to decide which side of the fence you stand on. The turtle on a fencepost just observing will be taking the side of evil. The middle will be where the lukewarm gather without any conviction one way or the other, and the Lord has some harsh words for those who do so. *"You who are lukewarm I will spit you out of my mouth"* (Rev. 3:16).

At the moment things look bleak to the believers as they read and watch the news. Satan seems to have the upper hand as many believers are being smashed to the rocks like a dinghy in a bad storm. Many families are enduring a trial of some sort. Some trials are small, others not so small. As we see the onslaught of filth and the mass of corruption around us, there is a 2,500 year-old letter where the Lord prescribed to the Prophet Jeremiah an antidote for what ailed Israel His people, and how to live in the midst of the trial. The Lord tells him obedience to the Commandments is necessary for blessings.

The Jewish people throughout history knew what exile meant with all its repercussions. In chapters 29 & 30 of Jeremiah, the prophet writes to those who had been exiled from Jerusalem and had to live under the tyrannical king Nebuchadnezzar. We can see time and again over a thousand years that the Lord reigned in His Chosen people often through a bad king. Weather and moral deterioration caused social problems from within, bending the will of His people to come back to Him. Whether or not it can be articulated as such, this is the cause of the anxiety around us. Nerves are tender and frayed and it will continue. The blessing and protective hedge has been removed from America due to its sin as America is under judgment. To give a blanket "no" to this thinking would make one scripturally illiterate. Now, the question is, how do believers conduct themselves and live a joy filled and peaceful life as we are asked to do amidst the moral degeneration?

As Jeremiah wrote, due to disobedience, through the permissive Will of the Lord, there was a prescribed 70 years of exile. The false prophet Hananiah predicted the exile would only last two years and he died shortly thereafter for *"preaching apostasy"* (Jer. 28:16). So from the beginning, it was the Lord who had ordained that Israel live in exile. *"When seventy years are completed for Babylon, I will come to you and fulfill my good promises to bring you back to this place. For I know the plans I have for you."* It was the Lord who allowed exile for the good of His people in the long term, yet it could not be seen at that time. The present is often the most difficult to discern. Hindsight is a wonderful teacher.

Jeremiah 29:5-15 provides instructions for His Chosen people and how they should live in exile. The Lord said,

"*build houses, settle down, plant gardens and eat what they produce, take wives and have sons and daughters, choose wives for your sons, find husbands for your daughters so that these can bear sons and daughters in their turn, you must increase and not decrease. Work for the good of the country to which I have exiled you; pray to the Lord on its behalf, since on its welfare yours depends. For the Lord says this, only when the seventy years to Babylon are over, will I visit you and fulfill my promise in your favor by bringing you back to this place. I know the plans I have in mind for you — it is the Lord who speaks — plans for peace, not disaster, reserving a future full of hope for you. Then when you call to me, to come to plead with me, I will listen to you. When you seek me you will find me, when you seek me with all your heart.... I will restore your fortunes and gather you from all the nations, and all the places where I have dispersed you...*" In the vernacular: go about the business of life and do what you need to do not only to survive, but prosper.

It was during this period of exile that the birth of a nation with its cultural and ancestral norms took root. It was during the Babylonian captivity that Israel moved away from the single temple concept in Jerusalem to a local community based synagogue society. A local expression of faith lived in community. What they learned in exile sustained them for several thousand more years — prospering and thriving in the midst of trials as a wandering people.

We have a mandate of our own. Pray through Jeremiah 29 & 30 carefully, and see how the Lord speaks to your heart. God has a plan and we must see that He is in control. The Blessed Mother gave birth to her Son in a cold dung heap only warmed by the heat of barn animals. The Holy Family left in the middle of the night to live in exile in Egypt for a period of years to avoid adverse circumstances, and chose the safe route for the protection of their Son Jesus.

Heaven knows the trials we are enduring, and it is not abnormal in Church history. We have reached the point in our history as a nation when we will see the separation of the sheep and the goats, and the wheat from the chaff. It is now unavoidable. We have crossed the Rubicon and sticking to the fundamentals of our faith will sustain us peacefully and joyfully. Reject the noise around you, and go about your business.

Prayer will be the key to our spiritual health. The Lord is in control.

JESUS I TRUST IN YOU

The Mind of an Unbeliever

I, as everyone else in life, encounter people with views other than my own. It is life. In my youth I never gave conservative versus liberal much thought, probably due to wise parents who arranged activities to keep their kids out of trouble rather than talk politics. However, as I grew older I became fascinated with how people develop intellectually, politically, socially, and spiritually, and how that becomes world-views that shape who we are, and what we do as a person, a family, and as a nation. What is it exactly that molds us into who we become? Is there a common denominator? What defines our actions? What is the thought process that develops so acutely that it defines what we do on a daily basis?

"The good person out of the good treasure of the heart produces good, and the evil person out of evil treasure produces evil; for it is out of the abundance of the heart the mouth speaks" (Luke 6:45). The treasure of the heart is the common denominator defining our actions on a daily basis. Jesus said, *"My sheep hear my voice... and they follow me"* (John 10:27). Obedience to His word is paramount for an ordered life. Jesus said, *"I come to give you life and give it more abundantly,"* and Satan is out to *"kill, destroy, and steal."* (John 10:10) Satan said, *"I will not serve,"* and then he led the rebellion of mankind. There is sin — and it has consequences, chaos, disorder, disorientation.

There are many forms of thought that define where we are on the political spectrum. We are what we think. Likewise, there are easily recognized words and terms for what could generally fall into the category or genre of liberal or conservative. Where is the intersection of disordered affections due to sin and a political philosophy that is either acceptable and civil, or one that flies in the face of what is contrary to Scripture and ungodly? We are living in times that Sister Lucia of Fatima labeled as *"diabolical disorientation."* Our present times are one of great confusion and division. There is little doubt that there are many well-intentioned people with liberal views. But at the very foundation of their thinking is an individual defined by rejecting the plan and order of God and His ordained word giving mankind a plan for civility and order in a fallen world. In their actions they say, "I will do it my way. I will not serve — I have a better way." That is what the fallen angels said *"My ways are not your ways"* (Is. 55:8). Jesus was clear when he said, *"Unless a seed falls into the ground and die, it cannot bear fruit"* (John 12:24). Man's rebellion is rooted in pride.

However, in political philosophy, words can mean a profoundly different thing than as they relate to our ideology. The term "militant secularism" for example has a profound ramification not only in how we act in the market place expressing our world-view but in our spiritual life. Spiritually, over a lifetime I have learned that every aberrant human behavior is due to a wound or a hurt. We act out our hurts or virtues in the market place whether we are aware of them or not. Behavior has an origin spoken or unspoken, acknowledged or not acknowledged, aware or not aware, confronted or ignored. Our hearts define our behavior.

Admittedly, no one is immune; not even the believer. But the unbeliever is neces-sarily more prone to liberalism. G. K. Chesterton called the liberal extreme of the political spectrum *"the modern and morbid habit of always sacrificing the normal to the abnormal."* The rebellion in the streets and in the hearts and souls of man is an alienation from God. If one is alienated from God, he or she is alienated from self, and thus others. The angry man is not even able to articulate why he is angry. His utopia is anarchy.

Chesterton also observed, *"When men choose not to believe in God, they do not thereafter believe in nothing, they then become capable of believing in anything."* Like-wise, if they believe in anything, they will believe in anyone. It is similar to the old adage, *"If a man doesn't stand for something, he will fall for anything."* As unbelievers march and vent their anger with the heel of their shoes, their pen, or their voice, they are rejecting tradition, virtue, the normal for the abnormal, something that works for something that doesn't work, and order for chaos. They supplant foundational Christian principles with new forms of *"social justice"* in all of its ill-formed think-ing. All the while the unbeliever is rejecting the tradition of the Gospel and the very words of Jesus, striving to build a new world with no foundations other than living by his or her glands.

The liberal is looking to replace any traditional thinking for the chaos of the unknown. In short, liberals want a world without God because they think they have a better way to order society. The liberal also wants to end any connection to the traditional normal, and desires to have the state supreme. The state cannot reform man's soul, but only the Lord can. It is for this reason that Jesus did not come as a political ruler. He came to change hearts—and no matter the politics, a person becomes better if his or her heart is changed towards God.

As a nation we are on the cusp of violence due to such radically differing views of the populace. The fruit of unbelief is tyranny. Reject God, and blood runs in the streets. No matter the subject there is great discord that has grown to hatred. What will be the spark that sends people over the edge into societal chaos? That is an unknown, but as the anger and animosity builds it may not take much for some form of eruption. Unfortunately, it will take more than blood in the streets to bring the Lord back into the classrooms of America.

As Archbishop Fulton J. Sheen often said, *"Marry the age and you become a widow in the next."* Man's whimsy is fleeting because "the grass withers and the flower fades, but the Word of God endures forever" (Is. 40:8). As Isaiah said, *"It has been your sin that has separated you from God"* (59:2) Sin alienates us from everyone and every-thing and the result is a life of chaos for individuals, families, cities, and countries. The only blueprint for peace of soul comes from God—nowhere else. That is the history of civilization. No matter the social activism, this will never change. Truth is timeless and not wrapped up into the ideology or the fancy of the culture of the day. Truth will always win. Sometimes it takes longer than we may desire, but truth always prevails.

JESUS I TRUST IN YOU

The Great Secret to the Heart of God

For many years I was puzzled reading several verses in Scripture. What the Lord said about King David was one of those: *"Then they demanded a king, and God gave them Saul, son of Kish, a man of the tribe of Benjamin. After forty years, he deposed him and made David their King, of whom he approved in these words, I have selected David son of Jesse, **a man after my own heart**, who will carry out my whole purpose"* (Acts 13:21-23).

What was so special about David that the Lord would say that about a premeditated murderer, adulterer, warrior boy/king, poet, musician, sinner, saint, lowly shepherd boy, and giant slayer? Why was it that God Himself would call David *"a man after my own heart?"* The writer of Acts is merely quoting from 1 Samuel 13:14 on attributes that the Lord was looking for in His future King of Israel *"who will carry out my whole purpose."*

The key to understanding David is in many places of Scripture, but in I Chronicles Chapters 15 and 16, David gives detailed instructions and preparations for moving the Ark of the Covenant. They are very specific on the general care and procedures to move the Ark to another location. It is clear that King David took great joy in doing this and he made sure it was a very festive time for the people of Israel. There was music, logistics, food, and a procession. Much of the traditions and rubrics of Judaism can be seen here in what evolved over time to become the practices of the Catholic faith surrounding the altar. The OLD became a NEW Covenant established by the Incarnation and the Death and Resurrection of Jesus, and we have our elder brothers in the faith to thank for laying the groundwork.

In I Chronicles 15:14-16, we read of *"approaching Him in the right way, with the duties of the kinsmen as cantors, with their various instruments of music, harps and lyres and cymbals, to play joyful tunes."* In I Chronicles 15: 28-29, the Ark was brought to Jerusalem and King David was dancing with joy in front of it as it was being processed to the Citadel of David. His wife was Michal the daughter of King Saul, who was deceased. As Michal watched David from a window dancing and exultant, *"She despised David in her heart."* David's dancing was wildly exuberant, caught up in the joy of the Spirit of God, yet Michal was critical of him dancing in front of his servants half naked wearing only a loincloth. As a result of her derision and mocking David's actions of joy (2 Samuel 6), David cursed her womb and she remained childless.

The Key to Understanding the Heart of David's Many Characteristics is His Joyful Praise.

Praising God is the way to the heart of God and David knew it. It is the absolute key to understanding who David was to carry out God's *"whole purpose."* David was not the type of person to be affected by what others thought of him if he felt God demanded something from him. In essence, peer pressure was not something that concerned him. Jesus is clear: the way to inherit the Kingdom of God is to have the heart of a little child. Children will sing no matter what they sound like and regardless of others think of them. Youth does some tender things compared to the so called "sophistication" that comes with older age. King David's goal was to please one person — and that was God.

Four Thousand Praised the Lord on the instruments David had Made

We get a little more understanding of just how profound and important praise is to God when we see how important praise was to King David, *"a man after God's own heart."* Several chapters ahead in Chronicles, there is detailed information given about the Temple, the Ark, and its rules. King David was now an old man and was bequeathing his kingdom to his son, Solomon. Verses 1-5 of Chapter 23 provide more instructions to give God His due. *"A census was taken of those Levites thirty years old and upwards. On a count of heads their number was thirty-eight thousand; twenty-four thousand of these were responsible for the service of the house of the Lord; six-thousand were scribes and judges; four-thousand were keepers of the gate; four-thousand praised the Lord on the instruments David had made for that purpose."* Then David divided the Levites for specific tasks servicing the temple.

This number of those in the Temple just praising God is mind-numbing. We are dealing with a jealous God who wants no others before Him — He demands exclusivity. Honoring God is also the very first Commandment.

Praise Wins Battles

Winston Churchill writing in his *History of the English Speaking Peoples,* said of Joan of Arc that *"She finds no equal in one thousand years."* Joan of Arc as a young woman led an army into battle with a simple three-pronged approach: 1. She did exactly as the Lord instructed her under strict obedience with no interpretation of her own; 2. She made her army go to confession before battle; and, 3. She made the army sing hymns of praise and worship in battle. Joan of Arc easily won every battle no matter the odds, altering the landscape of France and Europe until the politics of the French dauphin got involved. Mark Twain said his favorite book was the book he wrote on Joan of Arc. He felt so strongly about her that he said she was the greatest woman produced by the human race. King David and Joan of Arc knew that the key to the heart of God was praise.

Adoration is Praise of the Highest Order

The greatest thing we can do in our age of the New Covenant is to worship in the form of Adoration. Saint Mother Teresa said Adoration was the single most important thing she ever did in her order. Once they started Adoration as a part of a daily regimen, she said the Sisters of Charity grew.

As Jesus said in His hour of agony in the Garden of Gethsemane, *"could you not watch with me for one hour?"* When was the last time we had an hour of Adoration to worship Jesus? There are 168 hours in a week, 672 in a month, and 8,064 hours in a year. *Can we not waste one hour with Him?*

The greatest thing we can do to win the cultural battle and change the culture is to change ourselves. Praising God as if no one is watching will be a remedy for the cultural descent to Gomorrah where we are sliding. It will transcend the daily battles that bring joy and peace of soul in an increasingly fallen world.

As King David wrote, *"One thing I ask of the Lord, one thing I seek: to live in the house of the Lord all the days of my life, to enjoy the sweetness of the Lord and to consult in His temple"* (Psalm 27:4).

JESUS I TRUST IN YOU

Do You Produce Fruit in Your Life?

I n Matthew chapter 13 there is the parable of the sower throwing seeds on the ground. It is a parable with little ambiguity or confusing metaphors. The seeds landed on four different types of ground. Some seeds landed on rocky ground, others thorny, some trampled, and the last landed on fertile soil. Only one seed produced fruit, and that is the seed that landed on fertile ground. In other words, only one out of four seeds produced anything, while the other seventy five percent came up fruitless.

In that same parable the Lord clearly states with those fertile seeds, some produced 100 fold of crops, others 60 fold, while others produced 30 fold. And then He says, *"He who has ears, let him hear"* (Matt. 13:9). In the space of just several verses, Jesus is telling one of the most poignant parables in all of Scripture about the production of souls for the Kingdom of God, and how different it would be for some versus others concerning producing disciples. Truly a clear depiction of why some people live fruitful and abundant lives, while others are largely spiritually sterile. So, the question is why? This is a very big WHY.

All know a seed thrown on a rock cannot bear fruit. The same with thorns, as if it even did take root, it would be choked and before long not grow. The same is with the seed thrown on trampled ground, which has little chance for survival. But, the seed thrown on fertile ground can produce if the circumstances are right. The "why" of growth is complex, yet quite simple if the seed grows in the right environment.

The answer to our growth is how we manage our pride and how we view Jesus. Is He a teacher, a philosopher, a prophet, Man, God, a revolutionary, a pacifist, a social reformer, a promoter of social justice, or other endless ways we view Him. The fact is, based upon His life, He came to change people, and He did it with a very simple message when He said, *"Unless a grain of wheat falls into the ground and dies, it cannot produce fruit"* (John 12:24). Jesus is talking about death to self. It is death to our pride in so many of our views we hold dear. It is death to the believer always needing to be right in circumstances that don't really matter in the long haul of life. It is death to the believer who is continually in discord with others dividing the body of Christ as they hold onto the pride of their belief system. It is death to so many rigid believers thinking they have the sole possession of the Kingdom of God in their midst and everyone else is wrong. It is death to the liberal who thinks the same. And if you do disagree with a proud person often you are looked at like some juvenile belligerent child.

The fact remains in light of so many nuances of the Gospel, some produce 100 fold, others 60, others 30, and others 10, others 5, and others 0. We often fail to be disciples and all that entails because we believe we are the ones correct on matters of faith. Our view of being believers over the last several generations has been far too intellectual rather than developing a gospel message of a lifestyle. Often once someone attends the seminary, they come back to their families and congregations like they have inherited the Keys to the Kingdom, but have little sense to implement a plan other than spouting a gospel message from the pulpit with little practical experience of living. Jesus was able to touch a man like Matthew a tax collector, Peter Andrew, James and John — fishermen, a grinder like Zacchaeus, a wealthy man like Lazarus, a deep sinner like Mary Magdalene, and so the list goes on. No matter the background, Jesus touched because He was first and foremost a fisher of souls. There are different size hooks for different types of fish, and for unbelievers we must know what best hook to be a fisher of people for the Kingdom of God.

Jesus changed the world walking among the people. He is the Way, the Truth, and the Life. His appeal was universal because He lived love, and people were attracted to that; healing; teaching by the fire; walking in the rain and the sunshine from city to city; being the light on a hill; fasting; driving out demons; giving life to the woman at the well; and an untouchable due to race; even pardoning the thief on the cross as Jesus saw his heart; not condemning the adulterous woman, but saying, *"Go and sin no more."* You cannot find Jesus arguing to make His point anywhere in Scripture. All you will get by arguing is an enemy, not a potential disciple.

We bring a lot of intellectual baggage when meeting people. We expect them to immediately change upon hearing from us — and it doesn't work. The acorn doesn't grow to be an oak over night. How can people sit in the same pew for 10, 20, 30, 40 years, or more — with no change around them? The model of Jesus changing the world by pouring His life into twelve men for three solid years day after day, month after month, needs to be looked at much more seriously if we are to make headway with unbelievers — and thus change our culture. The way to reach the world is to first change ourselves — and then one person at a time. By touching one person, we can then transform the world. This is no easy task, and takes training.

The fact is the mission field is not Nigeria or the Amazon any longer. It is next door to you on your suburban or city street. We are fast approaching being a pagan state void of any resemblance to civility and normalcy. If people are not changing around us, there is sin in our life. Why? Because wherever Jesus and the apostles walked, *"Signs and Wonders followed"* (Acts 2:43). It was His life people decided to follow, because He in turn was obedient to the Father. The key for bringing change is obedience to His message. Surrendering your will. Not needing to be always project-ing your opinions, but listening to the cry of the heart of another. Knowing when you are with someone who is hurting, you need to ask the Holy Spirit *"What is the way to the heart of this person?"* He will answer.

Jesus said, *"The harvest is plentiful, but the workers are few"* (Matt. 9:37). The 20th century was marked by human progress in many forms. Science, medicine, technol-ogy, travel, flight, automobiles, engineering, and wide dissemination of information were all around us. Due to a spiritual abdication of faith by parents a generation ago, so their children could get an education at all costs, there was a neglect of the confessional and the teaching of faith. As a result, we now see a generation going forward in despair. Our challenge now is to change the paradigm. We need to be the only Bible people read if change is to take place.

JESUS I TRUST IN YOU

How We Arrived at Insane

"Whom the gods would destroy, they first make mad."

Greek Antiquity

For years now, people who have some sort of desire for virtuous living, tradi-tional moral values, a desire to uphold a Christian belief system, and maintain the rule of law, have watched the systemic eradication of all of the above in western civilization. How did this happen in a brief amount of time? Historians Will and Ariel Durant in the *Story of Civilization* said that great civilizations commit suicide by dying from within, not invasion from without. This principle also applies to the Church. We are watching in real time the auto demolition of the Church with a stealth agenda from within to remake the Church. There are radical godless forces working in the hierarchy to bring the Church in a new direction to a one world gov-ernment, a one world currency, and one world ruler. If people cannot recognize it for what it is now, they simply haven't been paying attention. Or worse, they deny its reality.

Many in the hierarchy of the Roman Catholic Church have been directly com-plicit behind the scenes aiding and abetting this agenda to a trusting, yet unsus-pecting gullible uninformed public. Faithful Catholics never would have dreamed clergy they admired, trusted, and respected, sold them out for a socialist agenda. Adopting the principles of Antonio Gramsci and Saul Alinsky, and using the strat-egy of infiltration from within for a socialist agenda, has ben their modus operandi. The National Education Association (NEA) in concert with liberal clergy has been the heart and soul of the democratic party for several generations. This method of control has been perfected by liberal and socialist leaders in the hierarchy of the Roman Catholic Church for several generations. Jesus Himself addressed this on numerous occasions when He spoke about the law-givers of His time, *"I am sending you out as sheep among wolves"* (Matt. 10:6). The most insidious enemy is the one within, and they are barbarians inside the gates.

What we are experiencing is nothing new for the world, but what is new is the drive to socialism hasn't been this ferocious in the United States since the Great Depression. However, globally the world is in a new place. Through a group of men led by Frank Buchman of Moral Rearmament (founder of the Oxford Group) using plays with Christian themes, the drive to communism was beaten into submission and people saw the lie of socialism/communism out in the open. The lumber camps around Seattle Washington is where Buchman first had his plays, as the area was precariously close to communist rule in the 1930's. The desire for the collective of Hegel, Marx, Engels, Lenin, Trotsky, Stalin and Mao, and many other nations throughout the world like present day Venezuela is at full throttle. The drive to socialism has now reared its ugly head again, this time with a vengeance, and now with a global blueprint that is well funded and well organized.

Socialism, if not curbed of its voracious appetite to have state control of people and industry, leads to collective communism. Revolutions are the norm in history when there is an imbalance in justice with unbridled capitalism — the only question is when does a spark ignite a blaze? Socialism is the slow but steady march to a communist godless state. It is a linear from one to the other. Yet, those who propose its ideology cannot point to a single success where its ideology works for the benefit of all, as it only shares the spoils with a few at the top. In time the leadership siphons off the largesse of the state as fast as they can, for as much as they can.

As much as the philosophy of Ayn Rand's Objectivism is fatally flawed (heretical and anti Christian) due to her atheism and lack of acknowledgment of God in the Divine Plan of mankind. However, she got it right on collectivism, and this is one element for her widespread appeal to this day. The evil of collectivism is about all she did get right, as her philosophy is for college freshman who don't t have the intellectual resources to think more broadly about the role of government, the state, and the individual, and how God designed them to interact. Rand had seen the Bolsheviik Revolution as a young girl in Russia and the Ukraine, and knew violence would precede the move from socialism to communism. As a result, she fled Russia and moved to New York, and remained in the United States for the rest of her life.

What the Future Brings

Some of the most accurate and descriptive writings on how a nation evolves to socialism come from a French economist, philosopher, statesman, and writer by the name of Frederic Bastiat (1801-1850). After the French Revolution of 1789, there was nothing but economic and political turmoil as hundreds of years of rule by the French Monarchy came to an end. Chaos ensued, and death was nearby for all who opposed the new system of governance under the Reign of Terror. The experiment of liberty, equality, and fraternity was untried in France as it never had lived under self-rule. The transition from monarchy to democracy was violent. To correct the wrongs of the Sun Kings and the Monarchy, the people revolted, and by the Revolution of 1848, France had installed a socialist government. This period was when Bastiat was in his intellectual prime writing about what he saw during this sixty-year transition phase.

Bastiat wrote a lot on matters of state and economics, but most of his best writing was in a book called, *The Law, The State, and Other Political Writings.* It is a series of essays from 1843 until his death in 1850. The phase of America and the West from the 1960s to today has many similarities to that transitional period in France.

Bastiat writes about the march towards socialism in his essay called, Baccalaureate and Socialism. Bastiat writes, *"Plato was the constructor of imaginary republics that were to serve as models for future teachers of peoples and fathers of nations."*

"Whoever, not knowing the social body is a set of natural laws, like the human body, dreams of creating an artificial form of society, and sets out to manipulate the family, property, rights, and humanity to suit his will, is a socialist. He is not engaging in physiology but statuary. He does not observe; he invents. He does not believe in God but himself. He is not a scholar; but a tyrant. He is not serving mankind; he is making use of it. He is not studying its nature; he is changing it in accordance with Rousseau's advice. He is drawing inspiration from antiquity and following on from Lycurgus and Plato. And, to sum it up, he has certainly obtained his baccalaureate" (page 193).

Bastiat's thesis is that when the state controls the narrative on education, it will inevitably lead to socialism because compliance with the state is necessary for funding. The state dictates what is taught because funding is provided by the state. The state promotes the state. In other words, you don't bite the hand that feeds you, and the state doesn't work against itself. Plato's Utopia was the ideal for a society with a working class, a ruling class, and a military class. This philosophy is like communism. It works in a classroom, but it just doesn't work on the street, the home, the Church, or in industry. It is an ideal that man has pursued, but is in direct conflict with sin and human nature, therefore, is always doomed from the start. No one can point to a socialist society that ever functioned as these atheist idealists hoped.

Rousseau (1712-1778) was a prolific writer who had an enormous contribution to the Age of Enlightenment pre and post the French Revolution, and the intellectual foundation for France and Western Civilization. Radical political philosophers like Rousseau soften the beachhead for soon to arrive political tyrants.

All who majored in history and the liberal arts know Rousseau's thinking, and his adverse foundational flaws have impacted philosophical thought that has rippled into classrooms to this day. We ended up here in this modern day dystopia because of men like him.

The liberal, the progressive, the ungodly, and the unbeliever have an agenda to:

1. Eliminate Christianity and see Christianity not as the solution, but the problem;
2. This is the old age humanistic solution that dates back when Satan said, *"I will*

not serve" (Jeremiah 2:20) and deny the influence and the reality Satan exists, thus denying sin;

3. It is not neutral towards God, it is anti God, they deny God exists, and do not want His presence in the market square;
4. Denies the belief in Original Sin;
5. Doesn't understand a utopia cannot work because of the horrible potential of sinful human nature, and wants the State to provide it;
6. Is not personally committed to sacrifice or self donation, and wants the State and others to do what they won't because of laziness and selfishness;
7. Desires the collective of Marxism, socialism, and communism, but once achieved, it becomes totalitarian and severely oppressive to dissenters and previous supporters;
8. It is all about diversity if you are on their agenda and platform. If you dissent from them, you are a bigot and intolerant, and in a short amount of time, a political enemy of the state;
9. They are unbelievers looking to take as much as they can, and contributing as little as possible;
10. They wish to piggy-back on the labor of others so they can promote equality, but do less work themselves;
11. They deny the reality of Scripture and the supremacy of an all loving God, but reject that it has been sin that alienates man from God (Isaiah 59:2);
12. It is a humanist manifesto at its finest;
13. It is a reactionary remedy that is not sustainable, and breeds class warfare and violence;
14. Programs are invented that are illogical and have no sustainability in the short or long term.

Bastiat said:

Everyone wants to live at the expense of the state. They forget that the state wants to live at the expense of everyone.

Government is a great fiction, through which everybody endeavors to live at the expense of everyone else.

When goods do not cross borders, soldiers will.

Writers note: This implies it is fair trade. The USA has not had fair trade with China and other nations due to corrupt U.S. politicians being played for greedy fools by foreign governments gaming the system working towards a world body for governance. Thus this group deliberately weakened America. All the while they prospered personally at the expense of the American worker.

JESUS I TRUST IN YOU

Keeping Focus on the Essentials

There are instances in Scripture where a story in the Gospels really stands out above all the rest. These stories are often referred to in literature, jokes, folklore and metaphors. One of these stories is the one when Jesus walked on water in Matthew 14. We know that Jesus has a Divine and human nature, but I have always had a hard time fully distinguishing His human nature from His Divine nature. The fact is that no person in all of history ever walked on water, turned water into wine, reproduced a few loaves and fishes to feed over 10,000 people, then as was prophesied thousands of years in advance, and rose from the dead. Our faith that Jesus instilled in us has elements of both the tangible and intangible as exemplified by the deep spirituality of the Sacraments. As much as we have a sacramental faith, we also have a very mystical faith.

Perfect loves casts out all fear. As we watch the turbulent seas batter people about from shore to shore, our safety lies in keeping our eyes on Jesus. Sticking to the fundamentals and rubrics of the faith will ensure our families safe passage. It is in these things we find comfort, peace, and solace, as storms swirl around us. The Twin Pillars of the Eucharist and the Blessed Mother from St. John Bosco's vision of safety for the Church in all ages, are as relevant today as they were centuries ago — now even more so.

How people will cope in our culture when business is no longer as usual will be interesting to watch in the coming years. The issues ripping apart families, education, communities, and churches are legion. Tempers are short and tolerance for differing opinions is shorter due to the extreme ideological divide. Everything with people is usually fine when they are flush with cash. But when that ends it will get ugly fast. Historical examples of this fact are many. We have seen a steady erosion of faith in the last generation and it is accelerating. What exactly will be that event will be to launch us into further chaos to and completely unravel is unknown. There is no shortage of possibilities. Where it will come from and what it will be is anyone's guess. As someone said years ago, *"Driving after a New Year's Eve party is always a risk, there is a problem out there you just don't know what direction it's coming from."*

In light of all the uncertainty, people need to have a plan for their family. The average American spends more time planning a vacation than planning financially for retirement. People also spend far more time on the entertainment and sports craze than in formation of their faith. I have heard many times that families don't have the time for spiritual instruction of their children. However, I am amazed as I watch little Johnny and Mary dedicating dozens of hours per week for every form of entertainment and sports under the sun, then being dropped off at ball fields and Tae Kwon Do facilities on Sunday mornings. The fact is that people don't see the spiritual formation of their children as something important. Yet, when the little tyke gets in trouble later on in life, the parent wonders how it happened. Even worse, without a foundation of faith in Jesus nurtured by the parents, how will that tyke once grown respond to the crisis that will inevitably arise? We reap what we sow. Many parents focus on everything but the most important; Eternal Life.

Matthew 14 is the story of Jesus walking on the water. I cannot think of any other figure in world history where multiple people witnessed someone walking on water. It was a night with turbulent seas, and Jesus was walking on the water towards the apostles boat. At first the apostles said, *"It is a ghost,"* but then they realized it was not a ghost, but Jesus. To quell their fear, Jesus said, *"Take heart; it is I, have no fear"* (14:26-27). Fear in such circumstances would have been a normal reaction. Even the Blessed Mother, at the appearance of an angel telling her the future role she would assume, was also humanly startled. The angel then said, *"Fear not, for you have found favor with God"* (Luke 1:30).

While in the boat, Peter was then summoned by Jesus to, *"Come."* Peter then boldly stepped out in faith and walked on the water to Jesus. When Peter *"Saw the wind, he was afraid and began to sink."* Only when Peter's focus was on Jesus did he do the miraculous. When the fear of the unknown gripped Peter, he took his eyes off Jesus, and he began to sink. Now even more so in turbulent times, we need to focus on only the most important — the words of Jesus.

JESUS I TRUST IN YOU

What Does It Mean to Fight for Your Faith?

"It is better that scandals arise than the truth be suppressed."

Pope Saint Gregory the Great (Pope from 590-604)

Many people say you have to fight for your faith. One person will say that we need more acceptance of homosexuality while another will say that we need to go back to the Traditional Latin Mass. One person dislikes one approach, but then another says that a still different approach will be better. It goes on and on. That leaves the faithful with a really significant issue. How are we to conduct our lives in relative tranquility and peace in tumultuous times? What exactly does it mean to fight for your faith?

Nancy Pelosi (D-CA) as Speaker of the U.S. House of Representatives believes that she is fighting for her beliefs which in many instances are not in keeping with her Catholic faith, and for which she remains unapologetic. During her tenure in the House, Pelosi was a good friend and advocate of liberal Jesuit Father Robert Drinan (D-MA), a representative from Massachusetts from 1971 to 1981, when Pope John Paul II demanded he resign that political office. Drinan was well educated, with an LL.B degree from Georgetown University Law Center and an LL.M from Gregorian University. Prior to serving in Congress he was dean of the Boston College Law School from 1956 until 1970. During his time in Congress, he espoused a variety of positions contrary to the Catholic faith, including the support of abortion and other ungodly causes. Somehow he managed to reconcile these positions while all the time in his view remaining a Catholic in good standing. Another politician who has managed to reconcile the irreconcilable is former Vice President Joseph Biden. He has similarly promoted abortion on the one hand while at the same time claiming he is a Catholic in good standing, no doubt pandering to the Catholic vote.

Many politicians are prone to cherry pick and cite Scripture verses to justify the chasm between their political views and the Catholic faith that they claim to espouse. But politicians are not the only Catholics who are living a duplicitous and inconsistent life of faith. There are millions of Catholics who call themselves believers who fall into this category. They have absolutely no problem promoting homosexuality, transgender, abortion, euthanasia and a host of other societal issues while believing thy are faithful to the Church. It may be that they were never properly catechized or more liable, and are simply obstinate. While for most of us it is incomprehensible to twist the Gospel to allow a mother to kill her child in the womb, others have managed to justify such sinful conduct on the basis of purported rights or situation ethics. There is not much that needs to be explained about the *"thou shall not kill"* prohibition in the Fifth Commandment. For that matter, the other nine Commandments are equally clear.

We are at the point where members of opposing parties can barely be in the same room any longer, so people are retreating to peaceful and harmonious relationships along ideological lines. Even the divisions among families and friends based on these cornerstone issues are increasing, and becoming more virulent. In the past two presidential elections the only group that voted more liberal than liberal Catholics were atheists. Dissent will always be with us, but with the divide increasing so dramatically, what does a person who desires to adhere to an authentic orthodox view of Roman Catholic theology do, when the general tide of the culture war is virulently attacking their belief system?

People have always had different ethnicities, education, personal preferences, work environments, neighborhoods, employment, gifts, views, sport likings, family dynamics and such. Yet, for centuries the Church operated with *relative tranquility* (these words were chosen carefully) at the state and ecclesial level. There wasn't as much for the laity to disagree about and generally the laity tended to walk more in unison with the Church hierarchy and follow the moral teachings of the faith. When Nixon debated Kennedy many views of both men were similar if not identical, with minor nuances. The extremes on both sides were fringe elements. This leaves the believer wondering how they are to conduct their affairs today in a hostile environment in a Church where many clergy and lay folks have veered terribly off course from long accepted magisterial truth.

Jesus said, *"My people hear My voice and obey."* Yet what voice are we really hearing?

The vast chasm between opposing sides on a host of moral issues begs the question. Are we hearing the voice of Christ or our own? Both sides cannot be correct. Truth is truth. Here too is a conundrum as those who dissent from the Church's teaching believe they are somehow on God's side as they pursue their own truth. Someone must be wrong. As Jesus said, *"Straight and narrow is the path and few find it."*

I remember once hearing in 1975 the radical political activists Angela Davis and Eldridge Cleaver on the same night saying, *"If you don't like it, throw a bomb at it."* Conversely, Jesus said, *"My ways are not your ways,"* and *"My kingdom is not of this world."* Violence begets violence. Amidst the confusion, believers and their families are making decisions consciously or subconsciously on how to proceed with a moral belief system that is conducive to practical and viable solutions consistent with what they believe to be true.

Be the Solution

Those critical of what they see happening need to provide an alternative to the moral slide. Rather than throw rocks at the problem, be the solution and fill the void. Many Roman Catholics will do nothing, others will blithely sit in the pews discussing current events and what is wrong, while others will just leave the Church rather than take a strong stand and fight for the Truth. Some leave the Church because they have chosen to live in a manner that is against the Church's teachings. They may go to another Church where Christ's teachings are watered down and compromised. More recently those who are leaving the Church do so in disgust and moral outrage given the wave after wave of Church sex scandals and the lack of attention and inaction on the part of the Bishops who for far too long were hoping that these problems just go away.

Saint Catherine of Siena, was a 14th Century laywoman, mystic and Doctor of the Church. In her famous Dialogue, the Lord told her about the priests' responsibility. *"O dearest daughter! Those miserable persons about whom I speak to you have no consideration for themselves. If they had, they wouldn't fall into so many vices, but would live like virtuous persons, who prefer death rather than offend Me, staining their soul or belittling the dignity to which I have raised them, but on the contrary, they increase their souls' dignity and beauty... But these spoiled persons, completely deprived of light, calmly pass from vice to vice, until they fall in the pit. They have turned the temple of their soul and holy Church, which is a garden, into a stable of animals.... O wretched man, to what a level you have dropped! What you are to hunt are souls for the glory and praise of My Name and be in the garden of the Holy Church, and not to go hunting through the woods. But you have become a beast; within you have the sins of many mortal sins...Your soul is full of weeds, and thorns, since you have acquired a liking for barren land seeking wild beasts."*

While the Lord continues in the *Dialogue* chastising unworthy priests who have been derelict in their duties as consecrated souls because they are more culpable than others on account of their vows and who they represent. He has never recommended that we leave the Church. On the contrary, He Himself has given to Saint Catherine a solution as to the age old problem of unworthy clergy: to fight within the Church to uphold truth. The Lord told St. Catherine that the priest who has abdicated his responsibilities before God and man is in grave error, but due to his role, he can do things no one else can. Our Lord said it was the treasure the priest brings that is most important — *The Eucharist. "The sacramental mystery cannot be lessened or divided by their sinfulness. Therefore your reverence for them should never fail — not for their own sake, but because of the treasure of the blood."* (Dialogue 118). This does not mean that the laity should accept the conduct of bad priests, but those who would seek to leave must understand that leaving the Church will leave a bigger void as the Church is the glue that holds culture together.

Martin Luther realized that the Catholic Church was corrupt, but opted to bolt and create his own set of beliefs. By contrast, a host of saints have sought to reform the Church, including Ignatius of Loyola, Saint Francis of Assisi, Catherine of Siena, and countless others who unabashedly from within proclaimed the truth to unworthy clergy. They sought reform while keeping the integrity of the Petrine Keys and magisterial truth intact. We are thus witnessing chaos today precisely because we have readily accepted evil and have abandoned God. Many of us are no longer speaking the truth given to us freely in Scripture and Tradition and make no excuses for not doing so.

Liberals are better at fighting for their views because they have historically had more passion for change no matter how illogical or immoral their positions may be. When you reject God, anything is possible. It is for this reason that liberals have made more progress in reshaping the Church over the last several generations than the faithful have made in attempting to keep Scripture and magisterial teachings upheld as the dominant truth. How can we start to turn this around?

Several practical solutions can be implemented:

We are in our present situation because we have had a lack of formation in the faith. A proper grounding in the faith should include Scripture, Tradition, the *Catechism of the Catholic Church* and key Church documents and encyclicals, rather than a watered-down broad-brushed approach that stresses social justice. First and foremost, the most necessary thing for us to do is read and teach Scripture as the foundation of the faith. The Lord gave us Scripture. A Bible-based program is the most critical beginning step. We can attend an existing Bible study, or if there isn't one available, we can start one. It is that simple, and profound at the same time. We know what we know (outside of private revelation) about Jesus Christ through Scripture. Scripture is the Eternal Word of God. We also need to learn how to properly interpret Scripture in light of Church teaching. Get a good Catholic study Bible with notes, or find a Catholic website online to guide a Scriptural study grounded in Catholic traditional teaching.

Gather in small groups to encourage one another. Where two or three gather the Lord is in the midst of those in prayer. The Lord does not work often with large numbers. Much to the contrary, He works with small numbers. The groups can be in the form of prayer groups or a gathering of like-minded people so that each family can see it is not alone. We can have gatherings in our homes, serving some food, praying together and conducting other activities that will greet people where they are emotionally and spiritually. People will always show up for a free meal. We can simply put in a DVD of some sort of educational tool with a wide appeal that sparks dialogue. There is no shortage of good movies that can provoke discussion. It can be a form of a tithe to put out some food before or after an event in our homes. Putting the food out last is a good way to go.

People are looking for leadership, so each of us can be the person who provides an alternative. Leaders change the narrative and the dialogue. Long-term isolation and inactivity can easily lead into depression or despair. It is easy for people to get into a state of woe to me, feeling that they are alone, as if they are the only righteous person around. Elijah thought the same and the Lord reminded him that there were seven thousand people around him who had not bowed their knee to Baal (I Kings 19:18). As the Church moves incrementally towards insolvency with false doctrines being taught, and scandals proliferating, the problems for the faithful will increase — especially young families needing fellowship and community. We need to begin seeing our home and community of believers as a domestic Church. Teaching of the faith is paramount to sustain a healthy and productive life. Taking a leadership role to provide more of a community approach is necessary while still maintaining a Catholic Magisterial identity.

The remnant is tiny and will shrink again as many are just walking away from the Church rather than thinking through the ramifications of the corruption they see in the clergy scandals. Since we are sinful people, the entire history of the Church shows that scandals are the norm rather than the exception — in all denominations. The Roman Catholic Church doesn't have a monopoly on sinful clergy and its members. Recently the press has been exposing extensive sexual abuse by Boy Scout leaders spanning several decades. The Church is centralized and large, so it is easier to observe her faults. Heresies have always been taught by the hierarchy, and they will continue to be taught by them.

We need to be careful not to fall into spiritual pride and this includes thinking that our particular type of ministry or spirituality is the best or better than others. If we talk to someone in prison ministry or working with the homeless, that person may be inclined to think that everyone should be doing as they do. Saint Paul dealt with this issue when one person thought his version of ministry was more important than another. He said, *"The eye cannot say to the hand I don't need you. And the head to the feet I have no need of you"* (I Cor. 12:21). The parts of the body need one another to be complete and fulfill the needs of the mystical body of Christ. If we doubt this, we have never broken a thumb to see how many things we can't do with one little thumb in a cast. We can often determine the level of maturity of individuals by observing what they choose to argue about. We need to support one another rather than taking digs at people because they do something differently than you do. The Gospel means **The Good News.** People have different gifts and the person not having your precise vision and gift must be respected as long as error is not being taught.

We need to start to contribute rather than to criticize what someone else is saying or doing. It is easy to be critical of the status quo without being a leader providing alternatives. Saints are made in hardship and crisis. The history of Christianity is about overcoming injustice and sin. There has always been a battle in the Heavens between the cohort of God and the cohort of Satan. It is a daily battle. The believer is fighting against sin. People are attracted to holiness even if they don't understand it. People are more attracted to a kind and harmonious spirit than one of contention. If people feel safe, they tend to return. The battle will be won by prayer and holiness of action. Prayer must precede action. Be a healer in gatherings, bring in a soothing balm while upholding truth, not division.

The only limit to change is our lack of imagination. There is a way to everyone's heart and soul. We need to ask the Holy Spirit how to reach those who have been away from God. The acorn does not grow to be an oak tree overnight, nor do people change quickly. The longer someone is away from the Gospel, the Scriptures and the Sacraments, the longer it will take him or her to live a life in Christ.

"It is better to light a candle than curse the darkness."

JESUS I TRUST IN YOU

The General and the Cardinal

Solomon, as the wisest man who ever lived said, *"Nothing is new under the sun"* (Eccles. 1:9). The more things change, the more things stay the same. The only guarantee for all of time is that change is inevitable. As things change in politics, economies, culture, technology, borders, nation states, the human condition, medicine and in every social index imaginable, the people of God need to be reminded that they were given a promise by Jesus Himself for the governance and endurance of His Church. Jesus specifically said that, *"The gates of Hell would not prevail against it"* (Matt. 16:18). This statement has stood the test of time in light of all the things that have changed in our midst over two thousand years.

Places, names, and circumstances may change over centuries and millennia, but events today are eerily similar to our past whether we know it, or like to admit it. The French Revolution of 1789 and its ramifications of change and beyond is arguably the single greatest event to cause a sea change of philosophical, political, and economic disruption since the formation of tribal lands and fiefdoms under the strong domineering leadership of Charlemagne in the beginning of ninth century. Charlemagne is known today as the Father of Europe, but one which the Holy Roman Emperor would have never imagined.

As we look around today, we see a world on the cusp of the annihilation of nations, something the Blessed Mother predicted in 1917 at Fatima would occur if her requests were not carried out. Mechanical engineering tells us the more the moving parts, the greater the complexity. We are now living in a world of enormous change and complexity with an unknown future. We see it all around us. We feel it, and we see it on the faces of our neighbors, friends, and colleagues if we look hard enough. Confusion, anger, uncertainty, and fear are apparent on hearts and minds. For some, it is anxiety and despondency bordering on despair.

If the Church had only been a human institution, it would have collapsed long ago. After the French Revolution ushered in the power and supremacy of Napoleon Bonaparte, the General said to Cardinal Ercole Consalvi, *"I will destroy your Church."* The Cardinal as the leading architect of Rome adapting to a new world said, *"If in 1,800 years we clergy have failed to destroy the Church, do you really think you will be able to do it?"*

As in generations before us, the Church has its ebbs and flows, good days and bad days, good years and bad years, bright days and dark days. We have had little wars and big wars. We have seen times of an abundance of heroic virtue, and at other times corruption and vice as we look at the dissolution of the past morphing into a new structure. And yet the Church has survived. There has been a surfeit of grace even when man has turned his back on God. We have seen the Church endure the Protestant Reformation 500 years ago, the Aztec human sacrifice that Our Lady of Guadalupe in 1531 turned on its head with millions shortly embracing the faith, and the victory at the Battle of Lepanto in 1571 due to a rosary campaign that saved modern day Europe and the western world from being overtaken by Islam.

What the future is remains to be seen. No matter the change, we have the promise of Jesus that the Church and thus our faith will endure. It may get tough as it has in countless times in civilizations that have preceded us, but the Church will come out whole and healthy in the end. A tree needs to be pruned on occasion for its continued health. It is nature's way. Although Mother Church is severely wounded with internal anarchy, it will come out a bright shining star no matter the circumstances. That has been her history, that will be her destiny.

As Solomon said, *"Nothing is new under the sun"*, and Jesus said. *"Nothing will prevail against the Church,"* — that is our promise.

JESUS I TRUST IN YOU

Saints Who Raised the Dead

With more bizarre happenings in our culture, we must remember that Heaven is in control. The Scriptures are clear that *"Jesus Christ is the same yesterday, today, and forever"* (Heb. 13:8). The world and our surroundings may change, but Jesus Christ never changes. His law is everlasting no matter the circumstances.

When we look at the life of Jesus, we see signs, wonders, and the miraculous following Him. Wherever Jesus walked, we see miracles that no one has ever done in the history of the world. His first miracle changed water to wine. We look at His life, and see miracles like Lazarus being raised from the dead, Mary Magdalene and Zacchaeus witnessing a complete transformation in their lives, Jesus walking on water, healings, prophecy, words of wisdom, words of knowledge, and the miraculous climax when Jesus Himself was raised from the dead. Throughout Christendom, many unique people have left themselves open to the will of God, we see the same. Is our time any different? The answer is no, if you are looking in the right places.

The fastest growing expression of the spiritual in America right now is various forms of the occult. There is the soft side of the occult like Ouija Boards and the hard-core side like animal sacrifice to human sacrifice. There is a lot of room in between those forms of extremes where people dabble and then get involved more heavily into the occult. Once involved, it is a like a cancer that devours its victims. The youth have been attracted to mediums and spiritualists through books like *Harry Potter,* largely because they have not witnessed life-changing principles in the Christian faith.

Trying to appease the youth with a light message the equivalent of sugar water has had the opposite impact. People have decided to leave the faith because they don't see the supernatural power of the Gospel of Jesus Christ. People want to be challenged, and they don't find that in many Churches where truth is watered down. Therefore, people leave and our Churches are empty. Just watching a young child's excitement of the biblical supernatural and the mystical will make one a believer. Heaven has placed this gift in our hearts, but the world in its cynical intellect rips faith from our spirit.

The writers of Scripture are clear that Jesus performed miracles. We see just several passages where many more could be provided.

> *"...And a great crowd of people followed Him because they saw the signs He had performed by healing the sick."*

John 6:2.

> *"God also testified to it by signs, wonders and various miracles, and by gifts of the Holy Spirit distributed according to His will."*

Heb. 2:4

"The signs of a true apostle were performed among you with all perseverance, by signs and wonders and miracles."

2 Cor. 12:12

"Everyone kept feeling a sense of awe; and many wonders and signs were taking place through the apostles."

Acts 2:43

"Why should it be thought a thing incredible, that God should raise the dead."

Acts 26:8

Jesus said, "Very truly I tell you, whoever believes in Me will do the works I have been doing, and they will do even greater things than these, because I am going to the Father" (John 14:12).

Jesus is saying that believers will come after Him who will do even greater works than He. We have had many people who have been declared saints who have raised people from the dead, and performed these signs and wonders that are spoken about in the New Testament. The problem is, these saints are seldom if ever spoken about from the pulpit; therefore few know about these people of all background and ethnicities. Supernatural events that promote and build faith are often concealed under a rock, and seldom if ever spoken about often because of fear of appearing simple minded in faith. If one were to sit and explain a complex doctrine, often it will be said, *"Wow, that person is brilliant."* Often that person will be the first to criticize the role of the supernatural.

Below are just several stories of hundreds that could be presented to illustrate the point.

Saint Ambrose (340-397) one of the four original Western Doctors of the Church raised a boy by the name of Pansopius from the dead.

Saint Patrick of Ireland (389-461). There is a lot more to Saint Patrick than parades and green beer. There is disagreement on whether he raised 33 or 39 from the dead. He raised people from the dead sometimes who had been dead for years. People who falsely accused him were often converted on the spot. One instance when he and his confreres were accused of stealing, they were sentenced to death. Saint Patrick raised the man from the dead, and the man clarified the case on exactly where the stolen goods were hidden, and several converted to the faith.

Another time falsely accused of killing a horse, he raised the horse from the dead and gave it back to its rightful owner. Over thirty years he consecrated 350 bishops, built 700 churches, and ordained 5,000 priests in Ireland. At the time of the Reformation, Ireland was largely untouched as other European nations, as Ireland sent thousands of religious as missionaries throughout the world over centuries due to its solid formation of its citizens in the faith.

Saint Malachy (1095-1148) of Ireland lamented he waited to long to give a woman the Last Rites, so he raised her from the dead to do it correctly.

St. Bernard of Clairvaux (1090-1153) raised a man from the dead so he could transform his life to one of virtue to the previous one of sin.

Saint Hyacinth of Poland (c 1185-1257) raised 50 dead people in Krakow, Poland alone. At his canonization it was declared that his miracles were *"almost countless,"* as he traveled an estimated 25,000 miles on much of it on foot evangelizing. He is called the Polish Saint Dominic as he established the Dominican Order in Poland.

Saint Anthony of Padua (1195-1231) was one of the greatest miracle workers of all time. He raised twelve people from the dead, with miracles attributed to him even after his death. His father in Portugal (St. Anthony was from Portugal, not Italy) was accused of murdering a man while Saint Anthony was living in Italy. St. Anthony bi-located to his father's trial, brought the murdered man into the court room, rose the dead man from his coffin, asked the man who killed him, the man pointed to a man not his father, and the man fell back dead. While the journey to Lisbon would have been several weeks or more by horse drawn cart each way, Saint Anthony was only gone from his monastery several days. Saint Anthony had one of the quickest routes to canonization lasting less than a year due to his numerous signs and wonders.

Saint Joan of Arc (1412-1431) raised a stillborn child from the dead so the baby could be baptized. At the age of 19 she became a martyr having transformed the geopolitical landscape of Europe.

Saint Teresa of Avila (1515-1582) of Spain is known as the Glory of Spain. She raised her six-year old nephew from the dead. She is a Doctor of the Church, in addition to being a great reformer of the Carmelite Order.

St. Catherine of Siena (1347-1380) raised her own mother from the dead. Her mother never took her faith seriously while alive, and Catherine prayed for her mother, and she returned to life. St. Catherine had the stigmata, and worked many miracles.

Saint Dominic (1170-1220), founder of the Order of Preachers (OP), or the Dominicans, raised three people from the dead. The Order sprouted wings throughout Europe and the world, producing some of the greatest saints in history.

Volumes are written on the daily occurrence of miracles in his life.

Saint Ignatius of Loyola (1491-1556) brought a man back to life.

Saint Philip Neri (1515-1595) raised a boy from the dead.

Saint John Bosco (1815-1888) raised two boys from the dead. The book on his dreams has become a classic. His vision is famous of the **Twin Pillars** of the Eucharist on a high column, and the Blessed Mother on a lesser size column, saving a ravaged Church symbolized by the Barque of Peter being tossed from stem to stern in the end days. His vision of the Twin Pillars provides **THE** answer to where we need to place our trust in these times.

St. Vincent Ferrer (1350-1419) is another unknown saint except in circles of Catholic scholarship. He is a giant in the Church of the dark Middle Ages when illiteracy was the norm, and illness could bring immediate death due to a lack of viable medicine. Miracles were used to convert the masses, and there are twenty-eight people that he raised from the dead, in stories so miraculous they illustrate what Jesus said, *"Greater works will you do than I."* Over 40,000 miracles are logged that are attributed to him.

He was in such demand as a man with the gift of healing, that St. Vincent had to be transported in an iron cage from town to town so he would not be crushed to death. He could walk through a town and people would just touch him and be healed. In his time, his faith manifested so many miracles, that many wondered if he was the *Angel of Judgment* written about in the Book of Revelation.

There are over 400 cases in the Church of saints raising the dead in all periods of time. The Church has elevated many to the level of saint because they were holy men and women who sought God first in their life. Tens of thousands more healings and miracles are not widely known because it is not the nature of saintly individuals wanting to bring attention to themselves. The Lord uses the miraculous to draw people to Himself. It is the Lord doing the healing, not the individual. The healer knows this because they are always speaking in the name of Jesus. To deny this power is to deny the authority of Jesus and His role of healing as an important part of His public ministry. But again, it is fear of what others may think that often prevent people from proclaiming the Gospel as Jesus commanded.

(The book *Raised From The Dead* by Father Albert Hebert, is the basis of this article).

JESUS I TRUST IN YOU

36

Out of Control—Again

The article below is a reprint that was written after the deadliest high shooting in U.S. history at Stoneman Douglas High School on February 14, 2018 in Parkland Florida. Parkland left 17 dead, surpassing even the 15 dead from Columbine. Still, few are addressing the root cause of these diabolical acts. Even most conservative media refuse to deal with the underlying reason for violence in our culture. There will be more like El Paso Texas and Dayton Ohio's in our future just as there was Parkland 18 months ago.

Since the original article was written, a group in the United Kingdom by the name of Yakult UK, conducted a poll (released August 5, 2019) and found 80% of people across all ages felt as if they were living without a purpose. A staggering 89% of youth from the ages 18-29 (Gen Z) felt as if their lives were meaningless and without purpose.

A t the moment, the issue of guns surfaces in many conversations with small or large groups of people. Just about everyone has an opinion and it is passionate. Those conversations will continue far into the future because another Nikolas Cruz (whose last name means Cross in Spanish) is on the near horizon. Whether or not the massacre of Parkland in Florida is a turning point in the debate is to be determined, but if history is our guide, it will be forgotten. What has amazed me is how the media on both sides of the issue are dealing with *"gun control"* in a very superficial manner. No one seems to be addressing the root causes of violence as the debate isn't bringing us any closer to actually solving the underlying problem.

Is anyone addressing the fact that of the 27 deadliest mass shooters in American history, 26 boys committing these crimes were raised since childhood without a biological father in the home? The single issue of a boy without a father in the home is the glaring statistic that no one is talking about in the mainstream media. Mass shooters share two common traits. 96.3 do not have a biological father in the home, and 100% are on some form of drug. Digging a little deeper one would find the kids are often into some form of the occult or worse, and believe man evolved from an ape (evolutionist). Boys and girls need fathers as much as they need mothers, as each parent has a beautiful and wonderful role ordained by God. To make matters worse, many liberals continue to push social policies removing the father from the home as an authority figure, and most often depict him as the bumbling village idiot on film.

Many speak of more security in schools, more scrutiny of who gets a gun, what constitutes mental illness, age limits, size of the clip, bullets per second, bump stocks, easy access to guns, the interpretation of the Constitution, gun free zones, what comprises liberty and freedom, and so forth. The way the Constitution is written and interpreted by many people, there will be no easy or peaceful compromise.

I am not sure that Jesus would be on CNN or Fox News addressing the gun debate. When He walked the earth He addressed the state of our souls in the light of Divine Truth. The roots of violence that we see in our streets and schools are to be found first in our hearts. Saint Teresa of Calcutta was often quoted saying that *"If there is violence in the womb, there will be violence in the streets."* Saint John Paul II said on many occasions *"A nation that kills its own children is a nation without hope."*

The solutions being bandied about in the gun debate are just ointment on the existing wound of our sinful culture. They are not treating the root cause of the problem. I have heard some say in conversations that going to the root of the issue will no longer work due to diversity and other civil concerns. If that is the case, there is no solution to the violence and dysfunction in the culture from just about anyone in the media, so why not try the obvious one that is **THE ANSWER**. If a person has cancer, it cannot be cordially coaxed out, it must be driven out. Will it take more blood in the schools and streets, so that people will demand that God be welcomed back in the classroom?

Maybe concerned educators and citizens should start demanding the ONLY way to stop this carnage which is for faith to be restored in the classroom. Several years ago I saw a story where a warden in a men's prison provided every single prisoner with a Father's Day card and a stamp. Not one prisoner sent the card.

Until we start to address the following we will not get to the root cause of gun violence.

1. The billions of hours people (not just kids anymore) spend playing violent video games originally designed for military use in combat situations;
2. All forms of psychiatric drugs kids are ingesting at alarming rates;
3. Music lyrics that are outright violent and sexual;
4. A culture of violence on TV and all forms of media breeding a lack of compassion;
5. A desensitization of youth to human pain and suffering;
6. The proliferation of pornography on the internet available to a young child;
7. Homes with no fathers;
8. Homes with a mentally, emotionally, or physically absent father and/or mother, where rarely a family meal is shared;
9. Multiple billions (there are a thousand million in a billon) of hours which youth have played banal, and time sapping video games (where they are now in their mid to late 30's doing the same thing they did as teenagers);
10. Addictive behavior such as pornography, drugs, alcohol, and incessant media habits that rewire a person's neural pathways;
11. A total lack of spiritual formation and instead pursuing immediate gratification. (If there is any spiritual formation, it is often so ill-formed teaching it makes no sense to them in their soul);
12. Parents taking their child's side in disciplinary issues at school;
13. Removal from public education of any moral or philosophical compass to society that has been beneficial to mankind for millennia;
14. Absent parents. (The day where a school board gets more calls than any day in the year is when school is cancelled due to snow. Why? Because it disrupts a parents work schedule. Teachers have become baby sitters as much as they are educators and they know it);
15. Teachers who have quit disciplining students because often higher administration will support the parents so the schools won't have to deal with hassles and potential lawsuits;
16. Many youth who see no purpose in their lives, and they lack family connectedness;
17. An LGBTQ carnal and sinful culture proliferating like a spring rose in a life without boundaries, and kids without a grounded moral structure;
18. Silence from the vast number of pulpits in America of all faiths and denominations on sin and its consequences or outright rejection of biblical and Christian thought;
19. The virulent diabolical agenda to remove God from the public square.

Guns are not the problem — a lack of values in our culture is the problem. The people who use guns as a weapon incorrectly are the problem. Until a value-based education is restored, we will see a great deal more violence because two generations of people haven't had any Christian spirituality or formation in their lives.

Spiritual things have been stripped from thought and action in our culture. The name Nikolas Cruz of Parkland doesn't matter because just like him there are tens of millions of these wounded lost souls walking the hallways today, albeit not many as violent as Cruz. The name Cruz is not important because the shooters in these heinous crimes share nearly identical emotional and psychological profiles. Cruz as others to come has the profile of PURE RAGE against the system because they cannot find meaning in their life. After the killing spree he was so casual that he sauntered to the local McDonald's and had a hamburger. This young man has been so desensitized to God's love and a plan for his life as God intended, that he is void of human emotion other than hate and rage, and a complete blank slate spiritually.

What these people have not received is love at home. They are acting out in anger, irrespective of all income brackets and social strata throughout the land. These people are screaming to be noticed at any cost and are desperately in search for a purpose for living. Prayers are desperately needed for our homes. Invite God back into our homes and schools, and the country will heal itself. It will take a great deal more blood to bring about change from our present spiritual neglect.

JESUS I TRUST IN YOU

What Tribe are You From?

In the Old Testament there were twelve tribes with direct lineage to Abraham, Isaac, and Jacob. Lineage was very important to the ancient Hebrews as it was a way of immediate identification through affiliation to one's ancestral tribe. This thinking continued into the New Testament, in which it was important to show that Jesus was descended from David through Saint Joseph.

The twelve tribes given to the Jews by the Lord were: Asher, Benjamin, Dan, Gad, Issachar, Joseph, Judah, Levi, Naphtali, Reuben, Simeon, and Zebulun. Before the patriarch Jacob died (Genesis 25:19-26), he prophetically foretold the destiny of each of his sons and the role each one would assume for millennia. The Lord had His hand on His chosen people from the beginning. Jacob imparted his blessing to each of his sons, for the specific charism each would bring to the Jewish people and the progeny of the race.

Each tribe had a specific gift or duty in Jewish culture that was important for self-governance, cultural advancement, administration and function. In the Old Testament there is a lot to read about the Levites. The Levites from the tribe of Levi were the priestly class. Reference to other tribes is more obscure, just like in a similar way there is more information in the New Testament about Peter, James, John, and

Paul than Nathaniel and Bartholomew. Probably hundreds of thousands of books throughout history have been written on the Jewish people mentioning the twelve tribes. During the 400 year Egyptian captivity of the Jewish people, much of the lineage was lost through slavery under the Pharaohs.

In the Old Testament the tribe of Issachar lived in near obscurity, with only one verse dedicated to it in the First Book of Chronicles. It says, *"Of Issachar men who had understanding of the times, to know what Israel ought to do, two hundred chiefs, and all their kinsmen under their command"* (1 Chron. 12:32). Issachar was one of the smallest tribes, yet it was the most spiritually, intellectually, and historically sensitive to what was happening in that era. King David surrounded himself with the tribe of Issachar because they **understood the times in which they lived.**

David was specifically given the throne by the Lord who removed King Saul, *"and when he had removed him, he raised up David to be their king; of whom he testified and said, I have found in David the son of Jesse a man after my heart, who will do all my will"* (Acts 13:22). There is no allegory or metaphor here. The Lord specifically anointed David as King because he would do the will of God. Here is King David being placed on the throne of Israel through a special anointing by the Lord, yet David sought guidance from this small obscure group of people with similar characteristics of believers throughout the ages.

Today, the modern day version of the tribe of Issachar are people who walk in our midst in relative obscurity as they have done for thousands of years. Yet these faithful people are the very glue of society. Remove these people and the world would descend into chaos in a fortnight. They are not the high and mighty in lofty positions, but the army of God walking the streets this very day being faithful.

They are the people in Eucharistic Adoration praying for the welfare of the country, those serving the poor selflessly, ministers bringing communion to the sick, catechists and teachers, and those who fast and do corporal works of mercy often on a daily basis. It includes those who take people into their homes, tithe, pray in secret, and so on. These are people devoted to the Blessed Mother. Many in this group are aware of the coming Warning and Miracle of Garabandal. They journey and make pilgrimages to Marian Shrines asking for grace and for the intercession of the Blessed Mother for intentions of loved ones who have lost their way. They are in cenacles of all kinds; they have introduced the writings of Saint Faustina and the wisdom of Divine Mercy to their parishes; and as a group they are fighting the tide of filth in our culture by trying to provide an alternative according to Scriptural principles. This group reads the lives of the saints for inspiration and they do a host of unknown things that no one sees but the Lord.

This group is the modern day version of the Tribe of Issachar and they know the signs of the times because they hear God's voice and obey it. They are God's chosen people — the remnant. Fidelity and obedience to God's law is their main focus. With that comes wisdom and guidance.

So this raises a question. Which tribe are you from?

JESUS I TRUST IN YOU

Is All Well, or Not Well?
What Rules You—Fear or Faith?

Have you ever noticed some people speak faith and others declare doubt? Have you ever seen some people continually have an attitude and speech of *"Woe is me,"* while others always seem joyful and live abundantly? There are two spiritual forces in the world, God and Satan. When we speak doubt we give authority to Satan. The opposite of doubt is faith. There are only two types of spiritual energy, doubt and faith. We speak what we dwell upon, and we either release doubt or faith — there is nothing in between. We release spiritual energy in one direction or the other. Out of the abundance of the heart, the mouth speaks.

Jesus was clear in the Gospels that if we have faith as big as the grain of a mustard seed we can move mountains. Where there is faith, the Lord can heal. If there is doubt and lack of faith, miracles will not happen. The French have a saying, *"Miracles happen to those who believe in them."*

There are many places in Scripture where we see faith operational, but few are as spectacular as the story of Elisha and the Shunammite woman in 2 Kings 4:1-37. Elisha was a disciple of Elijah, and Elijah's mantle has now fallen on Elisha as a member of the *"company of prophets"* who was granted the anointing of Elijah. It is a profound story of faith and works.

There is a woman who once had means and has fallen on hard times. Her husband was also a member of *"the company of prophets,"* and they are childless. When Elisha passed through her town, she and her husband would offer hospitality with a spare room and provisions to Elisha, and his servant Gehazi. She tells her husband, *"Look, I am sure the man who is constantly passing our way must be a holy man of God"* (10). Elisha is appreciative of their help and asks what he can now do for her. Elisha instinctively knows without her saying it that she wants a child. She responds, *"No, my lord, O man of God, do not lie to your servant."* Elisha then says, *"This time next year you will hold a son in your arms"* (15,16).

The son was indeed born and growing. One day in the fields he has some sort of a head ailment with no explanation of the trauma. The sick son is carried to the mother by a servant, and by midday the son is dead. The Shunammite woman (mother) retreats to the bedroom where Elisha used to stay and briefly laments the death of her son. She then boldly tells a servant to saddle a donkey and she and her servant go to see Elisha. She instructs the servant, *"Lead on, go, do not draw rein until I give the order"* (24,25).

As she meets Elisha's servant Gehazi, he asks her, *"Are you well? Is your husband well? Is your child well?"* (26,27). She answers, **"Yes, all is well"** (26). Here is a woman who is promised a son, conceived a son and felt as if she has been deceived by Elisha as the child has now been taken away from her for a reason she doesn't understand. She has traveled some distance on a donkey to meet Elisha face to face. Elisha tells

Gehazi, *"She has bitterness in her soul,"* and in essence she is so angry she is reading Elisha the Shunammitess version of a riot act saying, *"Did I ask my Lord for a son? Did I not say do not deceive me?"* (28). She feels she has been lied to by Elisha — and she is distraught. It would be a normal human emotion.

Elisha and Gehazi travel to the home where the dead boy lay. *"He went and shut the door on the two of them and prayed to the Lord. Then he climbs onto the bed with the boy, and stretches himself on top of the child, putting his mouth on his mouth, his eyes to his eyes, and his hands on his hands, and as he lowered himself onto him, the child's flesh grew warm. Then he got up and walked to and fro inside the house, and then climbed onto the bed again, and lowered himself onto the child seven times in all: then the child sneezed and opened his eyes. When she came to him, he said, take up your son. She went in and falling at his feet, bowed down to the ground; and taking up her son went out"* (31-37).

The story continues with the fidelity of Elisha to her family. In 2 Kings 8:1-6, Elisha tells the woman *"to move away because a famine is coming to the land for seven years."* She moves away, and the famine came and *"her family was spared."* She then had to *"lodge a claim of ownership of the house and land with the king upon her return."* The king upon hearing the story of the woman of Shunem was so impressed *"he restored the land to her, and all the revenue from her land from the day she left the country until now."* God is faithful to His servants beyond their expectations.

This by all accounts is one of the great stories of Scripture. Elisha was a disciple of Elijah and received the double portion of Elijah's blessing, as he too was a member of *"the company of prophets."* In the book of Acts, St. Paul raised a young boy by the name of Eutychus from the dead after he fell out of a three story window. The boy had dozed off because St. Paul delivered a teaching that *"went on and on speaking all night."* The boy was restored to life by St. Paul much in the same way Elisha raised the boy of Shunem to life by *"clasping him to his body"* (Acts 20:9-10).

The lessons of the Patriarchs of the Bible are eternal and they are for today and those who believe. They apply today as they did then as *"Jesus Christ is the same yesterday, today, and forever"* (Hebrews 13:8). Times for many are difficult and we will have to rely on faith that the Lord will prevail. If we remain faithful to the Lord, the Lord will remain faithful to us. The rules of faith haven't changed from the days of Elisha to today. If we have the faith the size of a mustard seed, we can say to that mountain be cast into the sea. But, do you speak faith or doubt?

The anxiety and pain in the world are palpable. People know in their gut a spark from any direction can cause a world-wide conflagration that can alter our way of life in an instant. When the Shunammite woman was asked by the servant of Elisha in the presence of her dead son, *"Is all well?,"* she answered, **"Yes — All is well."** There are very few people who would have the faith to give such an answer emotionally dealing with a dead child. However, we must realize the Lord is in control — He sees all and He knows all. Fear is the chief activator of our faults. Everything passes through the Lord's permissive Will. In the midst of a crisis we need to maintain the internal fortitude of the Shunammite woman and abide in faith.

According to your faith so be it unto you. We all could get a stronger dose of faith from the woman with no name from Shunem.

Yes, all is well.

JESUS I TRUST IN YOU

God + 1 = A Majority

"I can do all things through Christ who is in me."

Phil. 4:13

No matter where the believer goes today, they feel under spiritual assault. Name the venue and one finds a constant barrage of the carnal and ungodly. Whether it be in a film, the shore, the mall, or for that matter a walk on the local school grounds. There is a bombardment to our senses just about everywhere. Is this a recent phenomena, or is this a repeat of civilizations in the past? Is this a normal cycle of history, or is it more intense on our watch at this moment in time?

Jesus Himself dealt with this on a daily basis. It is difficult to find anyone with influence that came to the aid of Jesus in His hour of need. The Scriptures show that Jesus had a special relationship with Lazarus who in turn had influence with the Romans, but not enough to save Jesus from the cross. Joseph of Arimathea provided a burial site for Jesus, but nothing else is known about him. Nicodemus, a Pharisee and a member of the Sanhedrin, only visited Jesus under the cover of night for fear of what others may think of his stature in the community — the most common hindrance of why the Gospel is not preached with authority. It was the "anawim," or God's little people who sought Him because they had nowhere else to turn for truth and sustenance. As St. Paul said, *"Not many wise, not many noble inherit the Kingdom of God..."* (1 Cor. 1:26-29).

When we feel outnumbered, an inspiring story to read is the story of Gideon in Judges 6-8. It is an entertaining story for adults and children alike. While Gideon was out working in the fields, an angel spoke to him and said he would save the nation of Israel (6:4). Gideon responds humbly and tells God that he is from a poor family. At the same time he speaks boldly asking if God was on Israel's side, where is He now that the Midianites are looking to destroy their land? He asks if God has abandoned His people. God in turn was asking Gideon to lead the people into battle and save Israel.

The first thing the Lord asked Gideon to do was to overthrow the altar to Baal. Baal historically represented all the false pagan idols of Israel. He did so at night with ten men so no one would know it was him who did it. He is found out the next morning and God's chosen people are angry that Gideon has destroyed their altar. But Joash, Gideon's father, intercedes for him and counsels the people to let Baal contend for himself if he is a god.

Proving his obedience, Gideon next is told to build an army. Gideon had to be sure it was the Lord speaking to him, so he asks for a sheepskin (fleece) to be wet from dew, and the ground dry. The fleece is soaked sending a strong signal grace. Still not satisfied, he asks for something as bold for the next evening. He asks that the fleece be dry, and the ground wet. The Lord gives him the signs he asked for to go into battle.

The issue is now past an intellectual concept of the words of an angel, and moving to actuality. An inevitable battle is on the horizon and he knows it. He is now satisfied as the signs are so great. As a learned man in the ways of the Lord, Gideon knew the Lord could accomplish what He wanted.

Here is the lesson for those of us reeling from the weight of the onslaught of our culture. The Lord will prevail if He can find someone who will do His will, no matter the circumstances in front of them. Gideon assembled an army of 32,000 men. The Lord told him it was too many, and he had to thin the ranks. God instructed Gideon to tell the men that those who were fearful to go into battle could leave with no negative repercussions for their future welfare. The Lord was making it clear that the battle would be won on His terms. Twenty two thousand decided to go home, and 10,00 remained (Judges 7:2).

The Lord then told Gideon that these men should go down to the river and he should watch his men drink. Of the 10,000 men who went to drink, all but 300 knelt down and drank with their faces in the water unaware of their surroundings drinking without the wisdom of a warrior, watching for potential peril from the Midianite army of 135,000 around them (Judges 8:7). The Lord said that those 300 shall be your army. Gideon now had 300 men from the initial 32,000.

The Lord told Gideon to go into the camp of the enemy and listen. Gideon and a servant heard a soldier tell of his dream that a great barley loaf came into the camp and flattened a tent. Another soldier interpreted the dream that Israel would win. Gideon returned excited to tell his men that the Lord was going to perform a miracle through them. The Lord in His sequential pattern was telling them in advance that they would win the battle. The Lord dealt with them as he does with us by patiently sending us graces if we are willing to listen. Fear prevents us from moving in faith.

Gideon instructed his men to approach the enemy with trumpets, pitchers, and lamps, and to make as much noise as possible. The men were told not to engage the enemy and stand their ground. The noise created confusion and fear among the Midianites, and they turned on themselves in battle. Gideon won the battle and returned home to the Israelites a hero. The people wanted to make him king, and he refused, acknowledging it was the Lord who led his people. As a result of the events, the Israelites lived in peace and worshipped the Lord and not Baal for the next 40 years (Judges 8:28).

The above story is not like many others in scripture that are often allegory or metaphor. The story is clear that the Lord wanted to show Gideon and the Israelites that

He will win the wars if we do as He asks. Obedience is the key to victory in spite of all odds. God used a single man for His glory in spite of such enormous odds and peculiar circumstances. It was the Lord alone who won — not the pride of any man to declare victory.

In the fight for independence from England approximately 3% of the people from the young ill equipped, and financially strapped colonies were committed to the birth of a nation. They prevailed through hardship. In the American Civil War it was also approximately 3% committed to the ideals of the north under Lincoln. They prevailed through hardship. The key concepts history shows us is that a small group of **COMMITTED** people can do amazing things under the banner of the Lord, and accomplish what He asks.

The Lord tells us, *"The harvest is plentiful, but the laborers are few"* (Luke 10:2). People prefer to pontificate rather than get their hands dirty and join the battle. There are more arm-chair quarterbacks critiquing the game than participating. The believer most often is the philosopher at coffee shops and bars rather than actually rolling up their sleeves and out in the field hospital of broken humanity. Few are willing to till that ground; but more people give opinions, than workers toiling in the field for souls in need. It is easier and less costly to let someone else with faith to go forward and do the work. It was the obedience of Gideon that gave him faith to proceed as asked. The Lord will often provide a fleece if the decision is a major one to provide assurances to sustain us. These signal graces are embedded in our soul to go forward.

"Little children, you are from God and have overcome them,
for He who is in you, is greater than he who is in the world."

1 John 4:4

JESUS I TRUST IN YOU

The Power of One

On September 19, 2016, four Cardinals, Joachim Meisner (Germany), Carlo Caffarra (Italy), Walter Brandmüller (Germany) and an American, Raymond Burke, issued a formal request to Pope Francis asking that he clarify the language on several moral matters. That request is known as the *Dubia*. These four Cardinals alleged that Pope Francis had consistently used vague language on the interpretation of doctrine and Scripture, and asked Pope Francis for clarification. Among the Church documents that the Cardinals found to be unclear in its text and interpretation was the post-synodal apostolic exhortation, *Amoris Laetitia,* released by Pope Francis on April 8, 2016.

Two of the original *Dubia* signatories have since died, Cardinal Meisner and Cardinal Caffarra. This, coupled with silence from Rome on the matter, has made the *Dubia* and its signatories irrelevant. In 2016 Cardinal Burke was quoted as saying, *"But it is true that, for classical commentators, a Pope who departs from his office in dogmatic questions, that is to say, who is guilty of heresy ceases to be the Pope, automatically."*

On January 4, 2019 Brandmüller also said, *"It is statistically proven that there is a connection between homosexuality and sexual abuse. Society at large is being hypocritical in its condemnation of sexual abuse by priests. What has happened in the Church is nothing other than what is happening in society as a whole. The Church has failed to distinguish itself from the rest of society."* Brandmüller insisted that *"the sodomitic filth"* today is similar to the Church in the 11th and 12th century. Brandmüller has often referred to Saint Peter Damien who in 1049 delivered an address to the newly elected zealous reformer Pope Leo IX, which was an appeal to save the Church from the *"sodomitic filth that insinuates itself like a cancer in the ecclesial order, or rather like a blood thirsty beast through the flock of Christ."* Brandmüller also said that *"the homosexual crisis among clergy is almost epidemic."*

We can see that Brandmüller was correct, and how members of the Church hierarchy are complicit. On January 13, 2019, Cardinal Vincent Nichols of England on January 13, 2019 celebrated his second pro LGBT Mass honoring homosexual Catholics, parents, and families. On January 16, 2019, Pro Ecclesia Swiss, a lay group, launched a world-wide petition campaign asking the bishops to stop homosexual networks in the Church. This is a Church and world in crisis. One must remember the words of Saint Louis de Montfort who said that in the end days it would be the laity that would save the Church.

What should we expect moving forward from authority figures in the Church? In times of crisis should we expect the bishops to lead the people? Will we see moral courage? If history is our guide, there may be a few bishops who speak out, but don't look for large numbers to be bold. Bishops by and large ascend to the title by being fairly "vanilla," meaning that they don't tend to go to one extreme or the other so no one gets offended. The Japanese have a saying about business that I think applies to bishops, *"The nail that sticks out the furthest gets hammered in first."* This mentality breeds conformity rather than courage. One goes along to get along. One also gets along, to go along.

One historical case of supreme importance that took place nearly 500 years ago and altered European history to this day. King Henry VIII of England, who at one point was referred to by Rome as the Defender of the Faith. However, in time he placed his love life, lust and kingly ambitions over God. King Henry had married his first wife Catherine of Aragon with the Church's blessing. When he was unable to conceive a male heir to the throne with Catherine, he determined to marry another woman by the name of Anne Boleyn. To marry Anne Boleyn, Henry first needed to annul his marriage to Catherine. He then went to his Chancellor, Cardinal Thomas

Wolsey, the leading Catholic figure in England at this time. When Lord Chancellor Wolsey failed to secure the desired annulment, Henry had him arrested for treason and appointed Sir Thomas More as Lord Chancellor.

When the requested annulment still failed to materialize, King Henry simply took matters into his own hands and married Anne Boleyn in 1533, followed by the Queen's coronation, which Sir Thomas More did not attend. Since the King did not obtain permission from the Church of Rome, Henry then made himself the new Supreme Leader of the Church of England. Henry persisted and continually asked More for his approval to annul his marriage to Catherine. More refused. As a result, More was stripped of all authority as Chancellor of England, lost all of his property, saw the dissolution of his family that was relegated to poverty, and was thrown into the Tower of London. In July of 1535 More was decapitated, and his head was displayed on a spike on London Bridge. Like Joan of Arc, More's trial was a sham, and both trials were held by leading clergy pronouncing sentence with enormous pressure from the state. In the end, Henry married a total of six times and altered the social and religious fabric of nations to this day. You don't need to look much further than Northern Ireland to see the roots of religious division over the last five centuries.

ONLY ONE bishop in all of England stood by the side of Sir Thomas More and that was the Bishop of Rochester, John Fisher. Two weeks before More's death, he too suffered the same fate as More with his head ending up also being displayed on a spike on London Bridge. Henry had also repeatedly sought the intercession of Fisher with Rome on securing an annulment from his marriage to Catherine of Aragon, and once secured, to marry Anne Boleyn. Fisher never capitulated on magisterial truth, upholding the teachings of Scripture as to the indissolubility of marriage. The purpose of placing the heads of decapitated individuals on a spike for popular view was as a strong inducement for the English to comply with what Henry demanded. Again, **ONLY ONE** bishop in all of the British Isles was willing to speak truth to power — Bishop John Fisher. Both Fisher and More were declared saints in the Church by Pope Pius XI in 1935.

To have Catholic clergy in England comply with his wishes, he was prone to promise the largesse of the treasury, land, title, prestige, entitlements, and easy careers, if only they would capitulate to state demands. It has been a long practice of sovereigns not unique to any generation. Although the Catholic Church in England survived, albeit with the blood of many martyrs, discrimination against Catholics, tacit or otherwise remains. Now 93 years old, Queen Elizabeth II of England had never stepped foot in a Catholic Church on Irish soil until 2012. Her reign as Queen of England and the Commonwealth began in1952. Old habits and traditions die hard if it concerns the preservation of wealth and land. The king or queen of England is required to subscribe to the Church of England.

An equally disturbing example in our modern era was Germany under Nazi rule. When Hitler's evil politics became manifest, few leading clergy members spoke out. Some, but not many, spoke from the pulpit about the horror of Hitler's genocide, beginning with all of its social experimentation. Most clergy pledged allegiance to

Hitler under the banner of National Socialism early on, not understanding where their false fidelity to a temporal power would lead. Germany had suffered greatly from World War I, and the ensuing economic destitution of the Weimar Republic brought it to its knees. Once Germany had a leader with a vision, the people latched on and took bread over truth. The more things change, the more they stay the same.

Today

There are approximately 70.4 million registered Catholics in the United States. This represents about 22% of the U.S. population. What percent regularly or infrequently attend church, or just attend Mass on Christmas or Easter is not the point here. There are 32 Territorial Archdioceses with 145 Territorial Dioceses under U.S. jurisdiction. Comprising this vast stretch of land are about 300 (plus or minus) archbishops, bishops, retired, military, auxiliary or emeritus, still holding the title of bishop. How many bishops can you count on in the United States to provide clarity on magisterial truth as it concerns our great social issues of the day? Worldwide? The answer seems to be not many.

So this begs the question. If there are so few bishops in comparison to the general population of Catholics, why is it that America's favorite past time is to criticize the bishops (often valid) when the people do so little to remedy the situation in the Church? The ratio of Catholics to bishops with the above scenario is about 235,000 laity to **ONE**. Yes, we know some bishops and clergy have done horrible things and criticism is often justified, but it is the role of the laity now to build the believers from the ground up. Many bishops are either compromised or just unwilling to be vocal. This is an historical fact. For every one person looking to remedy the ills of our culture, there may be thousands of lay people using social media talking about the scandals rather than actually doing something constructive to bring a remedy to the Church.

Henry VIII drained all of the Catholic Church's resources throughout England and rendered it penniless amidst persecution. The beautiful abbeys scattered throughout the British Isles in his time were then bequeathed to the wealthy for fidelity to state loyalties. The Tree at Tyburn in London can attest to that. Ever seen Downton Abbey on television? If so, you saw the majesty of the estate and environs. There were hundreds like it scattered throughout the British Isles, because for hundreds of years they had been monastic centers of learning and propagation of the faith. With the Reformation and Henry's lustful pride, the landscape of Europe was altered as the Commonwealth eventually spread to India, Australia, Canada, and other locales. Pope Pius XI said of More:

*When he saw the doctrines of the Church were gravely endangered, he knew how to despise resolutely the flattery of human respect, how to resist, in accordance with his duty, the supreme head of the state when there were question of things commanded by God and the Church.... It was for these motives that he was imprisoned, nor could the tears of his wife and children make him swerve from the path of truth and virtue. **In that terrible hour of trial, he raised his eyes to Heaven, and proved himself a bright example of Christian fortitude.**

Saints Thomas More and John Fisher and others like them paved the way to the future for us. It could be argued that Thomas More changed English history more than any other man, much in the same way Joan of Arc did in France. Burned at the stake for speaking the truth as God gave it to her, Joan of Arc is now the Patron Saint of France. Winston Churchill called her the greatest figure in French history. They are models for truth in action.

JESUS I TRUST IN YOU

To the Seven Churches of the World

I n Chapters 2 and 3 of the Book of Revelation, Saint John the Evangelist, Jesus' beloved disciple, was writing in exile on the Isle of Patmos in Greece. During his time in an open-air prison, with the angels being John's source of inspiration, came the Book of Revelation. Revelation as a book in Scripture is considered alluring, symbolic, allegorical, eschatological, futuristic, bewildering, and confusing all wrapped up into one.

One thing throughout the ages that has remained a constant is the fact many serious Biblical scholars disagree on the topics addressed in Revelation and what its twenty-two chapters mean. Conformity of thinking is not the norm across the Christian world, especially as to symbolism. Even its very name is a source of contention among different Christian denominations. Some call it the Book of Revelation, others call it The Apocalypse, while others call it The Revelation to John. But not all of it is a mystery. Certain things are abundantly clear.

The angel told St. John, *"Now write what you see; what is and what is to take place hereafter. As for the mystery of the seven stars which you saw in my right hand; and the seven golden lampstands, the seven stars are the angels of the seven Churches, and the seven lampstands are the seven Churches"* (Rev. 1:19-20).

Chapter 2 of Revelation begins where the angel reveals to John what the future Churches of the world will look like in characteristics and attributes through the ages all the way to our modern era. There are a total of seven Churches addressed by city. They are: Ephesus, Smyrna, Pergamum, Thyatira, Sardis, Philadelphia, and Laodicea.

If one were to look at this another way, each city has a "spirit" that more or less defines it. When one thinks of New Orleans we may think of a carnal Mardi Gras filled with flesh and Cajun cuisine in a large port city. New York City is a liberal financial center while Washington, D.C. is a political power. Los Angeles and San Francisco are both lust and sex capitals. Some towns in the Midwest are still called Mayberry, and so forth. To each of the seven Churches in Revelation, Our Lord had something very encouraging to say, while to six of the seven Churches He also had something negative to say. The angel dictated:

To the Church of Ephesus, *"You have been patient and bearing for My name's sake... but you have left your first love."*

To Smyrna, *"I know your tribulation and your poverty.... Do not fear what you are about to suffer... The devil is about to throw some of you into prison... He who conquers shall not be hurt by the second death."*

To Pergamum, *"But I have a few things against you. You have some there who hold the teachings of Balaam... Repent then... To him who conquers I will give some of the hidden manna..."*

To Thyatira, *"I know your works, your love, your faith, service and patient endurance, and that your latter works exceed the first... But I have this against you, that you tolerate the woman Jezebel, who calls herself a prophetess and is teaching and beguiling My servants to practice immorality..."*

To Sardis, *"I know your works; you have the name of being alive, and you are dead. Awake and strengthen what remains for I have not found your works perfect... He who conquers shall be clad in white garments..."*

To Philadelphia, *"The words of the holy one, the true one, who has the key of David, who opens and no one shall shut, and shuts and no one opens... learn that I have loved you... I will keep you from the hour of trial which is coming on the whole world..."* The Lord has nothing against the Church that loves until the end. There is nothing negative said about this Church. It has endured the trials and maintained fidelity to the commandment of the New Covenant — Love.

To Laodicea, *"I know your works: you are neither hot nor cold... You are lukewarm... I will spew you out of my mouth...For you say I am rich, I have prospered and I need nothing.... For those I love, I reprove and chasten so be zealous and repent..."*

Each of those cited brief statements are part of a much longer narrative in Chapters 2 and 3. Several things are clear. All Churches have their tribulations. All the Churches fall short in some capacity except the Church of Philadelphia, as it is the sole Church that endures to the end loving God. It did not succumb to the wiles, whims, and false doctrine of the day while its ears were being tickled by the fancy of the age. Each Church in the age has its challenges, but an encouraging word is always given to those that do not falter.

These Churches have contemporaneous spirits throughout history. There has always been child sacrifice, suffering, the worship and pursuit of pleasure and wealth in its many forms, witchcraft, drugs/stimulants, immorality, loss of faith, the pursuit of the new while abandoning the old, false mysticism, the occult, deceivers and a sterile intellectualism, just like there were in those Seven Churches. The more things change, the more they stay the same.

Yet over the centuries God has raised up His saints — the overcomers. Among these are Saints Vincent Ferrer who worked thousands of miracles, Faustina, Anthony of Padua, Dominic, Francis, Clare, Padre Pio, Teresa, Therese, and a litany of others who fought the false doctrine of the age. God raises up His own to combat the evil of the age.

When one looks at the confusion of today, do we really see anything that has not been seen before? Revelation was written two thousand years ago and it is as relevant today as it was then. Human nature remains a constant. There is a theme that is consistent in all of the messages to the Seven Churches. First, it is imperative to remain steadfast to the end in spite of obstacles. Second, the remnant must remain faithful to obtain the eternal prize. Third, the devil is always active and is out to destroy Heaven's plan for mankind as the evil one's agenda is to *kill, destroy, and steal.* (John 10:10)

As King Solomon said one thousand years before Saint John was penning his Book on the island of Patmos, *"What has been will be again, what has been done will be again; there is nothing new under the sun"* (Ecclesiastes 1:9-10). Jesus tells us the gates of Hell will not prevail against His Church. Every generation has its trials, and at present we already have a *de facto* schism. We must endure as those before us did.

JESUS I TRUST IN YOU

The Blessing & Cursing of a Nation

The concept of an angry God based upon the readings in the Old Testament is not an original thought. For millennia laymen and theologians alike have debated the concept of a God who punishes people for their sins. Some have difficulty reconciling the loving and merciful God of the New Testament with His divine justice. The fact is that sin has had and continues to have profound consequences. Sinful man is the one who prompts God's justice. While God indeed is a loving God and loves the sinner, He is also a just God. God does not impose Himself on man's free will. When the sinner becomes obstinate and refuses God's love and mercy, he opens the door to God's justice. That justice can be meted during the sinner's lifetime or in the hereafter in the fires of Hell that so many believe is a fanciful dated concept.

At Fatima, Sister Lucia told the world the Blessed Mother said to her that *"War is a punishment for sins of mankind."* On another occasion Lucia was told that *"People were falling into Hell like snowflakes for sins of the flesh."* In a world of unhealthy political correctness that lacks the backbone and conviction of unvarnished truth, this Heavenly advice has fallen on the deaf ears. Many mired in sin prefer to ignore these stern warnings and focus instead on a watered down and sanitized version of God's love as if sin had no consequences.

God is a God of love and because He is God He can do no evil. He does not gratuitously punish. However, He is a God of justice (Is 61:8). It is humanity by its sinful conduct that invites God's justice to be exercised here on earth or in the hereafter. The sinful man has given the devil room to maneuver, to gain a stronghold, foothold, or toehold in his or her life. Sin is a separation from God and a refusal to do His will. Isaiah wrote that, *"it has been your sin that has separated you from God"* (59:2).

Obedience is a condition for God's blessings. God will still love us unconditionally even when we sin. He will never abandon us and is ready to accept the repentant sinner. However, we cannot expect for God's blessings to continue to flow when we have been obstinate in turning our backs to Him and His law.

Is America Under God's Judgment?

Jesus said, *"I did not come to abolish the law or the prophets, but to fulfill them."* (Matt. 5:17). Many people today are asking the question whether America is under God's judgment. Has His protective hedge been removed because of the sins of the nation? If God blesses a nation because of its virtue, is there a curse due to sin? Is there a consequence of sin that manifests itself in the welfare of a nation? Are there long-term repercussions for a nation that doesn't just allow abortion and homosexuality and other incalculable immoralities, but governmentally sponsors programs that actually promote these immoral acts? Moreover, in many ways our government is cooperating and funding with evil such as the public funding of abortion, which is an abomination in itself.

Chapter 28 of the Book of Deuteronomy presents a haunting dilemma on just this issue of a merciful yet a just God. It is a long Chapter with a total of sixty-nine verses. In its first two verses we read how the Lord gives a condition for blessings. *"But if you obey the voice of the Lord your God faithfully, keeping and observing all those commandments of His that I enjoin on you today, the Lord your God will set you high above all the nations of the earth. All the blessings that follow shall come with you and overtake you if only you obey the voice of the Lord your God."* While this was intended when written to apply to the people of Israel, it equally applies to us, the people of God.

Man has a convenient propensity to confound clear writing and twist scriptural passages to their personal interpretation and agenda. However, in the referenced verse there is little room needed for interpretation. Blessings are bestowed upon God's people when they are faithful to His statutes and commands.

Blessings Are Given

The first fourteen verses of Chapter 28 relate to the blessings given to God's people. *"You will be blessed in the town and the country, your children, your family, your livestock, your cattle, your flock, your soil, your bread, your comings and goings; with conquering your enemies, and with blessings for your barns and your undertakings, and on all your land I have given you... with a great store of things, opening the Heavens of His rich treasure; with seasonable rain for your land, and the fruit of the produce of your soil, and with all the work of your hands; ...with nations as your subjects and not serving other nations, bless all the work of your hands, not serving any other gods..."* and so forth. The blessings are very general and cover the broad spectrum of prosperous living under the protection and mantle of God.

However, beginning with verse fifteen there is a shift which describes blessings as being conditional on obedience. ***"But if my people do not obey the voice of the Lord your God nor keep and observe all those commandments and statues of His that I enjoin on you today, then all the curses that follow shall come up with you and overtake you."*** The IF THEN clause was given to the people of Israel time and time again, and the very issue of obedience to the Lord is a common theme for blessings. IF my people do this, THEN...

Curses

For the next fifty-four verses, until the end of the Chapter, dwell on how sin destroys the individual, the family, the culture, and the whole of society, and the destruction described is very specific. *"There will be droughts, blight, rain, fire, illness; enemies besieging you and foreigners taking over your land, invading, and taking delight to bring you to ruin;... no rest for the sole of your foot;... destruction, sons and daughters handed over to other people, destruction, no fruit from your soil nor for your offspring;... wars, famine, pestilence, disease;... strangers living among you taking over;... no respect for the old and pity for the young;... enemies will besiege you, plagues on your descendants, disease,"* as well as other curses rather than blessings. These passages provide us with just a small sample of the specific manner in which the Lord breaks a stiff-necked people.

If volume of text is an indication of the Lord trying to underscore a point, then the lengths to which God goes in describing the curses reflects its importance. There is four times the volume of text for curses compared to blessings in Deuteronomy. The curses are the stick rather than the carrot for the people to return to God.

Those who are intellectually honest will admit that the blessings on this country have eroded over the last generation. Is sin a factor? We can decide for ourselves based on facts and observation. *"The grass withers and the flower fades, but the Word of God endures forever"* (Isaiah 40:8). The fact is that the U.S. can no longer count on past blessings as if these somehow will continue forever despite the fact that with each passing year the nation drifts further from God. Blessings are being lost and we cannot presume that these will be restored if we remain adamant in our sin. Do we need to live in ruin before we come to our senses? The earth itself is groaning due to sin.

In the past couple of years, natural disasters have increased at alarming rates. We have seen entire communities in the West gutted by fires. In late August of 2017, Hurricane Harvey shortly thereafter affected the Houston area and inland Texas, while shortly thereafter Hurricane Irma devastated areas of Florida from Key West to the Georgia border and Alabama. The economic cost of these two hurricanes is estimated at more than $350 billion. One sad statistic is that Houston, which is the fourth largest city in terms of population in the U.S., has the largest abortion mill in the entire world. Beyond the economic and physical toll that these phenomena of nature have wrought, is the emotional and psychological toll of those whose lives have been upended. The latter may take generations to heal.

On September 20, 2017, after first being hit by Hurricane Irma, the entire Commonwealth of Puerto Rico, an American territory was pummeled and devastated by Hurricane Maria, a Category 5 hurricane. In its aftermath, over 3000 people lost their lives, and it is estimated that the devastation was of such magnitude that for the island to fully recover it will take some $139 billion. People lived literally in the dark for month on end as the electric grid failed. The island of Puerto Rico was already bankrupt and the anticipated federal bailout will be astronomical.

Since Hurricane Andrew in 1994, America has spent well over $1.5 trillion on natural disasters and that number is climbing fast. The hurricanes are just the most visible event wreaking havoc on America. In 2019, the number of tornados in the middle and southern parts of the country was unprecedented. In a period of just six hours, 41 tornadoes touched down in portions of Alabama, Georgia, Florida and South Carolina. Massive flooding and torrential rains have devastated the nation's farmlands which will have repercussions in financial markets. Sin has consequences.

JESUS I TRUST IN YOU

The Coming Food Fight at the Thanksgiving Day Table

Division Among Families: Politics and the Church

No matter where one travels, there is a near constant conversation from Catholics and non-Catholics alike about Pope Francis. Since the white smoke went up the chimney of the Sistine Chapel and Francis walked onto the balcony overlooking St. Peter's Square on March 13, 2013 and the words 'Habemus Papam' (we have a pope) were uttered, opinions on his papacy are all over the spectrum. Now into his fourth year as leader of the Church holding the Petrine Keys, the long knives are out. Many who sat on the fence as a courtesy and deference to the Office are no longer silent. If they held their tongues and pens in the past it is no longer the case.

Pope Francis is a lightning rod to most who study what he says and does. No matter the political or spiritual persuasion, the sentiments are profound on the future direction of the Church under Francis. Pope Emeritus Benedict XVI recently said that *"the Church is on the verge of capsizing."*

Controversy surrounds Francis, and many orthodox Catholics cringe in pain every time he boards a plane and speaks extemporaneously to the press. Former

Vice President Al Gore jokingly said recently that he is thinking of becoming Catholic because the pontiff holds so many views dear to his heart.

The chasm in thinking is far and wide and diverse on nearly any subject among the faithful and non-faithful alike. To many people, Pope Francis is a train wreck in slow motion. Others view him as the new Messiah in the flesh finally saving the world from its many ills and the wrong direction of the Church under previous popes.

This division leaves a lot of potential for a massive food fight around the table when family is together. When people are of the same mind regarding grave and sensitive subjects, there is comfort in knowing others share their view. *Today, the veneer of civility has eroded at a dizzying pace and it is open warfare among many friends and colleagues on spiritual and political subjects.* Topics like President Trump and Pope Francis are bombs waiting to go off among groups of people.

That leaves one with a need to discern the future for one's peace of mind and soul. How should we navigate the turbulent waters that swirl around us as we watch families get ripped apart by the culture? The division inside many families is now virtually explosive on just about any subject brought up. Some preserve a modicum of civility by avoiding family gatherings.

The topics over which may prompt heated debate and entrenched views runs the full gamut of issues and include immigration, abortion, radical Islam, education, anxiety on the global interconnected economy, North Korea, LGBTQ, gender issues, global warming, the judiciary, government policy, health care and dozens of other issues where one pegs the other as progressive, socialist, Democrat, conservative, or Republican and so forth. With sides chosen, many people 'opt to divorce' themselves socially from those with differing opinions. Yes, the division is great.

More Troubles to Come

This divide is going to increase in the future, not decrease, especially in the family. Liturgical reform now on its way will be the deciding factor for many still on the fence. As of October 2017, each diocese can now decide with little fear of Rome's influence how to choose to interpret many aspects of the Church's teaching on Communion for the divorced and those living in homosexual unions. In one diocese, Father Friendly will agree to one interpretation, and in the next diocese there will be a different interpretation and implementation on the exact same issue. Much greater confusion is on its way. *Sister Lucia of Fatima said the final battle in the Church would be over marriage and family.*

In many ways we are staring at the real time disintegration of the United States in terms of governance and cultural norms. America is fighting for its very soul and the forces of Hell have been unleashed to destroy it. If America fails, many other parts of the world will fail as well. We are on the threshold of the wholesale destruction of a way of life and the fight will not go away any time soon.

Revolutions begin when the economy sours. When people lose hope and can't see a way forward to make a living and provide basic needs for their families, that's when it starts to get ugly. The French and Bolshevik Revolutions are just two examples of that — and both of those events irrevocably changed those nations to this day. The American Empire is over, but as a country America will remain. Although the United States may look now like a strong economy, normal economic history suggests corrections are the norm.

We Can No Longer Be Silent

The day of people being the turtle on a fence post doing and saying nothing needs to change fast. Heaven has been warning us time and again where our safety lies, yet those admonitions have largely been ignored. There is a price to pay for ignoring Heaven's requests.

Saint Robert Bellarmine, a Cardinal and Doctor of the Church who fought during the Counter Reformation summed it up best when he observed during times of error and confusion: *"... It is also lawful to resist the one who attacks souls or who disturbs civil order, or, above all, who attempts to destroy the Church. I say that it is lawful to resist him by not doing what he orders and preventing his will from being executed."*

In Message 192 (N-T) of the Marian Movement of Priests, the Blessed Mother said:

"Pray that you may never doubt the love of the Father, who always watches over you and provides for you, and makes use of suffering as a means of healing you from the sickness of corruption, of infidelity, of rebellion, of impurity, of atheism. I now ask you for more prayer. Multiply your cenacles of prayer. Multiply your rosaries, recited well and in union with me. Offer me also your suffering and your penance. I ask you for prayer and penance for the conversion of sinners, that even my most rebellious and most distant children may return to God, who awaits them with the merciful eagerness of a Father. And then, together we will form a great net of love that will envelop and save the whole world. Thus my motherly and supreme intervention can be extended everywhere, for the salvation of all who have gone astray."

Truth, if not spoken with love, is not love at all. Believers have an obligation to transcend the temporal to the eternal in conversations.

"A gentle answer turns away wrath."

Proverbs 15:1

Every Mass and hour of Adoration for the intended cause is worth one thousand conversations falling on deaf ears.

JESUS I TRUST IN YOU

The Cult of Softness: We Forgot God

"Refute falsehood, correct error, call to obedience — but do all with patience and with the intention, of teaching. The time is sure to come when, far from being content with sound teaching, people will be avid for the latest novelty, and collect themselves a whole series of teachers according to their own tastes; and then, instead of listening to the truths, they will turn to myths."

2 Tim. 4:2-4

The last several generations have produced profound sociological, financial, political, and religious changes in America. Societies and cultures evolve into what they become for many reasons. But the facts remain that the United States of America today is not the same country that previous generations experienced based on just about any social index you choose.

Social scientists analyze these phenomena that play out in all the classrooms of the U.S on a daily basis. Socrates taught that every generation thought that those coming up after them is on its way to Hell due to lax moral standards. Parents today can surely identify with that statement as they look at the state of their kids' schools and their neighborhoods.

Did the parents of the depression era think that their kids had become soft due to an easy lifestyle in the new USA after victory in World War II? With two chickens in every pot, a new Chevy in the driveway, and with good free public education, the basics were covered and less and less families had to really toil for the bread they ate. In the post-World War II era of prosperity, materialism won over spirituality. America started to drift away from God. The children and grandchildren of millions of impoverished immigrants found themselves on easy street due to the unrivaled dominance of America.

By the 1960s, the fabric of America began to fray at the edges. It was in that context that in 1969 some 400,000 youths ended up on a farm in upstate New York at a music festival called Woodstock to celebrate the *Aquarian Exposition* with free pot on every blanket. That festival epitomized the sexual revolution and all that came with it, including the pill that spread like wildfire during the decade of the late 60s, altering life in America forever. Along with the ease of living over a period of time came the insidious philosophy and lifestyle of relativism and utilitarianism that we have today. For many Americans, absolute truth is no longer to be found. Each person is free to make up his or her own.

Where did America go wrong? How did we ever end up where we are today? The generation that won World War II, as well as their parents, had experienced economic austerity during the Great Depression (1929-1939) as well as privation during the war. Many tasted death firsthand, with many fathers, husbands, brothers and sons, not returning from war. The returning GI wanted tranquility and a better way of life after 60 million deaths in all the theaters of war. Yet these were individuals who had been honed by necessity and grew with toughness and integrity taught by their parents. Very little nonsense was tolerated in the home, and the word respect was understood by all.

The Greatest Generation made the mistake of placing education over faith. Upon returning home after WWII, the G.I.s placed a big priority on getting an education for their children and elevating family stature. During that process, they stressed a relentless pursuit of education, while neglecting faith. Much of the nation's secular education was a prescription for a false freedom, where questioning was instilled rather than affirming the very Christian principles upon which the nation had been based and wars fought. Education became the new doctrine. Grades were the be all and end all, while Church and religious instruction slowly became a ritualistic formality for many. As many families prospered on account of education, there was less reliance on God and if anything, demand for yet more material goods and worldly success.

Here is when the greatness of a civilization ends. Forgetting God is the common denominator in the failure of a people, because Scripture is clear that it is the Lord who raises a nation up due to fidelity to Him, and it collapses due to sin against Him. To a humanist devoid of scriptural knowledge, it is an absurd thought as he or she merely looks at a cycle of history and not the root cause. It is the Lord who raises a nation up, and the sin of its people that brings a nation to its knees. It is the Lord alone who puts up a protective hedge around His faithful people and blesses them.

When we see *"safe spaces"* now in schools for students to retreat to rather than listen to opinions other than their own, we know we are in a new place. The slogan **Hate Has No Home Here** is another way of saying, *"I want an ungodly agenda and don't bring any thought other than my own into my space. Stay away from me if you disagree with my diversity opinions."* It is a political statement that includes a liberal platform. It emanates from a mentality whereby those who disagree with their entrenched views are considered hatemongers. They can have an opinion, but just don't express your view if it is contrary to theirs because they don't want to hear it.

After the election of Donald J. Trump to the presidency, schools all over America created safe environments for students. Cornell University passed out large three-inch metal diaper pins (few use them anymore) so students who came unglued with the trauma of it all could wear them outside their clothing for all to know they were to be left alone due to the election outcome. Stanford had a room where students could pet puppies — and so it went throughout the land. Mind you, these "prestigious" higher education institutions charge over $65,000 a year to attend. While their mission may be to ensure that their graduates can get a financial edge in life over other kids, the stark reality is that they may do so to the loss of their soul.

Many do not understand the word "sacrifice" or an absolute standard of truth. The youth generally lack a basic understanding of theology, philosophy, or true and honest history. Revisionist history is the norm in many school districts. Many kids today have a disdain for the military and lack an awareness of the cost of freedoms their grandparents fought for that enable them to protest their views.

Most in the past lived simply and ascetically out of necessity. Today's entitled generation wants all of its creature comforts and desired economic status now, without toiling to achieve these over time. Most live in a utopian fantasy ignorant of human nature, preferring to commune with the latest electronic gadget or App rather than interacting in person with other human beings, not the least their own family members. Because of their false expectations, many fall flat on their faces leading to further frustration. History has shown that bad economics can make brutes out of the best of people. Jesus was clear when he said that we will find our life when we lose it for others. *"Unless a grain of wheat falls to the ground and dies, it cannot bear fruit."* Love thy neighbor as thyself was another admonition. True joy and peace of soul is only attained when one has faith and applies that faith in serving others. This is in stark contrast to the "#MeToo" movement marching in the streets; it exemplifies the "self" mentality.

Some are enslaved by their own ego and avoid suffering at all costs, although suffering that is part of the human condition as a result of original sin can even be redemptive. The result is the soft cult of "snowflakes" who want to progress through the wide avenue rather than the narrow road, largely void of personal responsibility, and do not recognize the fallen state of man as the root cause of violence in the world. Moreover, they are ignorant of the fact that only a personal encounter with Christ is the solution to what ails them. The solution is not on what the state promises as they have been brainwashed to believe, but life in accordance with God's precepts. When one removes God from one's problems and solution, as well as from culture itself, anything goes and chaos ensues.

What makes this present time and generation somewhat unique is the religious hatred and distrust in God. Previous generations never had the ubiquitous tools for knowledge at their disposal as people do today. Previously, error could be the result of lack of catechesis. However, many in today's generation have made a conscious choice to hate God and His law. They are burdened by a variety of serious problems, yet look for solutions exclusively on their own and in all the wrong places. The Founding Fathers were clear in all of their writings that a democracy can only work when there is a Christian belief system. As a result of this disintegration, we are rapidly descending into chaos.

In March of 2018, Bishop Robert J. McManus of Worcester, MA called for Professor Tat-siong Beny Liew, the chair of New Testament Studies at the Jesuit College of the Holy Cross to disavow "highly offensive and blasphemous" articles in which the professor claimed that Jesus was a "drag king" and that the relationship between God the Father and Jesus was homosexual in nature. This garbage coming from a reputed Catholic college had brought academe to a new low. Obviously someone chose to employ the professor. Parents for their part pay dearly for their child's education, incurring no doubt hundreds of thousands of dollars in debt, to be treated to this kind of blasphemy. In today's world, if the college your son or daughter is considering is run by the Jesuits, BEWARE. There is a very good chance that the education your child will receive is off base as to magisterial Catholic teaching, and as we have seen much too often, morally offensive as well.

We have arrived at a new place in America, and the country of old is getting harder to recognize.

JESUS I TRUST IN YOU

Spiritual Resolutions

Few will disagree that 2018 was a wild year for the Catholic Church; Cardinals McCarrick and Wuerl, the Pennsylvania grand jury report, whistle blower Archbishop Carlo Vigano, Bishop Malone of Buffalo and 60 Minutes, and the doublespeak of many in the hierarchy confusing the laity and clergy alike. Many disruptions in the Church were unprecedented. For example, never before in the history of the Church have we seen the promotion of an LGBTQ rainbow and environmental rosary, promoted by a priest no less. The priest is Father James Martin, S.J., and the only thing you need to know about him, is that he is as far out there as anyone can imagine. The LGBT rainbow rosary reminds me of what Sister Lucia of Fatima said: the world would go through a period of *"diabolical disorientation."* It appears that not a single Jesuit has reprimanded him in print, and there are approximately 12,000 of them in the world. The Jesuits as a body of men need a Reformation. A renewal. Historically, as an order of men they have done great good, however, in the last several generations they have done serious harm and lost their way. There are some good ones to be sure, but not many remain. As an Order, they have excessively stressed social activism over personal holiness and the supremacy of Scripture.

In the bible story of the adulterous woman (John 8), Jesus came to the aid of a woman who was about to be stoned. Jesus said, *"He who is without sin, cast the first stone."* Then it says, *"The oldest among them dropped their rocks first."* The accusers left, and Jesus was left alone with the woman. Then Jesus says, *"I do not condemn you, but go and sin no more."* Jesus does not condemn, but He instructs us to go and sin no more. He did not say, *"Who am I to judge?"* We are not called to condemn either, but we are to put forth the strength and strong words of the Gospel without compromise. There are clearly times where the Word of God cannot be altered, and the acceptance of this behavior is not scripturally or morally acceptable. Theologians may fiddle with encyclicals, but no one can change the Word of God.

Sin has become normalized, and we have grown accustomed to it. There is a fear to speak out. Not being outraged by an LGBT rosary defies all sensibilities. Martin is promoting a sacrilegious rosary, and leading Church authorities refuse to reprimand or discipline him. We know things in life by their boundaries, and this is way out of bounds. So, the question is, what will it take for moral outrage? Father Martin has been a darling of the Vatican under Pope Francis, and was even scheduled to speak on matters of the family in Dublin, Ireland, until he was canceled in 2018. This fact alone should tell you where the leading hierarchy want to bring the Church. There is an overt agenda to normalize homosexual sin under the false guise of diversity and inclusiveness. Out of the tens of thousands of priests in the world to speak on family matters, Martin was a scheduled speaker in Dublin at a Vatican approved conference. Darkened intellects are perpetuating an agenda today much the same way as when Saint Paul spoke about the pagan Romans as **"being given over to depraved minds."** Moral civility is absent their thinking.

The Church sex abuse scandal is coming from the top. This scandal will steamroll in 2019 as the state Attorney Generals coordinate to file suits against the Church. As of today, 45 state AGs are working with the Attorney General of Pennsylvania to plan a path forward. When finished, it may include all 50 states, Guam, Puerto Rico, and American Samoa. Pastors can expect to see donations shrink like never before, as the laity and people are no longer buying the lies and cover-ups. They have had enough. Donations will dwindle worse than most think, affecting the entire spectrum of social services. It is the conservatives who donate to the Church, and the liberals to groups like Planned Parenthood.

The last week of December 2018, Cardinal Sean O'Malley of Boston reported Cardinal Timothy Dolan of New York to the Vatican after reading a story in the New York Times about abuse. The New York Times reported about a known sex abuse incident by a priest that Dolan had lauded — after knowing of the situation. O'Malley would have known of Dolan's conduct for years, but this gave him an excuse to turn Dolan into Rome. This event is probably also a first as it was done in public. One is reminded of the prophecy of Akita, Japan that spoke of this in the early 1970's when it was first prophesied, *"Cardinals opposing cardinals, bishops against bishops, priests against priests..."* 2019 will see more of this division, and it will be even more public and virulent as both sides dig in to promote their view of how they would like to see their ideology promoted.

The Deep State of the entrenched Vatican curia is a club of close interlocking relationships that, like the political arena, that have helped promote each others careers for generations. Again, if you think 2018 was disruptive, 2019 will be more so.

All of the above leaves us with the question, how to achieve peace of mind and peace of soul? How best to love our family, friends, and those around us? ? A few practical suggestions:

Less Screen Time

The amount of time spent on screens by all social classes is enormous, and growing. It is not hard to be in a public place and not see the majority of people staring at a screen. For the most part, news is repetitive, inane, banal, and a time sapper. If a person is totally absorbed with social media, it would be reasonable to say there is little time left for a spiritual life. If a person is experiencing a time of crisis in their life, a good counselor, psychologist, or psychiatrist will tell that individual to stop watching the news. The news is designed for shock value (ratings) and this is terribly disruptive to our spirits. People say they have no time for spiritual development, but they do have time for up to four hours of TV on weeknights, and more on the weekend. Spend more time in prayer and Eucharistic Adoration. Saint Mother Teresa of Calcutta often said her order grew when it started daily Adoration.

Carve Out a Portion of the Day for Quiet

A quiet time is where we hear God speaking to us; it is where we get our guidance for our activities. If a person is unable to get to daily Mass, waking up a little earlier to get direction in a quiet time is a good start. There is no growth without spiritual reading. The Bible is the Word of God. There is nothing else like it. There are many great authors in world history, but the words of Jesus are the way, the truth, and the light. Jesus never wrote a word, never traveled more than probably about 75 miles from his hometown, but He is the central figure in all world history. His words bother many because they are beauty and truth in stark contrast to a world of darkness and sin. The apostle John addresses this when he says, *"the reason the world does not know us..."* (I John 3:1-2, 21-24). The world hated Him before they hated you (John 15:16).

Stick to the Fundamentals of the Faith

We know the fundamentals of the faith the same way we know we are not to eat carbs and sugar if we want to be healthy. We just don't follow through on the spiritual enough. Spending time with God for spiritual growth in prayer, fasting, scripture study, fellowship, frequent Mass, and confession. Start reading one chapter a day of the New Testament, and in one year you will have read it all. Develop new habits. In times of stress, it is best to stick to the fundamentals. Near where I live there are four different forms of martial arts and self-defense in a contiguous office complex. They cater to all age groups, and they are busy from early morning until 10:00pm on week-nights with older groups. This is all well and good for self-image and child development when balanced, but the odds are there is little time or effort being spent on spiritual growth in their most formative years. It is a total disconnect to what is most important in the life of a child. If a balance is struck fine, but usually it is not. We find practical atheism around us all day.

Be Honest About the Faith

"Study to show thyself approved" (2 Timothy 2:15). Study the word in 2019 like you never studied it before. Read it as a love letter not an academic document. Apply it to your self and make it a way of life. It was the little people who followed Jesus because He spoke to their hearts. People are screaming in their hearts for the truth, but few know how to present it naturally on a level the unbeliever can understand or follow. Start by building a relationship with a person before spouting scripture passages they can't hear. Once they know you care about them, they will listen. The acorn doesn't grow to be an oak over night, nor does a person. Go slow, be patient, and love them as a friend.

JESUS I TRUST IN YOU

The Mystical Rose
The Significance of the 3 Swords and 3 Roses for Today

For the last several decades, we have witnessed the way the laity view the clergy much differently than in the past — and even more so in the last several years. The Blessed Mother has addressed her priest sons at many apparition sites throughout the world. Based on the significant decline in Church attendance and donations going into the Sunday basket, all is not well. People are voting with their wallets, and it is noticed in Chanceries throughout the Western world.

Our Lady of Good Success in Quito, Ecuador in the early Eighteenth Century said there would be a crisis of faith starting in the middle of the twentieth century. The apparitions of Akita, Japan in the early 1970's spoke of a serious rift among clergy having strong differences of opinion, and what doctrine is taught in the Church. Akita has come alive before our very eyes. The Blessed Mother said at Fatima that apostasy (loss of faith) would engulf the Church. The Church is in great turmoil and there is confusion amidst dense darkness. Attorney Generals (AGs) throughout the country are suing dioceses for sexual improprieties of clergy. The laity would be more forgiving of past transgressions if they saw *leading hierarchy* willing to deal with the issue. It should not be forgotten the overwhelming majority of clergy are outstanding individuals. Unfortunately, it only takes one rotten apple to spoil a bushel basket. In addition, Catholic clergy do not have a monopoly on abuse. It is widespread in every denomination, and nearly every profession.

One apparition has largely gone unnoticed where Heaven tells us that clergy need great prayer to sustain them in their mission to promote the Gospel and live in fidelity to the truth. It is the apparition of Mary the Mystical Rose (Rosa Mystica) of Montichiari, Italy. Montichiari means "clear mountains" in English. It was in Montichiari the Blessed Mother appeared to a humble and obscure woman by the name of Pierina Gilli over a twenty-year period beginning in 1947 to 1966. Pierina was born in the Brescia province of Italy (in the area of Lombardy) on August 3, 1911, and died at the age of 79 in the year 1991.

The young Pierina Gilli had many difficulties in her life. Her father was a contract daily farm worker who died when she was just seven years old. As the oldest of three children, she was then placed in an orphanage for four years. Due to the inability of her mother to support her, she was then hired out as a housekeeper to the blind mother of a friendly priest. Her mother remarried, and Pierina moved back into a home that now had a total of eight siblings. She said that her step-father had been inappropriate with her, however she remained silent to keep peace in the home. She only confided this to her mother years later. Nothing was easy for Pierina materially, financially, or relationally. It was a life of hardship from the very beginning that continued throughout her life.

Always keeping a diary, she developed a deep spirituality, and at 32 years old she entered the Consecrated Life in an order called the *Handmaids of Charity* in Montichiari. Accepted as a postulant she studied nursing, yet became very sick with an intestinal occlusion which precluded her from further study. On November 23, 1946, the mystical began to take over that altered her life forever. The Blessed Mother appeared to her and she wrote in her diary, *"Then I see the most beautiful Lady, as if transparent, dressed in purple with a white veil that descends from her head to her feet; she held her arms open, and I saw three swords piercing her heart."* The Blessed Mother did not speak. At different times it was the Blessed Mother and Blessed Sister Mary Crucified as former head of the *Handmaids of Charity* who appeared to her.

Several months later on March 12, 1947 she was admitted to the local hospital and nearly died of heart failure. In July of 1947 she had another vision of the Blessed Mother identical to the first with three swords piercing her Immaculate Heart. In her diary she wrote, "At 3:15 AM on June 1, 1947 the Madonna said only three words to her, **"Prayer, Sacrifice, Penance."**

In what is called the First Grand apparition, Pierina wrote in her diary, the Blessed Mother said, *"I am the Mother of Jesus and the Mother of all of you. Our Lord sends me to bring a new Marian devotion for all male and female institutes, religious orders, and secular priests. I promise those religious institutes, orders and secular priests who venerate me in this special way my special protection, and increase in spiritual vocations, few betrayed vocations, and great sanctity among the servants of God. I wish the 13th day of each month to be celebrated as the day of Mary. On the 12 preceding days, special prayers of preparation should be said. She came with a white dress and with a white cape around her head that reached to the floor, and on the chest of the Virgin were three roses: one red, one white, one gold."*

The Three Swords And The Three Roses

Pierina would explain the meaning of the three swords and three roses. *"The **first** sword means the loss of the vocation as priest or a monk. The **second sword** means priest, monks, and the nuns who live in deadly sin. The **third sword** means the priests and monks who commit the treason of Judas. While giving up their vocation, they often lose their faith, their eternal beatitude, and become enemies of the Church. The **White Rose** means the spirit of **Prayer**. The **Red Rose** means the spirit of **Expiation and Sacrifice**. The **Golden Rose** (Yellow) means the spirit of **Penitence**."*

The Blessed Mother is asking for a devotion that protects the clergy and its institutions from evil. She also asked for the Catholic practices of Holy Hours of Adoration, Mass, the Eucharist, and the Rosary.

The Blessed Mother would say to Pierina on her final visitation on the premises of the *Handmaids of Charity,* *"For the last time I come to request the devotion already recommended at other times. My Divine Son wanted to leave proof by His most Precious Blood in order to witness how great is His love for all humanity, from which is returned great offenses. Get the purification cloth, and show it to all here present. Behold the drops of Blood of the Lord. Let it be covered by a white cloth, and then let it be exposed for three days in this chapel, together alongside the statue of Sister Mary Crucified of the Rose that will become miraculous for the sake of the devotion of the faithful. Have the coming factual test be referred to the Bishop, and say to him that conversions of revival of faith will verify it.*

I interpose myself as Mediatrix between all human beings and particularly for religious souls and my Divine Son who tired of continuous offenses, wanted to exercise his justice. I vitally desire that this Institute of the Handmaids of Charity may be the first to honor me with the title Mystical Rose. By such am I, as the protectress of all religious institutes, assuring my protection for a lively re-awakening in the Faith so that these elect souls may return to the primal spirit of their founders. Before departing, the Blessed Mother showed the three roses on her chest and said to Pierina, *"Live for the sake of love."*

On November 22, 1947, Pierina was told by the Blessed Mother to go to the Montichiari Church at 4:00pm. It was at this time Pierina was told about the **Hour of Grace** that would be given to the world. The Blessed Mother said, *"I have come down to this place because here will be great conversions."* The Blessed Mother said that she would appear at this Church on December 8th, which is the feast day of the Immaculate Conception when she would officially request the **Hour of Grace.**

Then at noon Mass with one thousand people in attendance for the feast of the Immaculate Conception, the Blessed Mother said to Pierina, *"I am the Immaculate Conception, I am Mary of Grace, the Mother of my Divine Son Jesus Christ. By my coming to the Clear Mountains, I desire to be called the Mystical Rose. Furthermore my desire is to see instituted the Hour of Grace for the whole world, by celebrating it on December 8th every year, in order to obtain graces and conversions; and to request the construction of railings for the custody of these cited four floor tiles, together with a statue that replicates the Mystical Rose."* At that moment two people were instantaneously cured. One was a young six-year old boy with polio, and a twenty six year old woman who had been mute for nine years who instantaneously burst into joyous praise. Heaven requested Pierina tell the people that each year at 12 noon on December 8th people celebrate the Feast of Rosa Mystica.

In the turmoil of our day with the scandals in the Church, this feast is now more important than ever. Jesus Himself had Judas as betrayer. Judas has always lived in the Church and walks among us. There have always been those that are operating in stealth, and those more open who spread false doctrine with intent to harm from the interior of the Church. This has always been the case, and it will continue due to Original Sin. That is why Heaven is asking for the **Hour of Grace** for the sins of clergy. It is precisely for this reason people should not be leaving the faith, but more strident in their prayer, fasting and penance for clergy.

JESUS I TRUST IN YOU

Index

Other Works by Ted Flynn

The Great Transformation
Findng Peace of Soul in Troubled Times, 2015
A description of how they world is being transformed in our time.

The Thunder of Justice
The Warning, The Miracle, The Chastisement, The Era Of Peace, 1993,
Updated and Revised, 2010
Ted & Maureen Flynn. An overview of the major and most impactful Marian
apparition sites in history.

Idols in the House, 2002
The destiny of a family and nation that abandons the first commandment of
honoring God first and foremost.

Hope Of The Wicked
The Master Plan to Rule the World, 2000
The political philosophy and ideology of rulers of the world in their own words
how they want to govern the world. We are now living what they proposed for us
generations ago. A book ahead of its time.

Key To The Triumph
The Final Marian Dogma of Co-Redemptrix, Mediatrix, and Advocate, 1997, DVD.

Prophecy and the New Times, 1995
DVD. Some of the major prophets of our age on film discussing the
Blessed Mother's agenda as the prophetess of our age.

Go to Sign.Org (Signs and Wonders for Our Time) for a greater selection of books
and other spiritual products.
703.707. 0799

About the Author

Ted Flynn is an author and the producer of several films. He is the Founder and President of MaxKol Communications (1994). He attended the University of Massachusetts (Amherst), American University, the University of Fribourg (Switzerland), and the London School of Economics (England).

He was Chief Economist of a government agency, been active in not-for-profits, real estate development, energy development, President and Founder of a publishing company, worked in Poland on energy development after the fall of the Berlin Wall, and in Belarus with food distribution for U.S AID and the Department of Agriculture during Glasnost of the former USSR. He has traveled to 50 countries in his career, and spoken over 1,000 times on television, radio, or speaking engagements on the types of subjects addressed in this book. He can be reached at: tflynn3@cox.net

"*People must recite the rosary every day.*

*Our Lady requested this in her apparitions, **as if to arm us in advance against these times of***

DIABOLICAL DISORIENTATION,

so that we would not let ourselves be fooled by false doctrines, and that through prayer, the elevation of our soul to God would not be diminished....
This is a diabolical disorientation invading the world and misleading souls."

Sister Lucy of Fatima on April 12, 1970.